ENGLISH HAMMERED COINAGE
Volume 2
THIRD REVISED EDITION

English Hammered Coinage

Volume 2
Edward I to Charles II
1272-1662

J. J. North

SPINK & SON LONDON
1991

First published in 1991 by Spink and Son Ltd

Reprinted 2006, 2017, 2020, 2023

A CIP catalogue record for this book is available from the British Library.

ISBN 10: 0907605346
ISBN 13: 9780907605348

Typeset by Columns Design & Production Services Ltd,
Caversham, Reading

Printed and bound by Gutenberg Press Ltd,
Malta

Spink and Son Ltd
69 Southampton Row
London WC1B 4ET

www.spinkbooks.com

CONTENTS

PREFACE TO THE THIRD EDITION

THE principal amendments to this edition have been in the coinages of 1279–1351 and the provincial issues of Charles I, both of which have recently been the subject of Sylloges dealing solely with the coins of Edward I to early Edward III and with those of Charles I respectively.

In the case of the Edwardian coins this has necessitated the rewriting of some sections, particularly those of classes 10 to 12 and the second coinage of Edward III, which have been the subject of considerable research in recent years. The first of these classes which covers nearly 40% of the pence of Edward I & II, has been completely revised and a new classification formulated to replace the Fox one, which has proved unusable for sub-classes c to f. This has resulted in a complex classification and a simplified version has been compiled for this volume. Readers requiring greater detail should consult SCBI 39, where the new classification is discussed and fully illustrated. A new plate of the pence of Edward I & II is included in this volume to facilitate identification.

The principal amendments to the coins of Charles I are to the attributions of certain groups of provincial coins, which have in the past been attributed to unattested mints now considered to be unlikely locations. A more logical grouping of the Civil War mints, formulated by Mr. George Boon and discussed in detail by him in SCBI 33, has been adopted in this volume.

Important studies have been published on the base shillings of Edward VI, the milled coins of Elizabeth I, the Tower shillings of Charles I and the mint of York of Charles I and the relative sections in this volume have been amended to take these into account.

Many of the new entries are due to metal detector finds, which have produced a number of unpublished coins over recent years. As one would expect, most of these are in the smaller denominations which do not normally appear in hoards but were easily lost.

Thanks are again due to numismatists who have kindly advised the author of unpublished coins. In particular Peter Mitchell has sent details of a number of new coins and omissions. Michael Sharp has kindly provided a copy of all the amendments which he has made to his copy of the second edition and advised on a number of points in the coinage of Charles I.

Unfortunately Howard Linecar, who was such a tower of strength in the publication of previous volumes, is no longer with us. The task of steering this volume through the press has fallen into the capable hands of his successor, Douglas Saville, who has given the author every assistance.

September, 1990   J. J. N.

PREFACE TO THE SECOND EDITION

DURING the fifteen years which have elapsed since the publication of the first edition of this volume, several basic studies of coinages during the period covered have been published. Notable are those of the reigns of Richard II to Henry V and Henry VII, which have appeared in the British Numismatic Journal. Some amendments to the classifications of Edward pence have also been made and a number of new coins published. All of these have been incorporated in the new volume, but the original numbering for each coin has been retained. This has entailed sub-dividing them in cases where there has been a basic reclassification of a series. In a few cases, such as Edward I Class X c-e pence, these do not equate precisely, but in the main the difference in numbering is so slight as to be insignificant.

Consideration was given to extending the illustrations, but, in the interests of economy, the same plates have been retained. However, the original one of Edward I has proved unsatisfactory for identification purposes and a new collotype plate of these pence has been inserted at the back. By special request the bibliography has been considerably extended and a number of additional footnotes inserted for minor articles and notes.

The author would like to thank all those who have so kindly drawn his attention to errors and omissions. It has not been possible to include all of the coins communicated to him, as many were varieties, which would have involved going into detail beyond the original scope of this book. He would especially record his indebtedness to Peter Mitchell, who has advised him of a number of new items and given much valuable advice, and Marvin Lessen, who has given the benefit of his expert knowledge of the coinages of the Commonwealth and Cromwell, together with a number of other suggestions. Michael Sharp has perused the section on Charles I and kindly allowed the author to incorporate a number of corrections arising from his unpublished study of the Tower shillings of that reign.

The Trustees of the British Museum have permitted coins from their collections to be utilised for the new plate of Edward I pence and Mr. K. A. Howes has again produced superb casts of these.

As with previous volumes, the author has had the benefit of Howard Linecar's expert advice on the production and presentation of this work and is grateful for his patient assistance with many points that have been raised.

August, 1975   J. J. N.

PREFACE

FOR many years the standard work on English coins has been Dr. G. C. Brooke's excellent book. Although this was brought up to date with a supplement in 1950, it was not possible to re-arrange the sections which had been altered by research since the original publication in 1932. As many readers are aware, a large number of important articles and books have been published in recent years, especially in the Anglo-Saxon section. The time therefore seems ripe to incorporate the results of these researches in a new book on the hammered series.

Basically this is an attempt to list every known type of coin struck in England from early Saxon times until the end of the hammered coinage in the reign of Charles II. Minor varieties and overstruck initial marks are normally omitted, as are mules except where no true coin is known of the type or the initial mark represented by the obverse or reverse.

In addition to the lists of coins, notes have been added to facilitate the identification of types in the more complicated series. Line drawings are used to emphasize points less clearly visible in photographs, and all the main initial markes for each reign are given.

The attempt to provide a book sufficiently detailed for the student and specialist, and yet clear enough for the general collector, presents a number of problems. In general the solution adopted has been to give minor details only where these are required for the classification of the coins.

The decision to divide the book into two parts has been largely influenced by the desire to present it in a format which is handy for reference. The first volume covering the early period down to the reign of Henry III is practically complete, and should be published in the course of the next year.

Some readers may feel that an undue amount of space has been devoted to the reign of Charles I. It has, however, proved impossible to condense further the numerous types of this coinage without sacrificing clarity and completeness. The classification of the Tower " portrait " silver has been slightly altered to correspond with the bust division of the gold coinage made by Mr. Schneider in his recent article.

One expert has justly remarked that the book tends to follow the ups and downs of numismatic literature. I can only hope that any deficiencies will encourage students to engage in researches on some of the neglected periods. The reigns of Richard II and Henry IV require further study and the privy marking of Mary has never received the attention it merits.

I am well aware that such an ambitious project is liable to contain a number of errors, although many of these have been corrected by the experts who kindly checked the lists before going to press. However, I trust that it may prove useful to collectors and students and that it will form a foundation upon which a complete corpus of English hammered coinage may be built. If any reader is fortunate enough to possess, or knows of a coin which does not appear in the lists, I should appreciate being advised of it on the card which accompanies this book.

HOVE   J. J. N.
September, 1959

ACKNOWLEDGEMENTS

THE following gentlemen have kindly read through the original manuscript with special reference to the sections shown against their names. Thanks to their suggestions and corrections, many improvements have been made and errors eliminated. Those which remain must be attributed solely to the author.

N. C. BALLINGAL, ESQ.	Charles I.
R. D. BERESFORD-JONES, ESQ., M.A.	Charles I (Oxford mint).
C. E. BLUNT, ESQ., O.B.E., F.S.A.	Henry IV, Edward IV.
I. D. BROWN, ESQ., B.SC.	Elizabeth I.
G. V. DOUBLEDAY, ESQ.	Edward III.
J. P. C. KENT, ESQ., B.A., PH.D.	Henry VIII, Mary, James I.
D. G. LIDDELL, ESQ.	Charles I.
D. MANGAKIS, ESQ.	Henry V.
W. J. W. POTTER, ESQ.	Edward III to Henry IV, Henry VII.
P. SANDERS, ESQ.	Elizabeth I (Milled).
H. S. F. SCHNEIDER, ESQ.	Gold (Edward III to Charles II).
B. H. I. H. STEWART, ESQ., B.A., F.S.A., Scot.	Edward I to Henry IV, Edward V.
E. J. WINSTANLEY, ESQ.	Henry VII.
H. K. HEPBURN-WRIGHT, ESQ.	Commonwealth, Cromwell.

In his exhaustive check of the gold, Mr. Schneider has rewritten certain reigns, notably that of Charles I (Tower mint), and the division of the " laurel " busts of James I is due to him. To Mr. Brown belongs the credit for the chapter on the hammered silver of Elizabeth I, which he wrote on the lines of his recent division of that coinage.

Mr. C. Wilson Peck has kindly allowed me to use his drawings of the privy marks found on the copper farthing tokens, and to base the lists of these on his B.M. catalogue.

Many of the above named gentlemen have also drawn my attention to unpublished distinctions on various coins, and allowed me to incorporate these in the text. I can only hope that this book, which owes so much to them, will in some small way express my gratitude for their generous assistance.

The officials of the British Museum have extended their usual courteous help, and all numismatists whom I have approached on various points have given unstintingly of their knowledge.

All the coins illustrated are in the National Collection at the British Museum. The Museum kindly supplied the necessary casts. Mr. R. A. G. Carson and Dr. J. P. C. Kent have given much of their valuable time in selecting the actual specimens, and Mr. K. A. Howes in preparing the plaster casts.

I would like to add a word of thanks to my publishers for their help and encouragement during the writing of this book.

GENERAL NOTES

LEGENDS. Except in the series where the obverse legend plays an essential part in the classification, the sovereign's titles in their longest form are given at the commencement of each reign. It will be appreciated that the obverse legend will only be found in this form on the largest coins, and that it is considerably abbreviated on the very small denominations.

No attempt has been made to reproduce the lettering, which is normally Gothic until the end of the reign of Henry VIII. Roman lettering is then used for a period and is finally adopted in the reign of Philip and Mary. The style of lettering is noted where it is used for identification.

ABBREVIATIONS. The following abbreviations and terms have been used.

Obv. and Rev.=Obverse and Reverse.

I.m. =Initial mark—the symbol placed at the commencement of the obverse and/or reverse legend. When the mark used does not appear in this position, the term mintmark is employed.

Mule =A coin struck from obverse and reverse dies of different issues.

RARITY. For the collector, degrees of rarity are shown against each type, and these are for the commonest coin of that type. It must be emphasized that these can only give an approximate idea of the scarcity of a type, especially in cases of those of extreme rarity. The use of the term "unique" has been avoided as further specimens have a habit of turning up as soon as a coin is thus classified. The terms employed are as follows.

ER =Extremely rare.

VR =Very rare.

R =Rare.

S =Scarce.

N =Normal.

C =Common.

PATTERNS. These are specimens of suggested designs for coins, and were not normally put into circulation. There are some borderline cases such as the groats of Edward I and the shillings of Henry VII. Patterns are often struck in a metal other than that in which the coin would have been made, and at times it is difficult to know the denomination intended, e.g. some silver and gold patterns of Charles II, which may be either shillings or unites. In the lists they have been placed under the metal in which the coin would have been, with a note by the denomination if they are known in another metal.

FORGERIES. This term is used only for imitations made at a later date with intent to deceive collectors, and, in most series of ancient coins, a large number of forgeries exist, especially of the rare pieces. Notes have been inserted in the lists where particularly deceptive forgeries exist, but it is obviously impossible to note them all. For further information readers are referred to L. A. Lawrence's "Forgery in Relation to Numismatics" (BNJ 2 ff.), which lists and illustrates a number of false hammered coins. From this article are taken the following notes on the main types of forgeries, but the instinct for distinguishing between a false and a genuine coin can only be really acquired by examining as many genuine coins as possible.

(1) ELECTROTYPES. As these are made from two halves, the join around the edge can usually be seen on thin coins. They are normally of light weight, and the surface is usually granular. They do not ring when dropped, but this applies to many hammered coins.

(2) CASTS. Of soapy appearance without sharpness of detail. There are often minute holes on the surface, but these can appear on genuine coins which have been corroded or badly cleaned. They are usually of light weight.

(3) FALSE DIES. The style differs from the genuine coins. The diameter and thickness of the flans is often incorrect.

(4) ALTERATION OF GENUINE COINS. Usually show marks of the graving tool where the alteration has been made.

There is an extensive collection of forgeries at the British Museum, to which students can refer in cases of doubt.

HISTORY

THE reign of Edward I has been chosen for the break of the hammered coinage into two sections, on account of the great change which took place in the system and control of minting at this time. The types which were adopted for the small silver were retained with little alteration until the time of the Renaissance.

The next important change took place in the time of Edward III, when gold was coined, and the groat and halfgroat were introduced into the regular coinage. Although the following 150 years present a rather monotonous series as regards types, the coins of this period have several interesting features. Many of them, especially the smaller denominations, provide fascinating problems of identification, and it is interesting to trace the slow development of the system of privy marking from the broken lettering of Edward III to the changing initial marks of Edward IV.

With the coins of Henry VII, the influence of the Renaissance begins to show. It is especially noticeable in the fine gold sovereigns, and the portrait on the late silver. The latter provides a refreshing change from the stylised facing bust which had been used for so long.

The decline in the fortunes of Henry VIII affected his coins, which became base and ill-struck at the end of his reign. Although his son ruled for only six years, the coinage in Edward's name is varied and attractive. The influence of Spain may be seen on the shillings and sixpences of Philip and Mary with their double portrait on the obverse.

During the long rule of Elizabeth I the coinage became more standardised, and the first experiments were made in this country in the use of machinery for striking coins.

The vast coinage of Charles I has many interesting features, and a number of problems. The varying fortunes of the king have left their mark on this complex and fascinating series.

The fine portraits on the hammered coins of Charles II provide a worthy finale to this method of striking.

The following pages summarise the main events of numismatic interest during each reign.

PLANTAGENETS

EDWARD I (1272–1307). This reign marks the beginning of a new era in the English coinage, when many of the traditions continued from Anglo-Saxon times were discarded. During the first few years the Long Cross pence in the name of Henry, with a new style of portrait, were struck, but in 1279 a new coinage was ordered. After a few experimental issues, a type was evolved which was to form the basic design of English pence and smaller denominations for the following two centuries. Round halfpence and farthings were struck at the end of 1280, abolishing the Saxon and Norman practice of normally making these denominations by cutting a penny into two or four parts. The attractive and rare groats of this king must be regarded as an experimental issue, although several varieties exist, and it remained for Edward III to make them an integral part of the coinage. Many of the specimens of Edward I groats which have survived are gilt and have brooch marks on the obverse, having been used as jewellery in medieval times.

The reorganisation of the coinage brought about a change in the responsibility for the purity etc. of the coins, and the name of the moneyer, which had so long formed a part of the reverse inscription, disappears. There is one exception—that of Robertus de Hadeleie, who struck pence at the Abbot of St. Edmund, Bury privilege mint.

The number of mints functioning was reduced to four or five normally, except in 1280–1 when ten were striking, and 1300–2 when the number was eleven.

On the occasion of the recoinage the question of the ecclesiastical privilege dies was examined. These were a most lucrative source of revenue to certain bishoprics and abbeys, the main ones being those of the Archbishops of York and Canterbury, the Bishop of Durham, and the Abbot of St. Edmund, Bury. Coins struck from privilege dies are usually distinguished by a special mark, such as the quatrefoil in the centre of the reverse of York pence, and the personal mark or crozier head used by the Bishops of Durham. The latter marks played a major part in the classification and dating of Edward I and II coins. Canterbury coins of the period bear no distinctive marks as the Archbishop received the profits from three dies at the Royal mint there in lieu of his own dies. Ecclesiastical marks appear on coins until the reign of Henry VIII, when Cardinal Wolsey exceeded his powers by placing them upon groats.

EDWARD II (1307–1327). Pence, halfpence, and farthings very similar to those of his predecessor were issued by this king. The pence are mainly distinguished by differences in the crown which are noted in the lists.

EDWARD III (1327–1377). During the early years of this reign minute quantities of pence were struck and the coinage consisted mainly of halfpence and farthings, debased in 1335. However, in 1344, an economic crisis caused a new coinage to be ordered. Gold was regularly coined for the first time since the seventh century, if one excepts the extremely rare gold pence of Henry III, which were probably experimental. The first gold coins, which are amongst the most beautiful in our coinage, are excessively rare, and consist of the florin (6s) with its half and quarter. In the same year, these were superseded by the noble (6s 8d) with its half and quarter. The obverse design showing the king standing in a ship, which appears on the noble and half noble, may commemorate the naval victory at Sluys in 1340. It is a type which is used on the noble and other gold coins until the reign of James I.

In 1350, severe penalties were introduced against the import of base foreign sterlings which flooded the country, and a year later the weights of the coins were reduced. The groat was re-introduced together with its half, and both became a regular part of the coinage, being still minted today as Maundy money.

The wars with France make their mark on the coins of this period when Edward III announced to the world his claim to the French throne by including REX FRANCIE amongst his titles. This title was retained on English coins until the reign of George III, two and a half centuries after we had lost our last possessions in France. During the currency of the Treaty of Bretigni, which was signed at Calais in October, 1360, the title of Duke of Aquitaine replaces that of King of France, but the latter reappears on the Post-Treaty coins. The treaty with its change of titles has been used to divide the fourth coinage into three parts—Pre-Treaty, Treaty, and Post-Treaty periods.

The ecclesiastical mints of York and Durham were again active and a mint was opened at Calais in 1363. Coins of the English types were struck there until about 1440.

RICHARD II (1377–1399). Coins of the same denominations and types as those of Edward III were struck during this reign. A mark, such as a lion, an escallop, or a crescent, was placed on the rudder of the ship on some nobles and half-nobles to distinguish the issues. This system of privy marking was developed during the reigns of Henry V and VI, until the changing initial mark takes its place on the coinage of Edward IV, and continues until the end of the reign of Charles I.

The coins of the York privilege mint were often struck from rather crude dies made locally.

LANCASTRIANS

HENRY IV (1399–1413). A further economic crisis, caused by the export of English coin, and the import of base foreign currencies, leaves its mark on the coinage of this reign. Very small quantities of gold and silver coin, of the same weight and types as those of Richard II, were struck during the first thirteen years, and consequently coins of this period are very rare. The first pence struck were from obverse dies of Richard II with the name mutilated, and reverse dies of Henry IV, which are distinguished by an extra pellet in two quarters. It is probable that certain half-groats with the name of Richard mutilated, and others from obverse dies of Edward

III and late reverse dies of Richard II, were also struck in the early years of Henry IV.[1] Unfortunately no groat which can be attributed to Henry IV's heavy coinage has yet been identified.

In 1412, the weight of the noble was reduced from 120 to 108 grains, and that of the penny from 18 to 15 grains. There was a large output, but, as the king died in the following year, specimens of his light coinage are also rare. It is possible, however, that some of the coins classified as early Henry V were in fact struck during his predecessor's reign.

HENRY V (1413–1422). The gold and silver coins struck by Henry V are of the same types and weight as those of his father's light coinage. Dies of the previous reign, with a privy mark stamped on them to distinguish the coins struck with them from earlier ones, were often used. These privy marks, a mullet, a broken annulet, or a trefoil, appear in the field of most coins except the last issue, and are the main factor in classifying the coins.

Although the designs of the coins remain unchanged, there is some variation in the busts. These commence with a realistic portrait, commonly known as the "emaciated" bust, and the coins bearing it are very rare. The following issues show a more impersonal bust, which, however, introduces one feature worthy of note—the sidelocks. These are tufts of hair protruding on both sides just below the crown, and are shown on most busts until the adoption of the profile portrait during the reign of Henry VII.

The final issue of the reign has no privy marks in the field, but bears a newly engraved bust of neat work. It is thought to be the work of Bartholomew Goldbeter, who was appointed Master of the Mint in February, 1422.

The privilege mints of York and Durham continued to strike pence, but the Calais mint remained inactive.

HENRY VI (1422–1461)—(Restored 1470–1471). The coinage of this king falls into two sections, those struck during his first reign, and the coinage of his brief restoration. During the first period the denominations and types are similar to those of the previous reign, and the system of privy marking enables them to be divided into eleven issues. This marking is effected by the means of symbols such as annulets, rosettes, leaves, pinecones etc., which are placed in the field, on the bust, and/or in the legend as stops. There is considerable muling, especially between the early issues.

The York royal mint springs into activity in 1423–4, striking groats and half-groats for the first time since the reign of Edward III, and gold for the first time ever. The privilege mint recommences placing a personal mark of the bishop on pence struck there, and at the end of the period the letter B (Laurence Booth) appears. This practice of placing an initial letter or letters of the bishop's or archbishop's name soon became customary at all three ecclesiastical mints. It continued until the suppression of such mints in the reign of Henry VIII, and has been of great assistance to students in the accurate dating of the various issues.

The production of the Calais mint reflects our brief tenure and loss of the French throne so gallantly won by the king's father at Agincourt. This mint was re-opened in 1424, and large quantities of coin of the early issues were struck there. In the later leaf-trefoil and trefoil coinages, only groats are known and these are rare. The mint was closed in about 1440 and, apart from the Tournai groats and half-groats of 1513, no English coins were struck in France again.

The coins of the restoration period are similar in type and denomination to those of Edward IV. Despite the short duration of the second reign—six months only—they are not as rare as might be expected.

YORKISTS

EDWARD IV (1461–1470; 1471–1483). On his accession, Edward continued to strike coins of the same types as the previous kings. They were, however, minted in very small quantities as the

[1] C. E. BLUNT. "Heavy silver coinage of Henry IV." Transactions of the International Numismatic Congress (1936) p. 360.

output of the mint had been low during the previous twenty five years. In 1464, the weight of the penny was reduced to 12 grains with a view to attracting gold to the mint, and reorganisation of the gold coinage took place in the following year, with the introduction of the Ryal or Rose-noble weighing 120 grains and worth 10 shillings. This fine coin bore the types of the old noble with the addition of Edward's personal badges, the rose and sun. The former was prominently displayed on the side of the ship, and in the centre of the reverse, where it was superimposed on a sun. The new coin proved especially popular on the Continent, where large numbers of imitations were struck, the majority being made later in the sixteenth century.[2]

In order to replace the old noble, which was the standard fee for many professional services, the Angel weighing 80 grains and worth 6s 8d was introduced. Its design of St. Michael slaying the dragon on the obverse, and the ship bearing a cross on the reverse, caused it to be used by the Tudor and Stuart monarchs as a talisman to be given to the sick, whom they had touched for the king's evil. This accounts for the large number of pierced specimens which exist, especially of James I and Charles I. Long after the angel had ceased to exist as a current coin, small medalets bearing similar designs were struck as touch pieces even by the Stuart Pretenders.

To cope with the great recoinage of gold, the royal mints at Canterbury and York were re-opened, and the mints were also opened at Bristol, Coventry and Norwich. However, the two latter mints were closed after two months, while York continued until September, 1471, and Bristol until July, 1472.

As mentioned earlier, a system of regularly changing initial marks to differentiate between each issue was introduced at the beginning of this reign, and this continued until the end of the reign of Charles I.

For the first time since the early fourteenth century, the Archbishop of Canterbury had the privilege of coining restored to him in 1465, and his personal mark appears on the coins. Although privilege mints had previously been restricted to the making of pence,[3] he was allowed to strike half-groats. The system of marking ecclesiastical coins with an initial or initials, introduced at Durham during the previous reign, now becomes customary at that mint and at York. The occasional use of locally made dies at these two northern mints is a sign of the troublous times.

The coinage of Edward's second reign is similar to that of his first except that no ryals or fractions thereof were struck. These denominations had been supplanted by the angel and its half during the first reign.

EDWARD V (1483). The few coins which can be attributed to this unfortunate king are extremely rare and bear the boar's head initial mark on the obverse with the sun and rose as reverse mark on the gold coins and the groats. The former mark is the personal badge of his uncle and supposed assassin, Richard III.

Long has the battle raged between learned numismatists as to whether the halved sun and rose initial mark should be attributed to this king or to his father. Messrs. C. E. Blunt and C. A. Whitton considered it to mark the last issue of Edward IV, and the majority of students now concur with this opinion. Obverses with this mark are therefore listed under that king, although they probably continued to be used at the beginning of Edward V's reign.

RICHARD III (1483–1485). The same denominations and types as in the second reign of Edward IV continued to be struck by Richard III. Except for the pence from the ecclesiastical mints of York and Durham and a few York groats, all coins were struck in London.

TUDORS

HENRY VII (1485–1509). After the somewhat monotonous types of the previous 150 years, the changes effected during this reign clearly mark the end of medieval art and the commencement

---

[2] J. D. A. THOMPSON. "Continental Imitations of the Rose Noble of Edward IV." BNJ 25 (1945–8) p. 183.

[3] There was an exception at Reading, which was allowed to strike halfpence and farthings as well as pence during the early years of Edward III's reign.

of the Renaissance in our coinage. The early change in the silver coins is slight, being confined to the substitution of a single or double arched crown for the conventional open one, which was still used on the earliest coins. However, on the last issue a fine profile bust engraved by Alexander of Brugsal[4] is used, and the normal reverse of a cross with three pellets in each angle gives way to the royal shield. The portrait is considered by many to be one of the finest in our coinage, and it is perhaps the first recognisable portrayal of a king since the time of Offa. The numeral (VII) appears after the king's name for the first time since its use on the Long Cross pence of Henry III.

A beautiful example of the art of this period is the gold sovereign, weighing 240 grains and valued at 20 shillings, which was first struck in 1489. On the obverse the king is depicted seated on a throne sometimes of highly ornamental style, while the reverse field is filled with a Tudor rose bearing the royal shield. A simplified version of the obverse of this coin is used on the pence of the last coinage, recalling the " sovereign " pence of Edward the Confessor and the gold pence of Henry III.

The king in ship obverse of the old noble was retained on the very rare ryals or half-sovereigns of Henry VII. The ship however flies two standards one of which bears the Welsh dragon, and the king is wearing a double arched crown. On the reverse is the Tudor rose with the three lis of France on a shield in its centre. Angels and half-angels continued to provide the bulk of the gold coinage, and only minor changes were made in the design.

Another new denomination was the silver testoon or shilling of 144 grains, which bore the same designs as the profile groat. There are several varieties of legend on this very rare coin which was probably only struck as a trial piece.

The ecclesiastical mints continued to strike coins bearing the initials or personal marks of the dignitaries responsible. Those of Canterbury and York were permitted to issue halfgroats and halfpence as well as the usual pence. The Archbishop of Canterbury's privilege was withdrawn in about 1490 A.D., and the king resumed control of the mint in that town. At the same time the royal mint at York was reopened for the coinage of half-groats. During the last quarter of 1500 the coinage of the privilege mints was suspended, but Archbishop Savage of York regained the right to mint halfgroats and halfpence in the following year.

HENRY VIII (1509–1547). The early coins of this king bore similar types to those of the last issue of his father. The sovereign, London pence, and halfpence are distinguished only by the initial mark, whilst the groats and halfgroats continue to use the profile portrait of Henry VII with the numeral in the obverse legend amended by the addition of the figure I.

Cardinal Wolsey was ordered to re-organise the coinage in 1526 by bringing its standard into line with that of the Continental countries. This was done in an attempt to stop the importation of French and Flemish gold coins, which were driving the English coins in that metal out of circulation. The first measure taken was to revalue the gold coins at 22 shillings to the sovereign, and to issue the Crown of the Rose of the same weight and standard as the French Ecu au Soleil (53 grains and 23 carat gold). Subsequently the entire gold coinage was adjusted by striking the larger coins from standard gold (23 ct. $3\frac{1}{2}$ grs.), and revaluing the sovereign at 22 shillings and 6 pence. Two new denominations were struck—the extremely rare George Noble and the Half George Noble (probably unique), both of which depict a spirited St. George on horseback spearing the dragon as reverse type. The extremely rare Crown of the Rose was replaced by the Crown of the Double Rose (valued at 5 shillings) and its half, both of which were struck of 22 carat gold. The coins are remarkable in bearing the initial of the king's name either with R. (REX) or with that of his queen at the time of their issue—K (Katherine of Aragon), A (Anne Boleyn), or I (Jane Seymour). The groats and halfgroats of this issue bear a good likeness of the young king. The customary titles on the pence and halfpence are replaced by the flattering legend H . D . G . ROSA SINE SPINA (Henry, by the grace of God, a rose without a thorn).

Before proceeding to the last issue of this king, it seems appropriate to write here about the ecclesiastical mints, whose varied fortunes abruptly ended during the period of the Wolsey

---

[4] It is probable that the dies were cut by his deputy, John Sharp (cf. BNJ 41 (1972) p. 89).

coinage with the dissolution of the monasteries. They had continued to strike coins bearing initial and other symbols during the first and second coinages. Of especial interest are the coins of Cardinal Thomas Wolsey as Archbishop of York. His vanity caused him to place a cardinal's hat as episcopal mark as well as his initials on the reverse of his coins, and this figured prominently in the draft indictment of 1529. He also struck groats at his privilege mint, and this assumption of the king's prerogative would have figured in the charges brought against him, had he lived to face his trial.

By 1542 Henry had come to the end of the fortune so carefully amassed by his father, and was searching for new sources of revenue. The slight debasement of the coinage effected in 1526 provided the clue to a lucrative source of wealth. Within four years the gold declined in fineness from 23 carats to 20 carats, and in weight from 240 grains (Wolsey coinage) to 192 grains per sovereign. The fall in the fineness of the silver coinage was even greater, from 10 oz. to 4 oz., and the weight of the groat was reduced to 40 grains. A new denomination in the gold coinage is the quarter angel, and in the silver the testoon became a regular issue. On the silver of the third coinage the full face bust reappears, and portrays the king bearded and middle-aged. It is a good likeness, but the low relief and bad striking usually make the details difficult to distinguish. Towards the end of the reign coins were being struck at the Strand (Durham House), Southwark, Bristol, Canterbury, and York to supplement the output of the Tower mint.

EDWARD VI (1547–1553). On the accession of the youthful Edward VI, the authorities were determined to restore the coinage to its former fineness. The disastrous state of the country's finances caused this to be deferred during the early years, and base coins continued to be struck bearing the name and portrait of Henry VIII. One series of half-sovereigns bear the name of Henry, but the enthroned figure has a youthful face. At the same time a number of coins were also struck bearing the name of Edward and on the silver his portrait in profile. The only denomination of these struck in any quantity was the testoon, which has the distinction of being the first English coin to bear a date.

In 1549 the first step to improve the standard of the coins was taken, when gold was struck of 22 carats. There was however no improvement in the silver, and 4 oz. fine was still used for the groats and lesser denominations. The shilling bearing the profile bust was subjected to a number of variations in weight and fineness. Those struck from silver 8 oz. fine weighed 60 grains while others struck from silver 6 oz. fine weighed 80 grains. As these testoons provided the revenue to meet the cost of the finer coinage, they were struck from even baser metal in 1550 and 1551— 3 oz. fine weighing 80 grains. Their value was reduced to ninepence in 1551, and later in the same year to sixpence. They continued to circulate at their reduced value until 1560, when the value of those struck from silver 3 oz. fine was further reduced to twopence farthing, and that of all others to fourpence halfpenny. They were countermarked on the obverse with a greyhound or a portcullis to denote their new values, and details of these coins will be found in the lists of Elizabeth I. The gold coins of this issue introduce the use of a profile bust on the fractions of the sovereign. Two busts are used, either crowned, or uncrowned, and both are charming portraits of the boy king.

During the third period (1550–1553) considerable improvements were made in the standard of the coins. Two finenesses of gold were used—23 carats 3½ grains for the sovereign of 30 shillings (240 grains) and the angel of 10 shillings (80 grains), and 22 carats for the sovereign of 20 shillings (174 grains) and its divisions. The latter coins show an attractive half-length figure of the king, crowned and in armour, and bearing a sword and sceptre. The greatest improvement was in the silver coins, most of which were struck from metal of 11 oz. 1 dwt. fine. A few profile shillings, most of the pence, and all half-pence and farthings were made from base silver. The "fine silver" coinage introduced several new denominations, the most notable of which were the crown and halfcrown. These fine coins have an obverse design of the king on horseback, and the date, which appears below the horse, is in Arabic numerals. The sixpence and threepence are struck for the first time, and these, together with the "fine" shilling, have a facing portrait with the value shown in pence on the left. A very few "fine silver" pence were struck, and these have the old "sovereign" type obverse with the king enthroned.

MARY (1553–1554). During the year before her marriage this queen struck sovereigns of 30 shillings, ryals, angels and half-angels in gold of 23 carats 3½ grains (Standard gold). The groat, half-groat, and penny in silver of 11 oz. fine bear a profile portrait of the queen of fine work but very low relief. The privy mark, which had for so long been the initial mark, is usually placed in the legend after the second or third word. The base penny of 3 oz. fine with a rose as obverse type continued to be struck.[5]

PHILIP AND MARY (1554–1558). The only gold coins struck during this joint reign were angels and half-angels of the usual type. In the silver, however, the shillings and sixpences are worthy of note as the only coins of our country to bear portraits of a king and queen facing one another. The type was copied from coins of Ferdinand and Isabella of Spain, which displayed the rulers' portraits in a similar manner, and it gave rise to the much quoted jingle:

> " Still amorous, cooing, and billing,
> Like Philip and Mary on a shilling. "

Unfortunately the shillings were often bent, and specimens in extremely fine condition are of considerable rarity.

The groat and lesser denominations in fine silver have a profile portrait of Mary alone, similar to that on such coins before her marriage, and base pence were also minted.

ELIZABETH I (1558–1603). It is to the credit of this queen that she finally restored the fineness of the coinage so shamefully debased by her father. A quantity of base coin was still in circulation when she mounted the throne, and in 1560 the nominal value of these was reduced. The testoons of Edward VI were countermarked to show their reduced value as mentioned in the history of that king. The withdrawal of these base coins was completed in 1561, and the silver was not again debased until 1920, when this was rendered necessary through the intrinsic value of the metal exceeding the face value of the coins.

Despite its length, this reign is more notable for the variety of denominations (nine in gold and eleven in silver) than of design. The coins of fine gold, i.e. Sovereign of 30 shillings, ryal, angel and its divisions, bear the conventional types. All other gold and silver coins, except the halfpenny, have a profile portrait on the obverse and the royal shield on the reverse. To distinguish between silver coins from the shilling downwards, a rose was placed behind the head on alternate denominations. This was essential to prevent confusion over the face value, especially in the smaller coins. Two remarkable values peculiar to this reign were the three halfpence and three farthings ($\frac{1}{8}$ and $\frac{1}{16}$ shilling), which were struck for about twenty years. The halfpence, which have a portcullis as obverse type, are worthy of note as they bear no legends. Towards the end of the reign the silver crown and halfcrown were re-introduced, and have been struck in every reign since.

A coinage in copper was considered for the first time since the days of the Northumbrian stycas, and, although the scheme did not materialize, patterns for such coins exist. A coinage in this metal was an urgent necessity, as the lack of small change had for a long time caused considerable hardship and prohibited small monetary transactions. From c. 1200 the need for such change led to the manufacture of anonymous pewter and lead tokens (cf. BNJ 53 (1983) p. 29 & 54 (1984) p. 86), later supplemented by Venetian base metal pieces known as " galley halfpence " together with billon coins of other continental countries. By the middle of the 16th century, shopkeepers were issuing tokens in lead or tin to facilitate trade, but few of these have survived. Some of the pewter jetons or medalets mentioned in the lists at the end of Elizabeth's coinage may have served as tokens, although it is unlikely that they were struck for this purpose.

Unfortunately an attempt to introduce machinery for striking coins failed because of the opposition of the mint workers, who feared unemployment. The new method of coining was brought to this country in about 1560 by Eloye Mestrell, a former workman at the Paris mint. He was eventually hanged for forgery in 1578, but numerous examples of his official work have survived. The comparison of a machine made coin of this reign with a hammered one will demonstrate the loss in beauty caused by sixteenth century opposition to progress. Nearly one hundred years was to pass before the " hammered " coinage was finally superseded by the " milled ".

---

[5] cf. footnote to No. 1964.

STUARTS

JAMES I (1603–1625). The first coinage of James is similar in denominations and fineness to the last issue of his predecessor, although the only coin struck in the angel series was the quarter. The royal shield is altered to incorporate the arms of the Scottish kingdom, which appear in the second quarter. That country's national emblem is used as an initial mark, and SCO is added to the royal titles.

The second coinage presents a large variety of denominations in gold; the Rose-ryal (30s) and Spur-ryal (15s), the Angel (10s) and its half, the Unite (20s) and its fractions, and a newcomer, the thistle crown (4s), with its simple types of a crowned rose and a crowned thistle. The thistle and rose also appear as the types on the halfgroat, penny, and halfpenny. The titles of King of England and Scotland are now amalgamated into that of King of Great Britain.

The third coinage is remarkable for the use of a Roman style bust, laureated, cuirassed, and draped, on the twenty shilling piece (known as the laurel) and its divisions. The values struck are similar to those of the previous issue except that the half-angel and thistle crown denominations are discontinued. There is no real break between the second and third coinages in silver, but they are divided in the lists to correspond with the gold issues.

During this reign many denominations were marked with their value, gold in shillings and silver in pence. After a brief appearance on the shilling and its divisions during the reigns of Edward VI and Philip and Mary, this practice had been discontinued, but it now became customary to mark most coins until the introduction of the milled coinage. The use of silver mined in Wales was indicated by plumes above the shield on reverses of coins struck from it.

The first attempt to introduce a copper coinage was made by the issue of royal farthing tokens, struck under letters patent by Lord Harrington, the Duke of Lennox, and finally the Duchess of Richmond. These poor little pieces, whose prescribed weight was only 6 grains, brought enormous profits to the patent holders, but did not prove popular with the general public. This is understandable in an age which still believed that the intrinsic value of a coin's metal content should be the same as its face value. The design of these tokens has little artistic merit, and their main interest is as forerunners of the fine series of copper coins which commences in the reign of Charles II.

CHARLES I (1625–1649). The vast and varied coins of this reign have always been of great interest to collectors. The emergency mints established in different parts of the country, and the coins struck by besieged towns and castles are reminders of the troublous times through which the country passed.

During the early years the coins were similar in type and denominations to that of the previous reign, the sole mint being that at the Tower. As will be seen from the lists, the coinage is divided into issues by variations in the busts and shields. The only major change in type was in 1630, when a bust was placed on the obverse of the halfgroats and pence instead of the rose.

Perhaps the most notable event during this period of peace was the employment at the mint in 1625 of Nicholas Briot, who was formerly with the Paris mint. Once again the mill was introduced into England, and some examples exist of coins being struck by it from current dies. However, it is more customary to find Briot's own dies used to strike coins by machinery. He was a great artist and, besides his beautiful patterns and proofs, he engraved dies for the majority of the York coins. His influence can also be seen in the busts and equestrian figures on some Tower coins as well as on a number struck at the provincial mints of York, Oxford, Truro, and " W ".

The striking of copper farthing tokens under letters patent continued throughout the reign. The Duchess of Richmond continued to hold the patent until 1634, when it passed to Lord Maltravers, who struck the tokens until 1649. In 1636 the reverse type was changed, and the farthings were struck with a brass centre to prevent forgery.

The provincial mints have recently been re-examined by Mr. George Boon in SCBI 33. He has amended a number of attributions and formulated a more logical arrangement, which has been adopted in this volume.

The first group consists of mints under the control of Thomas Bushell between 1637 and 1645. The first of these was Aberystwyth opened in 1638 for the purpose of coining silver from the Welsh mines. It was subject to supervision by the Tower mint, which supplied all of the dies. All denominations down to the threepence have the Welsh plumes on both sides, while the smaller values have them as reverse type. An open book was chosen by Bushell as his privy mark. The mint closed in 1642, but two further small issues are recorded in 1646, probably struck using old dies at the Silver Mills (Dover Furnace) about ten miles north of Aberystwyth.

In 1648 the mint at the silver mills was re-opened under the control of Edmund Goodere. The rare coins with the crown initial mark, once thought to have been struck at Combe Martin, are attributed to this mint.

In 1642 Bushell was ordered to move the mint from Aberystwyth to Shrewsbury. Although this mint remained open for only one year, it struck three new denominations—the gold triple unite and the large silver pound and halfpound. Coins minted there also introduced the "Declaration" reverse type. This famous instance of the use of coins for propaganda in wartime has the king's declaration, made at Wellington in 1642, inscribed across the field in an abbreviated form—REL(IGIO) PROT(ESTANTIUM), LEG(ES) ANG(LIAE), LIB(ERTAS) PARL(IAMENTI). No doubt his enemies also claimed the last two objectives as their reasons for the Civil War. It is possible that the mint at Shrewsbury may have re-opened in 1644 striking the coins marked "SA".

From Shrewsbury Bushell moved to Oxford, which became the king's main mint until it fell in 1646. The variety of coins struck there is too great for a detailed description here and readers are referred to the lists. Dies from Aberystwyth or Shrewsbury are sometimes used and the latter may normally be distinguished from true Oxford dies by the form of the plume. A number of dies were engraved by Thomas Rawlins, whose most famous work for this mint is the extremely rare pattern crown dated 1644.

In 1643 Bushell established his mint in the castle at Bristol. The coinage consisted mainly of silver, but there was a very small issue of gold probably for ceremonial purposes.

The next group of mints is those which were under the control of Sir Richard Vyvyan between 1642 and 1646. He had a roving commission to strike coins and commenced in November 1642 at Truro where he struck gold unites and silver crowns, halfcrowns and shillings. A finely engraved equestrian figure of the king, holding a baton and galloping over a pile of arms, appears on some rare halfcrowns, and this obverse is also used to strike coins at Exeter. A feature on some of the coins of this mint is that the mounted figure of the king has his face turned towards the viewer.

There are a number of coins which come late in the issues of this mint or early in those of Exeter and these are listed as "Truro or Exeter".

When Exeter capitulated to Prince Maurice in September 1643, Vyvyan moved his mint there and struck silver coins resembling those of Truro until the city was recaptured by the Roundheads in 1646.

The third group consists of other attested Royalist mints. At York the mint was active from 1642 until the battle of Marston Moor in 1644, probably using a rotary press to strike an attractive series of silver coins from dies by Briot. A number of base halfcrowns, previously thought to have been experiments for a debased issue, are now considered to be forgeries possibly made at the end of the eighteenth century.

Chester mint was active in 1644 striking mainly halfcrowns with a few shillings and threepences. A gold unite is also attributed to this mint.

Documentary evidence exists that there was a mint at Hereford, but no coins can be attributed to it with any certainty. Possible candidates are Nos. 2358–9, 2602 and 2627/2.

There are a number of unrecorded mints which struck coins with letters or symbols which cannot be interpreted with absolute certainty. It is now considered best to list these under the various marks with suggestions as to their possible attribution rather than under locations with which their association is not certain. The first of these "A, B and plumes" mint consists of a group of coins which have in the past been attributed to Lundy Island and later to Appledore and Barnstaple or Bideford. Current opinion favours Ashby de la Zouche and Bridgnorth as possible locations.

" H C " mint struck silver halfcrowns with the " pears " initial mark and was formerly attributed to Worcester. It was probably located at Hartlebury Castle near Kidderminster.

Coins of the " W " mint, consisting of a gold unite and silver halfcrowns (one dated 1644), were thought to have been struck at Weymouth. This seems highly unlikely and Worcester has been suggested as the possible location of the mint. Closely associated with these coins are those of the same denominations struck at the " S A " mint, formerly attributed to Salisbury. It seems likely that the mint at Shrewsbury (Salopia) was reactivated in 1644 and that these coins may have been struck there.

One of the halfcrown obverse dies has the " S A " erased by a large pellet (usually referred to as a cannon-ball) and may have been used to strike coins at Hereford in 1644.

A number of coins belonging to this group cannot be positively attributed to either mint and are listed under " W or S A " mint.

The " Garter " mint struck halfcrowns previously attributed very doubtfully to Combe Martin and now thought possible to have been struck at Hereford.

Among the irregular coins are two halfcrowns previously accepted as official issues. The first is of crude workmanship with a " Briot " obverse and an " Aberystwyth " reverse and was formerly attributed to Aberystwyth. It is now considered to be a forgery, as is the coin with interlinked CS as initial marks, formerly doubtfully attributed to Coventry or Corfe Castle.

In the patterns a " halfgroat " attributed to Aberystwyth is no longer considered to be a pattern and its mint and even its denomination (in view of its clipped condition) are doubtful.

Fascinating reminders of the Civil War are the siege pieces struck from roughly shaped fragments of plate to serve the monetary needs of besieged garrisons. The commonest are of Newark and consist of half-crowns, shillings, ninepences, and sixpences, all of which are lozenge shaped. The value in pence surmounted by a large crown dividing C R appears on the observe, while the reverse is inscribed OBS NEWARK with the date. The main issue of Pontefract consists of shillings, which have a representation of the castle gateway as reverse type. As the siege continued after the death of Charles I, some of these bear the name of his son Charles II, with the inscription POST MORTEM PATRIS PRO FILIO (After the death of his father, for the son). The silver three shillings and shillings of Carlisle are usually round, and their types resemble those of the Newark coins. The extremely rare gold half unites attributed to Colchester are probably concoctions. In Scarborough the value of the coin was decided by the weight of the rough piece of silver from which it was struck, and this produces some unusual denominations.

COMMONWEALTH (1649–1660). The puritanical outlook of this régime with its aversion to ornament produced coins of an austere design. All denominations except the halfpenny bear the same types, and they are only remarkable for being the sole coins in our history to be inscribed entirely in English. Despite the limited field of design imposed upon them, Blondeau and Ramage produced some fine patterns.

Coins bearing the dates 1658–1660 have the anchor initial mark, and some of these were struck during the reign of Richard Cromwell as Lord Protector. Doubtless the dies of Commonwealth coins were still used for a short time after the Restoration.

OLIVER CROMWELL—PROTECTOR (1653–1658). Although Cromwell refused the crown, the Parliament Council of State authorised the striking of coins bearing his name and effigy. They were engraved by Thomas Simon, and are beautiful examples of his work. Although they are all classified as patterns, it is possible that some were put into circulation as the halfcrowns of 1656 are normally found in worn condition.

After Simon's death, a number of his puncheons reached the Low Countries where they were used to make false dies from which various denominations were struck. In 1700 some of these puncheons and false dies were purchased by the Mint, and in 1738 specimens were struck from these.   As dies for the crown were cracked, John Tanner, the Mint engraver, made new dies for these and the half broad from Simon's puncheons.   A number of these imitations still exist and details are given in the lists by which they may be distinguished from the original strikings.

CHARLES II (1660–1685).   During the first two years of this reign, three issues of hammered coins in silver and two in gold were made.   There are several varieties of bust and punctuation, but these have not been noted in the lists.   The dies were engraved by Simon and the portraits are of his usual highly artistic standard.   However, in 1662 the superiority of the machine for striking coins finally triumphed and the hammered series ends.

EDWARD I

1272–1307

DENOMINATIONS—SILVER : Groat, Penny, Halfpenny, Farthing

COINAGE IN THE NAME OF HENRY III (1272–1278)

Obv. HENRICUS REX III. Crowned bust facing with sceptre in right hand.

Rev. Moneyer and mint name. Long cross voided with three pellets in each angle.

Penny
Class VI
1001 Very crude bust with pellets for eyes and realistic curls.   N
    LONDON—Renaud.
    DURHAM—Robert.
    BURY ST. EDMUNDS—Ion or Iohs.

Penny
Class VII
1002 New portrait of fine style with crown and side curls resembling   R
those of the next issue. Usually with Lombardic U.
    LONDON—Phelip, Renaud.
    DURHAM—Robert.
    BURY ST. EDMUNDS—Ioce, Ion or Iohs.

COINAGE IN THE NAME OF EDWARD (1279–1307)

Groat[6]

Obv. EDWARDUS DI GRA REX ANGL. Crowned bust facing within a quatrefoil with a small flower in each spandril; a flower at each side by hair.

Rev. DNS HIBNE DUX AQUT—LONDONIA CIVI (in two circles). Long cross with three pellets in each angle. Some reverses (probably late) have a pellet on the crossbar of the N in DNS.

1007 var. a (Fox 5). Flat crown with pellet ornaments. Small face   R
with short hair. Drapery two wedges with rosette below. Colon stops.

1008 var. b (Fox 6). Crown with four crescents carrying pearl   VR
ornaments. Large face with flat hair. Rosette in centre of drapery. Triple pellet stops.

1005 var. c (Fox 3). Crown with thick plain band and pearl orna-   VR
ments. Bushier hair. Curved drapery with rosette in centre. Colon or triple pellet stops.

1009 var. d (Fox 7). Crown with tall central lis and spearhead orna-   VR
ments. Smaller pointed face. Curved drapery with rosette in centre. Triple leaves in spandrels. Colon stops.

1006 var. e (Fox 4). Crown similar. Larger oval face. Thick curved   VR
drapery. Triple pellet or colon stops.

var. f (Fox 1 & 2). Crown with spread side fleurs. Broader face   VR
and shorter hair. Drapery of two wedges with three pellets below. Triple pellet stops. HBIN.

---

[6] Rearranged in accordance with the chronology formulated in SCBI 39, which illustrates all significant varieties of the silver coinage of 1279–1351. The groats were widely used as ornaments and are often found with solder marks on the obverse and traces of gilding on the reverse. Specimens in very fine condition are very rare.

1004   (1)   Quatrefoil of three lines. Minute pellets at each side of ER
                drapery. Trefoil below drapery.

1003   (2)   Quatrefoil of two lines. Line of three pellets below drapery. ER

1003/1   var. g (Fox —). Crown with bifoliate side fleurs. Similar face ER
          with wire-line hair. Annulet on breast? **ANG°₀** Colon stops.
          HBIN.

NOTES ON THE PENCE (cf. PLATE I)

Obv.   Royal titles. Crowned bust facing, drapery formed of two wedges usually. Initial mark.
          Cross pattée (usually).

Rev.   Mint name (except on early pence of Bury St. Edmunds, which have the name of the
          moneyer, Robertus de Hadeleie). Long cross pattéc with three pellets in each angle.

The pence of Edward I are divided into ten classes, the first nine being distinguished by the
trifoliate crown (three spikes to lis at each side) and the abbreviation of the king's name to **EDW**
(except on class 1b—**ED** and rare varieties of classes 6b and 8a—**EDWA**).

All Durham coins struck for Bishop Bek from class 4b onwards have a cross moline (*Fig.* 16
or 17) as initial mark on the obverse and also before **CIVI** until class 9b. Some of the coins of
that mint in classes 9b and 10 have a cross pattée as initial mark and were all formerly attributed
to the King's Receiver. Although a few in class 10cf may have been struck on his behalf, the
reason for most is uncertain.

There are also a large number of foreign imitations and forgeries of this series (Pollards,
Crockards, Lushbournes, etc.).[7] Those which bear the same bust and inscriptions as English coins
can often be detected by their blundered legends and light weight.

To assist quick identification of coins of this series, a chart showing some of the salient
features of each class is appended. Not all of them are present on every coin of the class, but the
presence of any one of them should help to indicate which section of the lists should be
consulted. The most common forms of lettering in class 10 are given, but there is considerable
variation within that class.

LETTERING

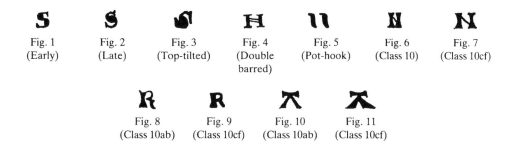

Fig. 1	Fig. 2	Fig. 3	Fig. 4	Fig. 5	Fig. 6	Fig. 7
(Early)	(Late)	(Top-tilted)	(Double barred)	(Pot-hook)	(Class 10)	(Class 10cf)

Fig. 8	Fig. 9	Fig. 10	Fig. 11
(Class 10ab)	(Class 10cf)	(Class 10ab)	(Class 10cf)

---

[7] N. J. Mayhew. Sterling Imitations of Edwardian type (RNS Special Publication 14; London 1983).

ABBREVIATIONS

Fig. 12 (Wedge) Fig. 13 (Crescent) Fig. 14 (Comma)

INITIAL CROSSES

Fig. 15 (Normal) Fig. 16 (Moline) Fig. 17 (Made up moline) Fig. 18 (Class 10) Fig. 19 (Class 10cf$_5$)

DRAPERY

Fig. 20 (Wedges normal) Fig. 21 (Class 3a) Fig. 22 (Class 3b) Fig. 23 (Class 3c) Fig. 24 (Class 4c)

CROWNS

Fig. 25 (Plain band) Fig. 26 (Broken lis—2a) Fig. 27 (Shaped)

SIDE FLEURS

Fig. 28 (Early Class 3) Fig. 29 (Class 3g onwards)

CLASS	CROWN	ON BREAST	A	LETTERING E & C	LETTERING N	S	REMARKS
1	*Fig.* 25	Annulet (Id) —rarely	Barred	Open	Lombard or Roman	Early (*Fig.* 1)	ED (W) REX (1a-c).
2	*Figs.* 26 *or* 27	—	,,	,,	Reversed Roman	,,	Small face, long neck (2b).
3	*Figs.* 28 *or* 29	—	,,	,,	Roman	Early or late (*Figs.* 1 *or* 2)	Drapery (*Figs.* 20–23). Abbreviations (*Fig.* 13).
4	*Fig.* 29	3 pellets (4e)	Unbarred (4d on)	,,	,,	Late (*Fig.* 2)	Abbreviations (*Fig.* 14). Pellets in legend (4d, e).
5	Spread	Pellet	,,	,,	,,	,,	Large spread coins.
6	,,	—	,,	Closed	,,	,,	Initial cross almost plain (6a).
7	,,	Rose (most)	,,	,,	Double bar (*Fig.* 4)	,,	Almond-shaped eyes.
8	Narrower	—	,,	,,	Roman	Top-tilted (*Fig.* 3)	
9	Flat	Star or pellet (many)	,,	,,	Roman or Pothook (*Fig.* 5)	,,	Small coins (9bc).
10	Bifoliate	Annulet (ER)	*Figs.* 10 *or* 11	,,	*Figs.* 6 *or* 7	Varied	Narrow face (10ab, cf. ₁) EDWA (RD) R.

MINTS

LONDON	CIVITAS LONDON	All classes except 3e and 9c.
BRISTOL	VILLA BRISTOLLIE	2b, 3bcdfg, 9b.
CANTERBURY	CIVITAS CANTOR	2, 3bcdfg, 4, 5, 6b, 7, 9, 10
CHESTER	CIVITAS CESTRIE	3g, 9b.
DURHAM (Plain cross)	CIVITAS DUREME	2b, 3bceg, 4ab, 9bc, 10a, 10cf 1, 2, 3, 5.
DURHAM (Cross moline)	CIVITAS DUREME	4bcde, 5b, 6b, 7b, 9ab, 10b, 10cf.
EXETER	CIVITAS EXONIE	9b.
KINGSTON-UPON-HULL	VILL'KYNCESTON	9b.
LINCOLN	CIVITAS LINCOL'	3cdfg.
NEWCASTLE-ON-TYNE	VILL NOVI CASTRI	3e, 9bc, 10ab.
BURY ST. EDMUNDS	ROBERTUS DE HADELEIE	3cdg, 4abc.
BURY ST. EDMUNDS	VILLA SCI EDMUNDI	4e, 5b, 6b, 7a, 8, 9, 10.
YORK—Royal	CIVITAS EBORACI	2, 3bcef, 9b.
YORK—Archiepiscopal (quatrefoil on reverse)	CIVITAS EBORACI	3ef, 9b.

BERWICK-UPON-TWEED — The coins of this mint do not conform with the classes struck at other mints and are treated separately on page 39.

Where a single number is shown in the above lists, all sub-classes are known.

LISTS

Penny
Class 1
(May to Dec. 1279)

Plain band to crown (*Fig.* 25). Roman **N**s sometimes reversed (except sub-class a). Abbreviation marks: Wedges (*Fig.* 12). LONDON only.

1010   (a)   **EDW REX ANGL DNS HYB.** (Lombardic **N** on obverse;   VR
                  distinctive **A**). Usually found muled with Class 1c.

1011   (b)   **ED REX ANGLIE DNS HYBN.** No drapery.   ER

1012   (c)   **EDW REX ANGL DNS HYB.** Small lettering.   C

1013   (d)   **EDW R ANGL DNS HYB.** Large lettering. (A scarce   C
                  variety with an annulet on the breast—Abbot of
                  Reading's die.)

Class 2
(Jan. to May 1280)

Crown with band shaped to ornaments (*Fig.* 27). **N**s usually reversed.

1014   (a)   Three varieties of face with short neck as on Class 1d.   C
                  Left petal of central lis of crown often broken off (*Fig.* 26).[8]
                  LONDON, CANTERBURY, YORK—Royal.

1015   (b)   High neck, small narrow face.   C
                  LONDON, BRISTOL, CANTERBURY, DURHAM, YORK—Royal.

Class 3
(1280–1)

Broad face, short neck. Abbreviations: Crescents (*Fig.* 13).

1016   (a)   Drapery curved with hook ends (*Fig.* 21). Pearl orna-   N
                  ments in crown. LONDON only.

1017   (b)   Drapery is a segment of a circle (*Fig.* 22). Pearl orna-   N
                  ments in crown.
                  LONDON, BRISTOL, CANTERBURY, DURHAM, YORK—Royal.

1017/1   (b/c) Transitional, face and crown of 3b, neck and drapery of 3c.   R
                  LONDON, CANTERBURY?

1018   (c)   Drapery hollowed in centre (*Fig.* 23). Early coins have   C
                  H with inturned foot as on Class 3b.
                  LONDON, BRISTOL, CANTERBURY, DURHAM, LINCOLN,
                  BURY—Robertus de Hadclcie, YORK—Royal.

1019   (d)   Drapery in two wedges (*Fig.* 20).   C
                  LONDON, BRISTOL, CANTERBURY, LINCOLN, BURY—
                  Robertus de Hadeleie.
                  N.B. The division of classes 3c and 3d by the drapery is
                  not entirely satisfactory and is difficult to apply in some
                  cases. Some numismatists prefer to classify all coins as
                  3c-d.

1020   (e)   Long narrow face. Sometimes pellet-barred **N**s.—   C
                  Northern mints only.
                  DURHAM, NEWCASTLE-ON-TYNE, YORK—Royal, YORK—
                  Episcopal (Quatrefoil in centre of reverse, and sometimes
                  on breast).

---

[8] cf. BNJ 28 (1955–7) pp. 294–9.

1021	(f)	Coarser work. Broad bust with large nose. Usually late S (*Fig.* 2). Abbreviations usually wedges. LONDON, BRISTOL, CANTERBURY, LINCOLN, YORK—Royal (Lombardic Ns), YORK—Episcopal (Quatrefoil on reverse; Lombardic Ns).	S
1022	(g)	New side fleurs to crown (*Fig.* 29).[9] Often small bust with narrow face. Early or late S. Stops vary. LONDON, BRISTOL, CANTERBURY, CHESTER, DURHAM, LINCOLN, BURY—Robertus de Hadeleie (a variety of crude style with Lombardic Ns may be an imitation).	C

Class 4
(1282–9)

Distinctly open C and E. Late S. Abbreviation marks: Large commas (*Fig.* 14).

1023	(a)	Spread crown with large side fleurs. Oval face with long hair. Very large S. (4a$_3$). Early varieties (4a$_1$ & 4a$_2$) have the face and crowns of late 3g with new short hair. Backward tilt to S. Tall narrow N. Late coins (4a$_4$) have a taller crown and incurved letters. Normal S. LONDON, CANTERBURY, DURHAM, BURY—Robertus de Hadeleie.	N
1024	(b)	Smaller smiling face with bushy hair. Sinister side fleur of crown usually damaged and appears to be bifoliate. LONDON, CANTERBURY, DURHAM (Plain cross; cross moline in one quarter (VR) or as initial mark on both sides), BURY—Robertus de Hadeleie.	C
1025	(c)	Crown with small nick between dexter jewel and side fleur. Larger oval face with longer hair. Drapery in one piece (*Fig.* 24). LONDON, CANTERBURY, DURHAM (Cross moline as initial mark on both sides),[10] BURY—Robertus de Hadeleie.	N
1026	(d)	Similar to 1025 with pellet before EDW and CIVI. Unbarred A. LONDON, CANTERBURY, DURHAM—Episcopal.	C
1027	(e)	Three pellets on breast (London and Canterbury only). Crown with spread fleurs and " ropy " hair (except on a few early coins which have the portrait of 4d). Pellet before LON and TOR or, rarely, TAS (Canterbury only). LONDON, CANTERBURY, DURHAM (made-up cross moline—*Fig.* 17), BURY (VILLA SEDMUDI).	N

Class 5
(c. 1289–91)

Very large spread coins. Pellet on breast. A normally unbarred.

1028	(a)	Bust similar to Class 4e. LONDON, CANTERBURY.	S
1029	(b)	Long narrow face. Tall narrow letters. Large initial cross. LONDON, CANTERBURY, DURHAM, BURY.	S

---

[9] There are three varieties of crown (cf. SCBI 39, Pl. 7 & 8).

[10] All coins of Durham until class 9b have the cross moline as initial mark on both sides.

Class 6[11]
(Between 1292
and 1296)

Smaller coins. Large crown with wide fleurs. Large oval face. C and E closed on this and subsequent issues.

1030	(a)	Rough execution. Initial cross almost plain. LONDON only. A variety of finer work has a squarer face and a thick initial cross pattée (ER).	VR
1031	(b)	Better execution. Initial cross pattée. Closed E. N rarely double barred (*Fig.* 4). LONDON (a rare variety reads EDWA), CANTERBURY, DURHAM, BURY.	R

Class 7[11]
(Between 1292
and 1296)

Rose on breast. Almond shaped eyes. N double barred.

1032	(a)	Crown as Class 6. Composite or non-composite S. LONDON, CANTERBURY, BURY (no rose, N normal).	S
1033	(b)	New crown. Longer hair. Non-composite S on obverse. LONDON, CANTERBURY (no rose, normal N), DURHAM (ditto).	VR

Class 8
(Between 1294
and 1299)

Full contractive marks including one after H on most coins. Slight notch in tail of H. Sometimes one or two Ns are double barred.

1034/1	(a)	New crown resembling that of class 7b with sinister petal of central lis usually broken. Normal S. LONDON (a very rare variety reads EDWA), BURY.	S
1034/2	(b)	Top-tilted S (*Fig.* 3). Wider neck and drapery. LONDON, BURY.	S
1035	(c)	Crown with very arched band. Face often small. Top-tilted S. LONDON.	S

Class 9
(c. 1299–1300/1)

New letter H without notched tail. Pellet eyes. Drapery of two wedges. Often a star on the breast.

1036/1	(a$_1$)	Crown of class 8b. Initial cross plain or very slightly pattée. Usually rough workmanship. LONDON, CANTERBURY, DURHAM—Episcopal.	N
1036/2	(a$_2$)	New flatter crown. Small neat initial cross pattée. LONDON, CANTERBURY, DURHAM—Episcopal, BURY.	N
1037/1	(b)	Smaller compact coins with shorter lettering having a new S (no longer top-tilted). N barred, unbarred or pothook (*Fig.* 5). The crown is either from the same punch as 9a$_2$ or a new one with a straight-sided sinister side fleur. Rarely a pellet on breast. LONDON, BRISTOL, CANTERBURY, CHESTER, DURHAM[12]— Plain cross, DURHAM[12]—Episcopal (cross moline on	C

---

[11] Classes 6 and 7 may be parallel issues (cf. BNJ 31 (1962) p. 82), and it is now generally accepted that class 7 was probably the earlier.

[12] Locally made dies are used at Durham either in combination or with regular dies (cf. BNJ 54 (1984) 74–80).

obverse only)[13], EXETER, KINGSTON-UPON-HULL, NEWCASTLE-ON-TYNE, BURY, YORK—Royal, YORK—Episcopal (quatrefoil on reverse).

1037/2   (c)   Similar to 9b with larger, crude lettering with barred **A**, s
variable **N** and contractive marks. Always muled with
dies of classes 9b or 10 (except Bury).
CANTERBURY, DURHAM—Plain cross, NEWCASTLE-ON-TYNE,
BURY.

Class 10   **EDWA(RD) R ANGL DNS HYB**. Bifoliate crown. Thin initial
(1301–10)   cross (*Fig.* 18) except in 10cf$_5$.

    (a) **EDWARD R**. Very narrow lettering with concave sides
(*Figs.* 6, 9 *and* 10). Long narrow face. Subdivided by
lettering.[14]

1038/1   10ab$_2$. Large lettering. Crown of 9b converted to bifoliate. N
All London coins have reverses of class 9.
LONDON, CANTERBURY, DURHAM—Plain cross,
NEWCASTLE-ON-TYNE.

1038/2   10ab$_3$. Small lettering. N
    (a) Crown of 10ab$_2$. Some London and Durham
coins have reverses of class 9.
LONDON (an extremely rare variety has an
annulet on the breast),[15] CANTERBURY, DURHAM
—Plain cross, BURY.
    (b) New taller crown.
LONDON (an extremely rare variety has a broken
annulet on the breast; another has a pellet on
the breast and each side of neck), CANTERBURY,
BURY.

    (b) **EDWAR R** (rarely **EDWR R** or **EDWA R**). Several
varieties as follows.

1039/1   10ab$_1$. Portrait of 9b with (a) trifoliate crown (b) bifoliate s
crown. London coins have reverses of class 9 and
very rarely read **EDWR R**. This issue precedes class
10a.
LONDON, CANTERBURY, NEWCASTLE-ON-TYNE.

1039/2   10ab$_4$. Portrait as 10ab$_3$(b) reading **EDWR R**. s
LONDON, CANTERBURY, BURY.

1039/3   10ab$_5$. Portrait as 10ab$_3$(b) reading **EDWAR R**. Lettering N
varies. Late coins have a larger and cruder crown.
LONDON, CANTERBURY, DURHAM—Episcopal[16], BURY.

1039/4   10ab$_6$. Portrait and lettering (with new stub-tailed **R** (*Fig.* 9) VR
and some variety in **S**) of late 10ab$_5$ reading **EDWA R**.
LONDON, CANTERBURY, BURY.

---

[13] On this and subsequent issues the cross moline no longer appears on the reverse.

[14] Reverses of early classes 10 are used with obverses of classes 9b and 9c at London (**ER**), Canterbury, Durham—plain cross and Newcastle-on-Tyne.

[15] Possibly struck for the benefit of the abbey of Reading (cf. BNJ 25 (1948) p. 239).

[16] Coins of Durham reading **EDWARR** with a plain cross inital mark were attributed to class 10b by the Fox brothers. These are continental imitations.

CROWNS OF 10c-f

| Crown 1 | Crown 2 | Crown 3 | Crown 4 | Crown 5 |

(c-f) **EDWA** R New crowns and lettering (cf. *Figs.* 7, 9 *and* 11). There is considerable variation in the letters. Except in class 10cf$_2$, Durham coins with a plain cross are rare and are possibly due to unmarked dies being sent to that mint in error.

1040   10cf$_1$.   Crown 1 (axe-shaped central lis; wedge-shaped petals   c and spearhead ornaments). Face and hair as 10ab$_5$. Some early varieties read **EDWAR R ANG** or **EDWA R ANG**.
LONDON, CANTERBURY, DURHAM (Plain cross or cross moline), BURY.

1041   10cf$_2$.   Crown 2 (well-shaped central lis; vestigial ornaments).   c Spreading hair.
LONDON, CANTERBURY, DURHAM (Plain cross or cross moline), BURY.

        10cf$_3$.   Crown 3 (well-shaped central lis which deteriorates; arrowhead ornaments, the dexter one inclined to right). The issue is primarily divided by the lettering.

1042/1   (a)   Lettering of 10cf$_2$ with broken E and H. This   c variety can be further subdivided by the hair.
LONDON, CANTERBURY, DURHAM (Plain cross or cross moline), BURY.

1042/2   (b)   New lettering with rounded E and curled tail to   c H (some straight-sided letters are used on late coins). Two sub-varieties can be distinguished by the face and hair.
LONDON, CANTERBURY, DURHAM (Plain cross or cross moline), BURY.

1042/3   10cf$_4$.   Crown 4 (neater with hooked petal to sinister side   VR fleur). Portrait as late 10cf$_3$(b).
LONDON, CANTERBURY, DURHAM (Cross moline), BURY.

1043/1   10cf$_5$.   Crown 5 (taller and more spread; dexter ornament   N inclined to left). The dexter side fleur becomes damaged and is repaired during this issue. On the reverse, letters I, M and (sometimes) N are straight-sided. Thick initial cross (*Fig.* 19), except on the earliest variety. There are three sub-varieties, the latest on smaller flans.
LONDON, CANTERBURY, DURHAM (Plain cross and cross moline), BURY.

1043/2   10cf$_6$.   Crown 3 with face and lettering of late 10cf$_5$.   VR
LONDON, CANTERBURY, BURY.

Halfpenny   Similar to the pence.

1044   Class 3b. Drapery a segment of a circle (*Fig.* 22).   R
LONDON only.

1045/1   Class 3c-e. Drapery hollowed (*Fig.* 23) or two wedges (*Fig.* 20).   S
LONDON, BRISTOL, LINCOLN, YORK.

1045/2   Class 3e. One pellet in each angle of reverse.   VR
NEWCASTLE.

1045/3   Class 3g. New spread crown as on pence.   R
LONDON, BRISTOL.

1046/1   Class 4c. Crown less spread. Smaller lettering.   R
LONDON only.

1046/2   Class 4d. Similar with pellet before LON.   R
LONDON only.

1046/3   Class 4e. Three pellets on breast. Pellet before LON.   VR
LONDON only.

1047   Class 6. Large crown of crude style. Small face. Short hair.   R
Small irregular lettering with closed C and E.
LONDON only.

1048   Class 7. Same crown. Larger face. Open C and E. Double-   R
barred N. Composite S. Small plain initial cross.
LONDON only.

1049   Class 8. Tall crown with sides almost vertical. Small neat   R
lettering with closed C and E. Initial cross pattée.
LONDON only.

1050   Class 10ab. EDWAR R. Long narrow face. Crown trifoliate   R
or, rarely, bifoliate (crowns 1 and 2 illustrated on p. 37). Long
narrow lettering (*Figs. 6, 8 and* 10).
LONDON only.

N.B. There are a number of halfpence which overlap the end of this reign and that of Edward II (cf. No. 1069/1).

Farthing   Types are similar to the pence.

1051/1   Class 1a. EDWARDUS:REX. Bifoliate crown without jewels.   R
Distinctive A.
LONDON only (LONDONIENSIS or LONDRIENSIS (ER)).

1051/2   Class 1c. Similar with trifoliate crown. Smaller lettering.   R
LONDON only (LONDONIENSIS).

1052   Class 2. EDWARDUS REX. Trifoliate crown with jewels.   R
Narrower face. Small lettering.
LONDON (LONDONIENSIS—reversed Ns), BRISTOL, YORK.

1053/1   Class 3c. Similar to No. 1052 with flatter, coarser crown and   S
larger face with bushy hair. Larger lettering.
LONDON (LONDONIENSIS), BRISTOL, YORK.

1053/2   Class 3de. E R ANGLIE (no inner circle). Crown similar to   S
No. 1053/1.
LONDON (LONDONIENSIS), BRISTOL, LINCOLN, NEWCASTLE, YORK.

1053/3   Class 3g. Crown with spread side fleurs.   R
LONDON only (LONDONIENSIS).

1054/1   Class 4de. Similar to No. 1053/3. Neat appearance.   R
LONDON only (CIVITAS LONDON).

1054/2   Class 5. Spread crown with tall fleurs. Large irregular lettering.   R
LONDON only.

1055   Class 6–7. Small crown. Conspicuous pellet or almond eyes.   R
LONDON only.

1056   Class 8. **E R ANGL DN.** Tall crude crown. Incurved letters   s
         with closed **C** and **E**.
         LONDON only.

1057/1   Class 9a. Flatter crown and smaller face. Short compact hair.   s
         Unbarred **N**. Initial cross almost plain.
         LONDON only.

1057/2   Class 9b. Wide flat crown with spreading side fleurs (used on   R
         ater halfpence. Crown 1 illustrated on p. 37). Small face.
         Short bushy hair. Small initial cross pattée.
         LONDON only.

1058   Class 10. **EDWARDUS REX(A).** Flat bifoliate crown with well   s
         shaped lis and no jewels. Oval face. Neat incurved letters.
         LONDON only.

NB. The farthings of group 10–11 overlap the end of this reign and that of Edward II (cf. No. 1070/1).

PATTERNS

Penny[17]   1059   *Obv.*   **ED'REX:ANGL'DNS HYB'E.** Undraped crowned bust   ER
                                  facing.
                         Rev.   **EDVVARDUS DEI GRA.** Long cross voided with rose in
                                  each angle.

---

[17] cf. NC (1923) pp. 56–9.

EDWARD II

1307–1327

DENOMINATIONS—SILVER : Penny, Halfpenny, Farthing

NOTES ON THE PENCE

The Pence of this reign are a continuation of the series of Edward I and are divided primarily by the different crowns. The details which distinguish the sub-classes are given in the list which follows.

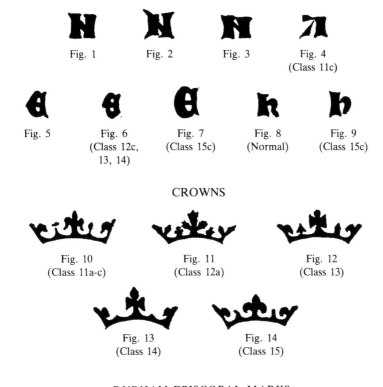

LETTERING

Fig. 1

Fig. 2

Fig. 3

Fig. 4
(Class 11c)

Fig. 5

Fig. 6
(Class 12c,
13, 14)

Fig. 7
(Class 15c)

Fig. 8
(Normal)

Fig. 9
(Class 15c)

CROWNS

Fig. 10
(Class 11a-c)

Fig. 11
(Class 12a)

Fig. 12
(Class 13)

Fig. 13
(Class 14)

Fig. 14
(Class 15)

DURHAM EPISCOPAL MARKS

Bishop Bek
(Initial cross
moline)

Bishop Kellawe
(Crozier end to long
cross on reverse)

Bishop Beaumont
(Initial mark:
Lion and lis)

MINTS

LONDON	CIVITAS LONDON.	All classes except 11d.
CANTERBURY	CIVITAS CANTOR.	All classes, except 12b and 12c.

DURHAM—No marks[18]	CIVITAS DUREME.	11a, 14, 15c.
DURHAM—Bishop Bek (cross moline)	CIVITAS DUREME.	11a.
DURHAM—Bishop Kellawe (crozier)	CIVITAS DUNELM.	11abc, 12a, 13.
DURHAM—Bishop Beaumont (lion)	CIVITAS DUNELM.	13, 14, 15abc.
BURY ST. EDMUNDS	VILL'SCI EDMUNDI.	All classes except 11d.

LISTS

Pence   Types as on pence of Edward I.

Class 11   Crown with broken pearl on left jewel (*Fig.* 10).
(c. 1310–   (a) Rounded back to C and E.
c. 1314)   1060/1   (1) Face and small lettering of late class 10 with stub-tailed R   s
and squat A. Often with "top-tilted" S and wide N.
Bushy wire-line hair. A few early coins have an unbroken
crown.
LONDON, CANTERBURY, DURHAM (Plain cross and cross
moline), BURY.

1060/2   (2) Larger lettering with scroll-tailed R and neater A.   N
Normal N (*Fig.* 1). S with swollen centre. Hair slightly
longer.
LONDON, CANTERBURY, DURHAM (Cross moline), DURHAM
(Crozier head on reverse),[19] BURY.

1060/3   (3) Similar with large open C and E.   R
LONDON, CANTERBURY, DURHAM (Crozier), BURY.

(b) Angular back to C and E (*Fig.* 5).

1061/1   (1) Similar to 11a$_3$, but with closed C and E. Fishtail S.   N
New shorter face.
LONDON, CANTERBURY, DURHAM (Crozier),[20] BURY.

1061/2   (2) Tall narrow lettering with incurved uprights and no serifs.   N
LONDON, CANTERBURY, DURHAM (Crozier), BURY.

1061/3   (3) Smaller lettering with large serifs to N (*Fig.* 2), sometimes   N
intermixed with letters of 11b$_2$. New smaller face.
LONDON, CANTERBURY, DURHAM (Crozier), BURY.

1062/1   (c) Variety of 11b$_3$ with distinctive A (*Fig.* 4). Often muled   s
with 11b and, very rarely, with 12 and 13.
LONDON, CANTERBURY, DURHAM (Crozier), BURY.

1062/2   (d) Crown of 10cf$_3$ with face and lettering of 11b$_3$. Initial   R
cross of four wedges.
CANTERBURY.

---

[18] As in late class 10, this is probably due to unmarked obverse dies being sent to Durham in error.
[19] Coins exist with a cross moline obverse and a crozier head on the reverse (VR).
[20] One reverse die has an additional crozier head before ELM (ER).

| Class 12 (c. 1314– c. 1317) | 1063/1 | (a) | Crown with wedge-shaped petals (*Fig.* 11). Central lis fourché. Trefoil or pellet ornaments. Thick initial cross. Lettering of 11b$_3$. Transitional coins have the initial cross and lettering of class 12b.
LONDON, CANTERBURY, DURHAM (Crozier), BURY. | R |

1063/2 (b) Crown with small diamond-shaped petals. Cruciform VR central fleur. Spearhead ornaments. Larger lettering with incurved uprights and no serifs. Thin initial cross of four wedges.
LONDON, BURY.

1063/3 (c) Crown with small heart-shaped petals and ornaments. VR Normally straight-sided uprights to lettering. Sometimes broken E (*Fig.* 6). Initial cross pattée.
LONDON, BURY.

Class 13
(c. 1315–
c. 1317)
1064 Crown with straight-edged central fleur and arrowhead left ornament (*Fig.* 12). The right-hand side fleur is nicked and becomes broken. The letter E becomes broken at the back. Thin initial cross pattée.
LONDON, CANTERBURY, DURHAM (Crozier), DURHAM (Lion i.c.), BURY.[21]

Class 14
(c. 1317–
1320)
1065 Crown with tall lis and no ornaments (*Fig.* 13). Larger face with smile and pointed chin. Sometimes with broken E. Thick initial cross on most coins. Rarely stops in obverse legend.[21]
LONDON, CANTERBURY, DURHAM (Lion or plain cross (ER)), BURY.

Class 15
(1320–
c 1333)
Smaller, flatter crown with spearheads inclined to left (*Fig.* 14).
1066 (a) Face and lettering of class 14. N
LONDON, CANTERBURY, DURHAM (Lion), BURY.

1067 (b) Smaller face. N
LONDON, CANTERBURY, DURHAM (Lion), BURY.

1068 (c) Larger face resembling that of 15a but squarer. Distinctive N large E with flat back (*Fig.* 7) and h with incurved tail (*Fig.* 9).
LONDON, CANTERBURY, DURHAM (Lion or plain cross (ER)),[21] BURY.[21] (One ER coin has a lion mark obverse with a London reverse and may be of that mint or of Durham.)

CROWNS ON HALFPENCE

1   2   3

Halfpenny

Type as on pence. LONDON only.

Class 10–11[22]   1069/1 (1) ANG. Trifoliate crown of 10ab (crown 1). S

1069/2 (2) A or AN. Bifoliate crown of 10ab (crown 2). R

1069/3 (3) ANGL' or ANGLI. New trifoliate crown with battle-axe R central lis (crown 3).

---

[21] A few coins have small marks in the obverse legend—Pellet: London (cl. 14); Durham (cl. 14, 15c), Bury (cl. 13, 14, 15c). Wedges: Durham (cl. 14), Bury (cl. 14, 15c).
[22] Dies of this variety probably continued to be used until c. 1335.

Farthing   Type as on pence. LONDON only.

Class 10–11   1070/1   A or AN. Tall, crude crown with wedge-shaped petals.   N
                              Small crude lettering. Almost plain initial cross.

Class 13   1070/2   REX, REX A or REX AN. Crown with uneven petals to central   S
or later[22]   lis. Pointed chin. Neat lettering with unbarred Ns. Initial cross
                               pattée.

EDWARD I, II AND III

BERWICK-UPON-TWEED MINT.[23]

The coins minted at Berwick during the periods 1296–1318 and 1333–1344, whilst bearing the same types as the English coins, do not fall into the same classes as most are from locally made dies.

Pence   Type as English pence of Edward I and II.

Class 1[24] (1296–7)	1071	EDW R (Lombardic E). Trifoliate crown. **VILLA BEREVVICI** (Roman E).	N
	1072	Similar reading **HYD**.	N
Class 2 (1297–8)	1073	Closed Lombardic E on both sides. Crude workmanship. (a) **EDW(A) R**. Bifoliate or trifoliate crown with large pellet ornaments. **BERREWYC, BERREVYCI or BEREVICI**. One die reads **HYBE**.	S
	1074	(b) **EDW R**. Bifoliate crown. Less crude style. Often with pellets in legend. **BEREVVICI**.	R
	1075	(c) **EDWA R**. Bifoliate crown. Pellet on breast. Very crude.[25]	VR
Class 3 (c. 1298?)	1076	**EDWA R**. Portrait resembles that of class 1. (a) Lombardic N in **DNS**. "Wide" face of class 1 or new narrow face with long neck. **WILLABEREVICI**.	S
	1077	(b) Roman N in **DNS**. Narrow face of class 3a.	S
Class 4 (c. 1300– c. 1310)	1078	**EDWA R**. Late V and W with large serifs. (a) Trifoliate crown. Usually pellet on breast. Lombardic N in **DNS**.	C
	1079	(b) Bifoliate crown. Pellet on breast. Lombardic N in **DNS**.	C
	1080	(c) Similar to 1079 but cruder portrait with prominent eyes (often solid). Roman N in **DNS**.	C
Class 5 (c. 1312)	1081	**EDWA(R)R**. London made dies of class 11a$_3$ (cf. No. 1060/3). Bifoliate crown with broken jewel. **:VILLABEREWYCI**. An extremely rare variety (class 5*) has the face, neck and drapery inserted with crude local punches.	S
Class 6	1082	**EDWAR R**. Trifoliate crown. Crude copy of class 5. One reverse die has a retrograde legend.	VR
Class 7 (Before April 1318)	1083	**EDWA(R) R**. Trifoliate crown. Very crude style with spread hair (usually wire-line).	VR

---

[23] cf. NC (1931) pp. 28–52 and B. H. I. H. Stewart, The Scottish Coinage pp. 128–131.
[24] This class is now subdivided by the face. cf. BNJ 47 (1977) pp. 141–4.
[25] These coins may be imitations.

Class 8a (c. 1344)	1084	EDWRADUS.ANGL D HB. Bifoliate crown. Bear's head in one quarter of reverse. BERWICI.	ER
Halfpenny		Types similar to the pence.	
Class 1	1085/1	Similar to No. 1071.[26]	ER
Class 2	1085/2	Similar to No. 1074.	VR
Class 3	1086	(a) Similar to No. 1076. Reads HB.	S
	1087	(b) Similar to No. 1077. One die has a star on breast.	S
Class 5	1088	EDWARDUS REX AN. London dies as No. 1069/2. Colon before VILL.	VR
Class 8[27]	1089	(a) EDWARDUS (ANGLIE D or DEI GRA R). Bear's head in one quarter of reverse.	R
	1090	(b) EDWARDUS D(EI) G(RA). Bear's head in two quarters.	R
Farthing		Types similar to the pence. EDWARDUS REX (Nos. 1091 and 1093).	
Class 1	1091	Style as No. 1071 with " wide " and " narrow " face.	ER
Class 3b	1092	Style and legends as No. 1077.	ER
Class 5	1093	London dies as No. 1070/1. Colon before VILL.	ER
Clas 8b	1094	EDWARDUS D(EI) G(RA). Bear's head in two quarters.	R

---

[26] SNC 83 (Feb 1975) pp. 56–7.
[27] Class 8b is now considered to precede class 8a and is dated c. 1333–42.

STANDARD TYPES

During the 14th and 15th centuries, certain standard types were used for the various denominations. To save space, a general description of each one is given here and is quoted in the lists as "Standard Type—" followed by a list of any variations.

The obverse legend is always the king's name and titles and the form shown at the beginning of each reign is that found on the larger gold coins. It is considerably abbreviated on the smaller coins, especially on the very small silver. The reverse legends are also abbreviated on many coins but in both cases the legends are only quoted in the lists where they have some bearing on the classification of the coin.

GOLD

A.	**Noble**	*Obv.*	King standing facing in a ship. He is crowned and wearing armour, and holds in his right hand a sword and in his left a shield quartered with the arms of England and France.
		Rev.	IHC AUTEM TRANSIENS PER MEDIUM ILLORUM IBAT. Floriated cross with a lis at the end of each limb and an ornamented compartment (containing the king's initial) in the centre; in each angle, a lion passant, guardant, with a crown above; all within a tressure of eight arches.

B. **Half-noble**   Similar to "A" but reverse legend DOMINE NE IN FURORE TUO ARGUAS ME.

C.	**Quarter-noble**	*Obv.*	Shield quartered with the arms of England and France within a tressure of eight arches (six arches on early coins).
		Rev.	EXALTABITUR IN GLORIA. Floriated cross with a lis at the end of each limb; in each angle, a lion passant, guardant; all within a tressure of eight arches.

D	**Angel**	*Obv.*	St. Michael standing facing on a dragon, which he pierces with his spear.
		Rev.	PER CRUCEM TUA SALVA NOS XPC REDEMPTOR. Ship with a large cross as mast from which hangs the Royal shield.

E. **Half-angel**   Similar to "D" but reverse legend O CRUX AVE SPES UNICA.

SILVER

F.	**Groat &** **Half-groat**	*Obv.*	Crowned bust facing within a tressure of arches.
		Rev.	POSUI DEUM ADIUTORUM MEUM — CIVITAS (name of mint) in two concentric circles. Long cross pattée dividing the legends; in each angle, three pellets.

G.	**Penny & infra**	*Obv.*	Crowned bust facing.
		Rev.	CIVITAS or VILLA (name of mint). Long cross pattée dividing the legend; in each angle, three pellets.

EDWARD III

1327–1377

DENOMINATIONS—*FIRST COINAGE* (1327–1335).

     SILVER : Penny, Halfpenny, Farthing.

     SECOND COINAGE (1335–1343).

     SILVER : Halfpenny, Farthing.

     THIRD COINAGE (1343–1351).

     GOLD : Florin, Half-florin, Quarter-florin, Noble, Half-noble, Quarter-noble.

     SILVER: Penny, Halfpenny, Farthing.

     FOURTH COINAGE.

     Pre-Treaty Period (1351–1361).

     GOLD : Noble, Half-noble, Quarter-noble.

     SILVER : Groat, Halfgroat, Penny, Halfpenny, Farthing.

     Treaty Period (1361–1369).

     GOLD : Noble, Half-noble, Quarter-noble.
     SILVER : Groat, Halfgroat, Penny, Halfpenny, Farthing.

     Post-Treaty Period (1369–1377).

     GOLD : Noble, Half-noble.

     SILVER : Groat, Halfgroat, Penny, Farthing.

Obv. legend: EDWAR D GRA REX ANGL Z FRANC DNS HIB.

(See lists for legends on coins of the Fourth Coinage).

INITIAL CROSSES

Pattée   Cross 1   Cross 1a

Cross 2   Cross 3   Potent   Plain

LETTERING

1	2	3	4	5

6	7	8	9	10

11	12	13	14

15	16	17	18

LETTER E.

1 Open (Series B).

2 Closed (Series C and D).

3 Flat-topped (Series E).

4 Broken (Series E).

5   ,,   (Series E).

6   ,,   (Series F).

7   ,,   (Series Gbc).

8   ,,   (Series Gd).

9 With cross-bar (Series Gg).

10 Open (Series Gh).

LETTER R.

11 Wedge-tailed (Series B and C).

12 Normal (Series D, E and F).

13 Wedge-tailed (Series E).

14 Forked tail (Series E).

LETTER X.

15 Normal.

16 Curule (Treaty).

17 Treaty.

18 St. Andrew's cross (Post-Treaty).

NOTES

The first three coinages of this reign are small and fairly easy to identify, but the vast fourth coinage is far more complex. Basically it is divided into three periods by the Treaty of Bretigni. On the larger coins the French title is used during the Pre-Treaty period; this is changed for that of Duke of Aquitaine for the Treaty period, and both titles are used for the Post-Treaty coinage.

The Pre-Treaty coins are divided into seven sub-classes, and these are identified by means of the initial marks and the lettering. There is much muling between the various sub-classes and these played a most important part in the original classification of the series. In the lists the only mules shown are for classes for which no true coins are known, but a list of the known mules is appended below.

In order to avoid confusion the letters used for sub-classes by L. A. Lawrence in his standard work on the series have been employed in the lists. This accounts for the apparent gap in the letters in some denominations for which no coins of certain sub-classes are known.

The following chart shows some of the striking features found on coins of various classes. The presence of one or more of them will indicate which section of the lists should be consulted.

SERIES	INITIAL MARK	LETTERING	REMARKS
PRE-TREATY			FRENCH TITLE
A	Cross pattée	Round with Lombardic **M** and **N**.	London pence in A to E have an annulet in each quarter.
B	Cross 1	Open **C** and **E**. Roman **M** and **N**. Wedge tail **R**. *Figs.* 1 *and* 11.	
C	Cross 1	Closed **C** and **E**. Lombardic **M**. Roman **N**. Wedge **R**. *Figs.* 2 *and* 11.	
D	Cross 1 or 1a.	Normal **R**. *Figs.* 2 *and* 12.	Roman **E** in **EDWARD** on some half-groats.
E	Cross 2	**C** and **E** broken at bottom. Wedge, forked or normal **R**. *Figs.* 3, 4, 5, 12, 13 *and* 14.	Roman **E** in **EDWARD** on some groats and pence. Annulet in each quarter on some pence.
F	Crown	**C** and **E** broken at top. Normal **R**. *Figs.* 6 *and* 12.	
G	Cross 3	Broad arched **M**. Various forms of **E**. *Figs.* 7, 8, 9 *and* 10.	Eight sub-classes *some* with the following: Gold: Annulet or saltire before **EDWARD**. Silver: Annulet below bust. **TA·S**. **T·A·S**. Annulet or saltire in one quarter. Annulet in each quarter.
TREATY			AQUITAINE TITLE
A	Cross potent	Abnormal sized **I**, **H**, **P**, **F** or **N**.	Gold: Annulets or pellets by central panel. Silver: Annulets on two cusps. Annulet in two top quarters of i.m.
B	Cross potent	Gold—Curule **X** (*Fig.* 16). Silver—Treaty **X** (*Fig.* 17) Curule **X** (very rarely).	Saltire, annulet, nothing, or quatrefoil before **EDWARD** or annulet after **EDWARD**.
POST-TREATY	Cross potent, pattée or plain.	Tall thin lettering. St. Andrew's cross **X** (*Fig.* 18). Reversed **F** for et. Often bar over last **N** in **LONDON** (Silver). Some early gold use Treaty lettering but are distinguished by French title.	FRENCH AND AQUITAINE TITLES Gold: Usually annulet before **ED**. Silver: Row of annulets on breast. Pellets by central lis. Annulet, lis, cross, or quatrefoil on breast.

N.B.—A crescent appears on the forecastle of some later Treaty period and early Post-Treaty period nobles.

MULES
(Occurring in fourth coinage)

Nobles:—B/A, B/C, C/B, C/D, C/E, E/F, E/G, F/E, F/G, G/E, G/F, Ga/Gbc, Ga/Gd, Ga/Gf, Gbc/Gd, Gbc/Gf, Gd/Gf, Gf/Gg, Gg/Gf, Gh/Gg.

Half-nobles:—B/A, C/A, C/E, Gab/Gc, Gab/Gf, Gc/Gab, Gg/Gh, Gh/Gg.

Quarter-nobles:—B/C, B/E, B/G, G/E, Ga/Gd, Gf/Gg.

Groat:—B/C, C/B, B/D, D/C, D/E, E/C, E/D, E/F, E/G, F/E, F/G, G/F, Ga/E, Ga/Gb, Gb/Ga, Ga/Gc, Gb/Gd, Gd/Gc, Gbc/Gef, Gd/Gef, Ge/Gd, Gf/Gd, Gbc/Gg, Gd/Gg, Ge/Gg, Gf/Gg, Gg/Gef, Gh/Gg.

Halfgroat:—B/C, C/B, C/D, D/E, E/D, E/F, E/G, F/E, F/G, Ga/F, Ga/Gb, Ga/Gc, Ga/Ge, Gb/Ga, Gb/Gc, Gb/Gf.

Pence:—A/C, C/A, C/D, D/C, E/F, F/C, F/E, F/G, E/Ga, F/Gb, Gc/Ga, Gb/Ga, Gb/Gc, Gc/Gd, Gc/Gf, Gd/Gh, Gf/Gg.

FIRST COINAGE (1327–1335)

SILVER

Penny[28]
(Class 15d)

Similar to No. 1068 (Class 15c) but with pellet stops on the obverse and usually Lombardic Ns. Coins of York and some of Canterbury have a pellet in the centre of the initial cross and three pellets in one quarter of the reverse.

1095	LONDON—a variety has a Roman N in LON.		ER
1096	CANTERBURY—a variety has a Roman N in DNS.		VR
1097	DURHAM (CIVITAS DUNELMI with Roman or Lombardic N). Small crown in centre of reverse.[29]		VR
1098	YORK—Quatrefoil in centre of reverse. Very rarely four pellets around the initial cross. A variety (ER) has Roman Ns on the obverse.		R
1099	BURY (VILL SCI EDMUNDI).		ER

N.B.—Mint records show that a very small amount of halfpence and a considerable quantity of farthings were struck during this period. They have not been distinguished from coins of those denominations attributed to Edward II and were probably struck from similar (if not the same) dies (cf. n. 22).

SECOND COINAGE (1335–1343)[30]

SILVER

Halfpenny

Standard type " G " usually with a star in the legends. Crown punches of earlier issues used in classes 1–3 are illustrated on p. 37.

LONDON mint.

Class 1	1100/1	AN. Six-pointed star after AN and before LON. Trifoliate crown of No. 1069/1. Unbarred Ns.	ER
Class 2	1100/2	Similar with bifoliate crown of No. 1069/2. Some coins read ANG. Rarely with Lombardic Ns on obverse and/or reverse.	R
Class 3	1100/3	Similar with trifoliate crown of No. 1069/3 (central lis recut during issue). Some coins read ANG. Letter N sometimes barred on obverse and/or reverse; rarely Lombardic (reverse).	N

---

[28] This coinage is examined in detail in SCBI 39, pp. 54–66.
[29] It is uncertain whether these coins were struck by Beaumont or Bury (cf. SCBI 39, pp. 61–2).
[30] Classified in accordance with the arrangement formulated in SCBI 39, pp. 66–78.

Class 4		ANG (star of six or eight points). New tall crude bifoliate crown (except 4d–e). Star on reverse variously placed.	
	1102/1	(a) Star of eight points after DON. Very large G.	C
	1102/2	(b) Star of six points before CIVI. Very large G.	S
	1102/3	(c) No star on reverse. Normal G.	VR
	1102/4	(d) Crown from same punch as class 2. Star before CIVI or none (possibly 4d/c mule).	VR
	1102/5	(e) Crown from same punch as class 1. Star before CIVI.	ER
Class 5	1102/6	No star on obverse. Bifoliate crown (probably an old punch recut). Star of six points before CIVI or LON.	ER

READING mint (Scallop shell in one quarter).

Class 3	1103/1	VILLA (star) RADINGY. Similar to London coins.	ER
Class 4	1103/2	VILLA RADING (star). Similar to London coins (class 4c).	ER
Class 5	1103/3	VILLA RADING (star). Similar to London coins.	ER
Farthing		Standard type G. LONDON mint only.	
Class 1	1101	A(N). Six-pointed star after AN (omitted on a few dies) and before LON. Low crown without intermediate jewels.	N
Class 2	1104	ANG (star). Tall crown. Very large G. Star before LON or after DON.	VR

THIRD (FLORIN) COINAGE (1344–1351)
GOLD

JAN.–AUG. 1344				
Florin	1105	*Obv.*	King enthroned beneath a canopy.	ER
		Rev.	IHC TRANSIENS PER MEDIUM ILLORUM IBAT. Royal cross with a quatrefoil, with a leopard in each angle.	
Half-florin or Leopard	1106	*Obv.*	Leopard sejant with a banner.	ER
		Rev.	DOMINE NE IN FURORE TUO ARGUAS ME. Type as No. 1105.	
Quarter-florin or Helm	1107	*Obv.*	Helm surmounted by a leopard on a fleured field.	ER
		Rev.	EXALTABITUR IN GLORIA. Floriated cross with quatrefoil in centre.	
1344–1346				
Noble	1108		Standard Type " A " with L in centre of reverse cross. Large lettering with Lombardic N. Weight: 136·7 grains.	ER
Quarter-noble	1109		Standard Type " C " with L in centre of reverse cross. Large lettering with Lombardic N. Tressure of six arches on obverse.	ER

1346–1351

Noble 1110 Standard Type " A " with closed **E** in centre of reverse cross. VR
Large lettering with Lombardic **N**. Weight: 128·6 grains.[31]

Half-noble 1111 Standard Type " B " with closed **E** in centre of reverse cross. ER
Large lettering with Lombardic **N**.

Quarter-noble 1112 Standard Type " C " with closed **E** in centre of reverse. Tressure R
of six arches on obverse.

SILVER

Penny Standard Type " G ". Bust has bushy hair, and broad neck
and shoulders. Crown with neat broad fleurs. **EDW (A)
RANGLDNSHYB**.

Key to Reverses:
 I Lombardic **N**s.
 II Roman **N**s.
 III Reversed Roman **N**s.
 IV Reversed double-barred Roman **N**s (doubtful).

LONDON.
Normal Types.
1113[32] Type 1 **EDW**. (Annulet stops, Lombardic **N**). Reverse I. N

1114 Type 2 **EDWA**. (Annulet stops, Lombardic **N**). Reverse I N
and II.

1115 Type 3 **EDW**. (Annulet stops, Roman **N**). Reverse I, II N
and III.

1116 Type 4 **EDW**. (No stops, reversed Roman **N**). Reverse I, N
II, III and IV.

Unusual Types.
1117 Type A **EDW**. (Annulet stops, Lombardic **N**, low crown). VR
Reverse I and II.

1118 Type B **EDW**. (Pellet stops, one Lombardic and one ER
Roman **N**). Reverse I.

1119 Type C **EDWARREXANGLDNSHYB** (No stops. Narrow R
lettering. Reversed Roman **N**s). Reverse I and III.

1120 Type D **EDW**. (Annulet stops, Lombardic **N**. Composite ER
bust). Reverse I.

1121 Type E **EDW**. (Pellet stops, Lombardic **N**). Reverse I. VR

CANTERBURY (Lombardic **N** on reverse).
1122 Type 2 Obverse as No. 1114. VR

1123 Type 4 Obverse as No. 1116. R

---

[31] Light coins from heavy dies exist and may have been struck in accordance with the order of 1351
(cf. NC (1963) 113–6).

[32] Early coins have a crown with hooked petals.

DURHAM[33]

Key to reverses (usually Lombardic M and N):

1. CIVITAS DUNEL (Lombardic M or reversed N). No marks.
2. CIVITAS DUNOLM. No marks.
3. CIVITAS DUNOLM. Pellet in centre of cross.
4. CIVITAS DUNELM. Crozier before CIVI.
5. CIVITAS DUNOLME (H for M). Crozier before CIVI.
6. VILA DUNOLMIE. Crozier after VIL; pellet in centre.[34]

1125	Type 4. Obverse as No. 1116. Reverse 1.	S
1126	EDWAR R ANGL DNS YB (one Lombardic and one reversed Roman N). Reverse 2.	ER
1127	EDWAR R ANG DNS HYB (Lombardic Ns). Reverses 2, 3, 4 and 6.[35]	VR
1124	EDWARDUS REX AIN (Lombardic N). Reverses 4 and 5.	ER

READING

| 1129 | Type 4   Obverse as No. 1116. VILLA RADINGY. Escallop in one quarter. | VR |

YORK

| 1130 | Type 4   Obverse as No. 1116. Quatrefoil in centre of reverse. | S |

Halfpenny   Standard Type " G " with bust similar to Pence.

LONDON

| 1131 | EDWARDUS REX. Two saltires, two pellets or nothing before REX. | N |
| 1132 | EDWARDUS REX AN. Two pellets or nothing before REX. Some have a pellet or small saltire at each side of crown. Often a pellet or small saltire in one quarter of reverse. | N |

READING. VILLA RADINGY. Escallop in one quarter.

| 1133 | EDWARDUS REX. | VR |
| 1134 | EDWARDUS REX AN. (Saltire before N). | VR |

Farthing

| 1135/1 | Standard Type " G " with bust similar to Pence. EDWARDUS REX. LONDON. | R |
| 1135/2 | Similar to No. 1135/1. Reverse as No. 1134. READING. | ER |

FOURTH COINAGE

Pre-Treaty Period (1351–1361)

Obverse legends:

NOBLES: EDWARD DEI GRA REX ANGL Z FRANC D HYB.

HALF-NOBLES: EDWAR D GRA (DEI G) REX ANGL Z FRA (NC) D.

---

[33] BNJ 29 (1958–9) pp. 326–33 and BNJ 30 (1960–1) pp. 363–5.

[34] Coins with the obverse reading EDWARDUS REX ANGLIE and this reverse (No. 1128 in previous editions) are Pre-Treaty A/Florin mules.

[35] This obverse is also found muled with a Pre-Treaty A reverse which reads VILLA DURREM.

QUARTER-NOBLES: EDWAR (D G) R (EX) ANGL Z FRANC (D HYB).

GROATS: EDWARD D G REX ANGL Z FRANC D HYB.

HALFGROATS: EDWARDUS REX ANGL (I) Z FRA (NCI).

PENCE: EDWARDUS REX ANGLI (Z).

On the Nobles and Half-nobles of this period there is a tiny lis by the lion in one quarter of the reverse.

On the groats the cusps above the crown have fleurs in Series B, C, Ga and Ge-f.

SERIES A (1351)

I.m. Cross pattée. Round lettering with Lombardic M and N. Annulet or saltire stops.
(Gold Nobles and Half-nobles are only known as reverse die mules with Series B and C. See below Nos. 1139, 1140, 1145).

SILVER

Penny

Standard Type " G ".

1136	LONDON. Annulet in each quarter.		R
1137	DURHAM (VILLA DURREM). Pellet in centre of reverse and annulet between pellets in each quarter. Crozier after VIL.		VR

SERIES B (1351)

I.m. Cross I. Roman M and N (reversely barred or unbarred), open Lombardic C and E, wedge tailed R. Annulet stops (gold). Pellet, annulet, or no stops (silver).

GOLD

Noble

Standard Type " A " with open E in centre of reverse cross.

1138	Double or single annulet stops. Reverse legend sometimes omits AUTEM or reads IBAT AM.		R
1139	Mule B/A. Reverse has closed inverted E in centre, omits AUTEM, and has double saltire stops and a saltire at each side of lis terminal of cross.		ER

Half-noble 1140 Standard Type " B ". Only known as a mule with a reverse of Series A with closed E in centre of reverse cross.   R

Quarter-noble 1141 Standard Type " C " with pellet below shield. Closed E in centre of reverse cross. Reverse legend sometimes ends A or AN.   S

SILVER

Groat 1142 Standard Type " F ". LONDON only. An early reverse die (probably unique) has a crown in each angle of the reverse instead of three pellets.   R

Halfgroat 1143 Standard Type " F ". LONDON only.   R

SERIES C (1351–1352)

I.m. Cross 1. Lombardic M, closed C and E, Roman N reversely barred, wedge-tailed R. Annulet stops.

GOLD

Noble	1144	Standard Type " A ".	S
Half-noble	1145	Standard Type " B ". Only known as an obverse mule with a reverse of Series A or E.	VR
Quarter-noble	1146	Standard Type " C ". Only known as a reverse mule with an obverse of Series B.	S

SILVER

Groat	1147	Standard Type " F ". Open C in CIVITAS. LONDON only (DI . G, DEI G., D . G).	N
Halfgroat	1148	Standard Type " F ". LONDON only.	C
Penny		Standard Type " G ".	
	1149	LONDON. Annulet in each quarter.	N
	1150	DURHAM (CIVITAS DUNELMIE). Crozier before CIVI.	N

SERIES D (1352–1353)

I.m. Cross 1 or 1a. New plain lettering with small serifs. Lombardic M, closed C and E, Roman N usually unbarred, normal R. Annulet stops. Where Cross 1a is used it is more frequently on the reverse.

GOLD

Noble	1151	Standard Type " A ". Only known as a reverse mule with an obverse of Series C.	ER

SILVER

Groat		Standard Type " F ".	
	1152	LONDON. Sometimes LONDOM, LOMDOM. Some have C for E in EDWARD. (Stops omitted on one die).	N
	1153	YORK. (Normally found as a mule. True coins are ER).	N
Halfgroat		Standard Type " F ".	
	1154	LONDON. Sometimes Roman E or Lombardic C as initial letter in EDWAR.	C
	1155	YORK. Roman E or Lombardic C as initial letter in EDWAR.	R
Penny		Standard Type " G ".	
	1156	LONDON. Annulet in each quarter.	N
	1157	YORK—Royal. No marks on reverse.	N

| | 1158 | YORK—Episcopal. Quatrefoil in centre of reverse. | R |
| | 1159 | DURHAM (CIVITAS DUNELMIE). Crozier before CIVI. | N |

SERIES E (1354–1355)

I.m. Cross 2. Lettering similar to Series D, but C and E are often broken at bottom, and V often has a snick in the right limb. Letter R may be as Series D, wedge-tailed, or with a forked tail. Annulet or saltire stops (gold). Annulet stops (silver).

GOLD

Noble	1160	Standard Type " A ".	N
Half-noble	1161	Standard Type " B ".	ER
Quarter-noble	1162	Standard Type " C " with pellet in centre of reverse cross. Only known as a reverse mule with obverses of Series B or G.	VR

SILVER

Groat		Standard Type " F ".	N
	1163	LONDON. Sometimes LOMDOM, LONDOM, LOMDON. Some have Roman E in EDWARD. Obverses have fleurs or lis on cusps, and some have a lis on the breast. There are also two obverse dies with lettering and a bust of an unusual form (perhaps unofficial).	
	1164	YORK.	N
Halfgroat		Standard Type " F ".	
	1165	LONDON.	N
	1166	YORK. Some have a lis on the breast.	C
Penny		Standard Type " G ".	
	1167	LONDON. One die has a Roman E in EDWARD. Sometimes an annulet between the pellets in each quarter.	N
	1168	YORK—Royal. No marks on reverse.	N
	1169	YORK—Episcopal. Quatrefoil in centre of reverse.	S
	1170	DURHAM (CIVITAS DUNELMIE). Crozier before CIVI.	N
Halfpenny	1171	Standard Type " G ". EDWARDUS REX AN. LONDON only.	VR
Farthing	1172	Standard Type " G ". EDWARDUS REX. LONDON only.	ER

SERIES F (1356)

I.m. Crown. C and E often broken at top. Normal R. Saltire/annulet stops (Gold). Annulet stops (Silver).

GOLD

Noble	1173	Standard Type " A ".	VR

SILVER

Groat	1174	Standard Type " F ". LONDON only—sometimes **LOMDOM**.	N
Halfgroat	1175	Standard Type " F ". Lis on all cusps. LONDON only.	N
Penny		Standard Type " G ".	
	1176	LONDON.	N
	1177	DURHAM (**CIVITAS DUREME**). Crozier before CIVI. (A crude " local " obverse die is sometimes used).	N
Halfpenny	1178	Standard Type " G ". **EDVARDUS REX**. Only known as an obverse mule with a reverse of Series G. Annulet in one quarter of reverse. LONDON only.	ER

SERIES G (1356–1361)

I.m. Cross 3. M with broad arched top, C and E often with a piece cut from the top. Many varietes and mules.

GOLD

Noble		Standard Type " A ".	
	1179	(a) Annulet before **EDWARD**. Small annulet stops/large annulet stops. Large E in centre.	N
	1180	(b) or (c). Small annulet stops or saltire stops with a saltire before **EDWARD**/small or large annulet or saltire stops. Small E in centre.	N
	1181	(d) Large annulet stops or saltire stops with annulet or saltire before **EDWARD**/saltire stops. Pellet or annulet at top end of royal cross.	S
	1182	(f) Saltire stops sometimes with saltire before **EDWARD**. Small E in centre of reverse cross and pellet at each side of lis end of top limb.	N
	1183	(g) Similar to (f) but large E in centre of reverse.	N
Half-noble		Standard Type " B ".	
	1184	(a) or (b). Annulet stops sometimes with an annulet before **EDWAR**.	S
	1185	(c) Mule only. Obverse die of (a) or (b)/saltire stops.	R
	1186	(f) Saltire stops. Pellet at each side of lis end of top limb of royal cross. Trefoil fleurs on reverse in cusp angles.	S
	1187	(g) Mule only. Obverse die of (f) or (h)/late E. Three pellets as fleurs. Sometimes pellet at each side of top lis.	VR
	1188	(h) Open E. Usually a pellet at each side of top lis.	R
Quarter-noble		Standard Type " C ".	
	1189	(a) Mule only.[36] Annulet stops/reverse die of (d).	VR
	1190	(d) Mule only.[36] Obverse die of (a)/saltire stops. Annulet to right of upper lis.	VR

---

[36] Nos. 1189 and 1190 are the same coin entered twice to represent each sub-series.

| 1191 | (f) | or later. Saltire stops. Small E in centre of reverse, and pellet at each side of upper lis. | N |
| 1192 | (g) | Saltire stops. Large E in centre of reverse. Obverses are indistinguishable from No. 1191. | R |

SILVER

Groat

Standard Type " F ". Usually an annulet in one quarter of reverse except (c). LONDON only.

1193	(a)	Annulet stops. Usually an annulet below bust. All arches fleured. Rarely LOMDOM.	N
1194	(b)	Annulet stops. Top arches not fleured. Rarely LOMDOM.	N
1195	(c)	Annulet stops/saltire stops. Usually a saltire in one quarter.	N
1196	(d)	New bust and letters. Large annulet stops. Pellet in TA · S.	S
1197	(e)	Large annulet stops. Pellet over crown. Two pellets in T · A · S.	S
1198	(f)	As (e) without pellet over crown.	S
1199	(g)	Late E (*Fig.* 9). Saltire stops. Lis or cross on neck. Two pellets in T · A · S.	S
1200	(h)	Open E. Saltire stops. Two pellets in T · A · S. (Although excessively rare as a true coin, only scarce as a mule with a Gg reverse).	ER

Halfgroat

Standard Type " F ". Usually an annulet in one quarter of reverse of (a) and (b). LONDON only.

1201	(a)	Annulet stops. Annulet below bust.	N
1202	(b)	Annulet stops.	N
1203	(c)	Mule only. Obverse die of (a) or (b)/saltire stops.	R
1204	(f)	Mule only. Obverse die of (a) or (b)/large annulet stops. Two pellets in T · A · S.	S

Penny

Standard Type " G ". Usually an annulet in one quarter of reverse on (a) and (b).

LONDON.

1205	(a)	Annulet stops. Usually an annulet below bust. Rarely LOMDOM.	N
1206	(b)	Annulet stops. One die has an annulet in each quarter of reverse.	S
1207	(c)	Saltire stops. Usually a saltire in one quarter of reverse.	S
1208	(f)	Mule only.[37] Large annulet stops/reverse die of (g).	S
1209	(g)	Mule only.[37] Obverse die of (f)/saltire stops. Two pellets in T · A · S.	S

YORK (quatrefoil in centre of reverse).

| 1210 | (a) | Small annulet stops. | R |

---

[37] Nos. 1208 and 1209 are the same coin entered twice to represent each sub-series.

1211/1	(c)	Mule only. Saltire stops/reverse die of (d).[38]	ER
1211/2	(d)	Large annulet stops usually with annulet on breast. One pellet in TA·S. (Some coins with an obverse resembling (d) have no pellet in TAS).	N
1212	(f)	Obverse as (d)/two pellets in T·A·S.	N
1213	(g)	Saltire stops with saltire on breast/two pellets in T·A·S.	S
1214	(h)	Open E. Two pellets in T·A·S.	ER

DURHAM (CIVITAS DUREME except h). Crozier before CIVI.

1215	(a)	Annulet stops with annulet on breast. Sometimes an annulet in one quarter.	N
1216	(b)	Small annulet stops.	S
1217	(c)	Saltire stops. One die has a saltire in one quarter.	S
1218	(d)	Large annulet stops.	S
1219	(f)	Annulet stops. Two pellets in T·A·S.	R
1220	(g)	Late E (*Fig.* 9). Saltire stops. One has a trefoil of pellets on breast. Two pellets in T·A·S.	N
1221/1	(h)	Saltire stops. Open E. CIVITAS DURELMIE.	R

N.B.—A variety placed between d and f, and numbered ** by L.A.L. has large annulet stops and a large annulet on each shoulder. It is also known muled with a reverse of Gf.

Farthing 1221/2 Standard Type "G". EDWARDUS REX. Annulet in one   ER
quarter. LONDON only.

Treaty Period (1361–1369)

TRANSITIONAL SERIES (1361–1363)

I.m. Cross potent. Often with letters I, H, P, F and N of abnormal size. Saltire stops.

GOLD

Noble 1222 EDWARD(US) DEI GRA REX ANGLIE DNS HYB Z ACQ.   R
(rarely Z AQUTA DNS . . . or D E). Standard Type "A" with large pellets or annulets at corners of central panel.

Half-noble 1223 EDWARD(US) DEI G REX ANGL (D HIB) or rarely ED DEI   N
GRA REX ANGL DNS HIB Z ACQ. Standard Type "B" with large pellets or annulets at corners of central panel. Some of the latter have an annulet over the crown on obverse.

Quarter-noble 1224 EDWAR DEI GRAC ANGL (D) or rarely EDWR R ANGLIE   N
Z DNUS HY. Standard Type "C" with pellets, annulets or trefoils on cusps of obverse tressure. In centre of reverse, a small cross potent with annulets or large pellets in the angles and in the centre. Varieties of reverse centre are (i) Large E in panel with pellets in angles, (ii) Voided quatrefoil in centre of small cross potent with annulets in its angles, (iii) Large pellet in panel with annulets at angles.

---

[38] cf. BNJ 44 (1974) p. 77.

SILVER

Groat 1225 EDWAR DEI GRAC REX ANGL (D). Standard Type " F " with annulet on cusp at each side of crown which has a high central fleur. LONDON only. R

Halfgroat 1226 EDWARD REX ANGLIE DNS HIB. Standard Type " F " with obverse similar to No. 1225, but seven arches to tressure. LONDON only. R

Penny EDWAR(D) ANGLIE DNS HIB. Standard Type " G ". Annulet in the two upper quarters of the initial cross.

1227 LONDON. VR

1228 YORK. Quatrefoil enclosing pellet in centre of reverse. R

1229/1 DURHAM (CIVITAS DURENE). Large pellet stops. (ANGLE DN). ˉCrozier after CIVI[39]. ER

1229/2 DURHAM (CIVITAS DORELME). Crozier before CIVI. R

Halfpenny 1230/1 EDWARDUS REX AN. Standard Type " G " with two pellets above the inital cross. LONDON only. ER

Farthing 1230/2 EDWARDUS REX ANG. Standard Type " G ". Annulet in one quarter.[40] ER

TREATY SERIES (1363–1369)

I.m. Cross potent. New lettering with curule-shaped X on gold and " Treaty " X (or rarely " curule ") on silver. Often one or all As unbarred.

GOLD

Noble EDWARD DEI GRA REX ANGL DNS HYB Z AQT. Standard Type " A " with double saltire stops.

LONDON (E in centre of reverse).

1231 (a) Saltire before EDWARD. N

1232 (b) Annulet before EDWARD. N

1233 (c) As (b) with crescent on forecastle. R

CALAIS (C in centre of reverse).

1234 (a) Saltire before EDWARD. Some have a flag at stern. R

1235 (b) No mark before EDWARD. Some have a flag at stern. R

1236 (d) Quatrefoil before EDWARD. Flag at stern. R

1237 (e) Annulet after ED. R

Half-noble EDWARD DEI G REX ANGL D HYB Z AQT. Standard Type " B " with double saltire stops.

LONDON (E in centre of reverse).

1238 (a) Saltire before EDWARD. N

---

[39] The reverse is also used with a Treaty obverse (cf. BNJ 44 (1974) pp. 77–8 & SNC 93 (1985) p. 39).

[40] The reverse is probably Pre-Treaty G.

	1239	(b)	Annulet before **EDWARD**.	N

CALAIS (**C** in centre of reverse).

	1240	(a)	Saltire before **EDWARD**. Flag at stern.	VR
	1241	(b)	No mark before **EDWARD**. Some have a flag at stern.	VR
	1242	(d)	Quatrefoil before **EDWARD**. Flag at stern. Sometimes a crescent on forecastle.	VR

Quarter-noble   EDWARD DEI GRA REX ANGL. Standard Type " C " with double saltire stops.

LONDON (Lis in centre of reverse).

	1243	(a)	No mark before **EDWARD**.	N
	1244	(b)	Annulet before **EDWARD**.	N

CALAIS.

	1245		Annulet in centre of reverse with cross in circle or nothing over shield.	R
	1246		Voided quatrefoil in centre of reverse with cross or crescent over shield.	VR

SILVER

Groat   EDWARD D(EI) G REX ANGL D(NS) HYB Z AQT.
Standard Type " F ".

LONDON

	1247	(a)	Double saltire stops.	R
	1248	(b)	Double saltire stops/single saltire stops.	R
	1249	(c)	Single annulet stops/double saltire stops.	R
	1250	(d)	Single annulet stops/single saltire stops.	R
	1251	(e)	Double annulet stops/single saltire stops. (But see i to k).	R
	1252	(f)	Double annulet stops/double saltire stops.	N
	1253	(g)	Stops as (f). Pellet at the tail of the R of **ADIUTOREM**. Sometimes an annulet on breast.	N
	1254	(h)	Stops as (f). Long narrow head with hardly any relief. Coarse lettering.	S
	1255	(i)	Stops as (e). Letters in **AQT** wide apart. Barred **A** in **ADIUTOREM**.	S
	1256	(j)	Stops as (e). Annulet before **EDWARD**. Unbarred **A** in **ADIUTOREM**.	N
	1257	(k)	Stops as (e). Annulet before **EDWARD**. Barred **A** in **ADIUTOREM**.	N

CALAIS (**VILLA CALESIE**).

	1258	(g)	Double annulet stops/double saltire stops. Annulet on king's breast.	R

Halfgroat   EDWARDUS REX ANGL DNS HYB. Standard Type " G " with double annulet stops/double saltire stops.

LONDON.

	1259	(f)	No marks.	N

	1260	(g)	Annulet on breast.	S
	1261	(j)	Annulet before **EDWARDUS**. Unbarred **A** in **ADIUTORE**.	N
	1262	(k)	Annulet before **EDWARDUS**. Barred **A** in **ADIUTORE**.	N

CALAIS.[41]

| | 1263 | (g) | Annulet on breast. | VR |

Penny   **EDWARD ANGL R DNS HYB**. Standard Type " G ".

LONDON.

	1264	(f)	Double annulet stops/saltire or annulet after **DON**. Unbarred **A** in **TAS**.	N
	1265	(k)	Double annulet stops/annulet or nothing after **DON**. Pellet before **EDWARD**. Barred **A** in **TAS**.	N

CALAIS.

| | 1266 | (g) | Double annulet stops/pellet after **LA**. | VR |

YORK. Quatrefoil in centre of reverse.

	1267	**EDWARDUS DEI G REX AN**. Single annulet stops on obverse.	VR
	1268	**EDWARDUS REX ANGLI**. Pellet stops on obverse.	N
	1269	Similar to No. 1268 but voided quatrefoil on breast and before **EDWARDUS**. Some are from local dies.	N
	1270	Similar to No. 1268, with annulet before **EDWARDUS**.	R
	1271	Obverse legend and stops as on London pence. Sometimes a pellet before **EDWARD**.	S

DURHAM.   **EDWARDUS REX ANGLI** (single annulet stops).

	1272/1	**CIVITUS DURENE**. Crozier after **CIVI** (Same die as No. 1229/1).	ER
	1272/2	**CIVITAS DUREME**. Crozier before **CIVI**.	N
	1273	**CIVITAS DUNELMIS**. No crozier.	S

Halfpenny   **EDWARDUS REX AN**. Standard Type " G ". LONDON only.

	1274	(f)	Double pellet stops/pellet after **DON**. Unbarred **A** in **TAS**.	N
	1275	(k)	Annulet stops/annulet after **DON**. Pellet before **EDWARDUS**. Barred **A** in **TAS**.	R

Farthing   1276   **EDWARDUS REX**. Standard Type " G ". Pellet stops. LONDON VR
only.

Post-Treaty Period (1369–1377)

I.m. Cross potent, cross pattée or plain cross. Tall thin lettering with reversed **F** for **ET** (previously **Z**), and **X** shaped like St. Andrew's cross. Saltire stops except on London farthings and some York pence.

---

[41] A die-link with London exists.

GOLD

Noble

EDWARD DEI GRA REX ANGL Z (or Ꝣ) FRA DNS HYB Z (or Ꝣ) AQT. Standard Type " A ".

LONDON.

1277   Same style as Treaty Period with French title added. Annulet   R
before EDWARD. Some have a bowsprit and a crescent on the
ship's forecastle. Treaty Period reverse.

1278   Post-Treaty lettering. Annulet before EDWARD and over sail.   S
Battlemented turrets to ship. Pellet or saltire before E in
centre of reverse. (One die omits the annulet before EDWARD).

CALAIS.[42]

1279   Group I. London obverse die (cf. No. 1277). Annulet before   VR
EDWARD. Crescent on forecastle. Treaty Period reverse with
C in centre.

1280   Group II. Post-Treaty lettering. Battlemented turrets to   ER
ship, flag at stern, and quatrefoil over sail. Reverse dies as
London dies of the Treaty Period (E in centre).

1281   Group III. Obverse as No. 1280. Reverse dies with Post-   S
Treaty lettering and E and pellet in centre.

Half-noble

EDWARD DI GRA REX ANGL Z FRANC D. Standard Type
" A ".

1282   LONDON. Mule only. Treaty obverse No. 1239/Post-Treaty   ER
reverse with E and pellet in centre.

1283   CALAIS. Flag at stern. Voided quatrefoil over sail. E in   ER
centre of reverse. (Those with C in centre are Post-Treaty/
Treaty mules).

SILVER

Groat

Standard Type " F ". LONDON only. Usually a bar over N in
DON.

1284   EDWARD DI G REX ANGL Ꝣ F DNS HIB Ꝣ A.   (Saltire   ER
stops). Four pellets around obverse i.m. Row of annulets
under the bust (Chain mail).

1285   EDWARD DI G REX ANGL Ꝣ FRANC D HIB.   (Double   ER
saltire stops). Initial mark and bust as 1284.

1286   EDWARD DI GRA REX ANGL Ꝣ FRANC (IE).   I.m.   S
Cross pattée. Often a pellet each side of central lis of crown,
or pellet above central lis and at either side of fleur on breast.
One die has a row of pellets across breast.

Halfgroat

Standard Type " F ". LONDON only. Usually a bar over N in
DON.

1287   EDWARD DI GRA REX ANGL Ꝣ FR. Pellet each side of   ER
central lis of crown. Row of pellets on right side of breast
(Chain mail).

---

[42] Nos. 1279–81. cf. BNJ 24 (1941–4) pp. 110–2.

| | | |
| 1288 | EDWARDUS REX ANGL ꟻ FRANC.   Pellet each side of central list of crown. | R |

| 1289 | EDWARD REX ANGL ꟻ FRANC(IE).   Large or small bust. | R |

| 1290 | EDWARDUS REX ANGL ꟻ FRAC.   Small head and long neck. (See also Richard II No. 1324). | S |

Penny   Standard Type " G ".

LONDON.

| 1291 | EDWARD R ANGL ꟻ FRANC.   Pellet on breast.   Or EDWARDUS REX ANGL ꟻ FR.   Nothing on breast.   Roman Ns usually reversed in LONDON. | R |

| 1292 | EDWARDUS REX ANGLIE.   Cross, annulet, quatrefoil, or nothing on breast.   Lombardic, reversed Roman, or unbarred Roman Ns in LONDON.   Usually extra pellets on reverse. | R |

YORK.   Quatrefoil in centre of reverse.   Sometimes a plain cross before CIVI, and rarely extra pellets on reverse.

| 1293 | EDWARD REX ANGL ꟻ FR(ANC).   Double annulet, large pellet, or saltire stops.   Some have a cross or annulet on the breast. | N |

| 1294 | EDWARD DI GRA REX ANG.   Saltire stops. | S |

| 1295 | EDWARDUS REX ANGLIE (ET).   Saltire stops.   Usually an annulet (sometimes a cross or nothing) on breast.   One die has a lis on breast and small pellet stops.   Another die has a cross and four pellets as initial mark. | N |

DURHAM (CIVITAS DUNOLM).   Reverse i.m.   Plain cross. Crozier before i.m.

| 1296 | EDWARDUS REX ANGL ꟻ FR.   Mixed stops (double annulets and saltires. | S |

| 1297 | EDWARDUS REX ANGLIE.   Annulet, lis, or nothing on breast. | N |

Farthing   EDWARD REX ANGL.   Standard Type " G " with head without neck.   Pellet stops.   LONDON only.

| 1298 | Lombardic Ns. | ER |

| 1299 | Roman Ns.   Reversed/unbarred. | ER |

RICHARD II

1377–1399

DENOMINATIONS—GOLD : Noble, Half-noble, Quarter-noble.

SILVER : Groat, Halfgroat, Penny, Halfpenny, Farthing.

Obv. legend: RICARD DEI GRA REX ANGL Z FRANC DNS HIB Z AQT.

BUSTS

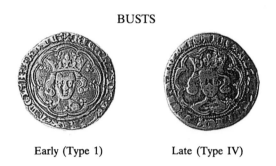

Early (Type 1)   Late (Type IV)

MARKS

Crescent	Escallop	Lion	Lis	Trefoil

Quatrefoil	Quatrefoil (voided)

LETTERING

As Edward III	I	N	R	X	𝔥 (ET)
Type I (Straight sided)	I	N	R	X	Ƨ (ET)
Type II (Fishtail)	I	N	R	X	
Type III (Small irregular) —mixed with other types	I I	N	R	X	

NOTES

The nobles and half-nobles are classified by the four types of lettering found thereon, specimens of which are shown above. Although there are variations in the lettering on the quarter-nobles, the distinction is not so systematic and it is usual to divide them by the symbol in the centre of the reverse cross. The lettering on the silver also varies, but other criteria are used for its classification (cf. BNJ 29 (1958–9) p. 334 and BNJ 31 (1962) p. 88).

GOLD

Noble   Standard Type " A ".

LONDON.

1300	With obverse or reverse die of Edward III, usually altered to **RICARD** or shewing R over E in centre of reverse.	VR
1301	Lettering of Edward III. Lis over sail.	VR
1302	Lettering I. Annulet over sail. With or without French title. Sometimes four pellets about the initial cross.	S
1303	Lettering II. Variants: 1. No marks. Without French title; 2. Lis on rudder; 3. Lion on rudder; 4. Trefoil by shield. Some have annulets instead of quatrefoils at forecastle.	R
1304	Lettering III. Variants: 1. Escallop on rudder; 2. Trefoil over sail. Without French title; 3. Crescent on rudder. Some of 1 and 2 have trefoil by shield.	R

CALAIS. Flag at stern.

1305	As No. 1300.	VR
1306	Lettering I. Voided quatrefoil over sail. With or without French title. One specimen possibly has an annulet on the rudder.	R
1307	Lettering II. Variants: 1. No marks; 2. Lion on rudder, sometimes with a pellet above and/or below the shield. With or without French title.	R
1308	Lettering III. Variants: 1. Escallop on rudder; 2. Trefoil over sail. Without French title; 3. Crescent on rudder.	R

Half-noble   Standard Type " B ".

LONDON.

1309	As No. 1300. One die has an annulet over the sail.	VR
1310	Lettering I. Annulet over the sail.[43]	R
1311	Lettering II. Lion on rudder (sometimes annulet stops on reverse).	R
1312	Lettering III. Crescent on rudder.	VR

CALAIS. Flag at stern.

1313	As No. 1300.	VR
1314	Lettering I. Voided quatrefoil over sail.	VR
1315	Lettering II. Lion on rudder.	R

[43] Known as a mule with Edward III reverse (No. 1282). The obverse die is possibly an altered Edward III obverse (cf. Doubleday colln. Lot 314).

1316	Lettering III. Variants: 1. Escallop on rudder; 2. Trefoil over sail; 3. Crescent on rudder; 4. Saltire behind rudder.	VR

Quarter-noble Standard Type " C ". French title usually omitted.

1317	R in centre of reverse. Nothing over shield.	VR
1318	Lis in centre of reverse. Variants (over shield): 1. Quatrefoil; 2. Slipped trefoil; 3. Cross; 4. Nothing—sometimes four pellets about the initial cross.	S
1319	Pellet in centre of reverse. Variants (over shield): 1. Trefoil of annulets; 2. Escallop; 3. Quatrefoil; 4. Nothing. (Obverse die of Edward III altered to RICARD.)	R

SILVER

Groat Standard Type " F ". LONDON only.

1320	Early bust as Edward III.	
	(a) Type 1. Copula **Ⴈ**. Lettering as Edward III.	VR
	(b) Type II. Copula **Ƽ**. New regular lettering.	VR
1321	New busts with hair wide at left or both sides. New waisted lettering with curved serifs.	
	(a) Type III.	VR
	(b) Type IV. New crown. Crescent on breast.	ER

Halfgroat[44] Standard Type " F ". LONDON only.

1322	Type II. Similar to No. 1320(b) with or without FR(ANC).	S
1323	Type III. Similar to No. 1321(a). Without French title except one die reading FRA.	ER
1324	Obverse dies of Edward III muled with reverse dies of No. 1323. (This coin may have been struck in the reign of Henry IV— Trans. I.N.C. (1936) pp. 362–3.)	VR

Penny Standard Type " G ".

LONDON.

1325	Type 1a. Early bust. RICARDUS without French title. Reversed Roman Ns in LONDON.	VR
1326	Type Ia. Early bust. RICARDUS with French title. Lis on breast. Reversed Roman Ns in LONDON.	VR
1327	Type IV. Late bust. RICARD without French title. One die has a quatrefoil after obverse legend. Lombardic Ns in LONDON.	VR

DURHAM (DUNOLM).

1328	Type Ia. Early bust. Lis or cross on breast.	

YORK (EBORACI). Quatrefoil in centre of reverse.

1329	London dies.	
	(a) Type Ia. RICARDUS REX ANGLIE. Lis, cross or nothing on breast.	C

---

[44] Possible Type IV halfgroats purporting to have a crescent on the breast were published in BNJ 29 (1958–9) p. 347 and BNJ 30 (1960–1) p. 149. Both were in worn condition and a better specimen from the same obverse die shows that there is no crescent (BNJ 34 (1965) p. 168).

(b)	Type Ib. **RICARDUS REX ANGLIE Z.** Pellets by shoulder. Cross on breast.	VR
(c)	Type IIa. **RICARDUS REX ANGLIE.** No marks on breast. Breastline indicated.	R
(d)	Type IIb. Similar to (c) but without breastline.	N
(e)	Type IIIa. **RICARD REX ANGL Z FRAN.** " Coarse " bust. Mark after **TAS.**[45]	R
(f)	Type IIIb. Similar but " fine " bust.	R
(g)	Type IV. **RICARD REX ANGLIE** or **RICARDUS REX ANGL Z F.** " Bushy hair " bust.[46]	S

1330 Local dies. Cross (usually with pellets by shoulders) or nothing on breast.

(a)	Group A. **RICARDUS REX ANGLIE.**	S
(b)	Group B. **RICARDUS REX ANGLE.**	S
(c)	Group C. **RICARDUS REX ANGILE.** Some reverse legends have retrograde **E** or **EB.**	S
(d)	Group D. **RICARDUS REX ANGILIE.**	VR
(e)	Group E. **RICARDUS REX ANG(L) FRAN.**	R
(f)	Group F. **RICARDUS REX ANGL DNS EB.**	R

Halfpenny   Standard Type " G ". LONDON only.

1331 Early bust.
RICARD REX ANGL (Types I and II).

(a)	Early. Annulet or saltire on breast. Reversed Roman **N**s.	N
(b)	Intermediate. Nothing on breast. Lombardic **N**s or (rarely) normal Roman **N**s on reverse.	C

1332 Late bust.

(a)	Type III. **RICARD REX (ANGL (F)** or **ANGLIE).** Tall thin " fish-tail " lettering.	S
(b)	Type IV. **RICARD REX ANGL(I).** Thicker and dumpier lettering. Taller thinner bust.	R
(c)	Type V. **RICARD REX ANGL F.** Round face and sloping shoulders.	ER

Farthing   Standard Type " G ". LONDON only.

1333 Early bust (Small head with slight bust). Usually double pellet stops. (rarely a rose after **REX**).[47] Roman or Lombardic **N**s in **LONDON.**

(a)	**RICARDUS REX ANGL.**	VR
(b)	**RICARD REX ANGL.**	VR

1334 Late bust (Large head without bust). **ANGL(IE).** Lombardic **N**s in **LONDON.** | VR

Farthing **1335** *Obv.* **RICARD . REX . ANGL.** Crowned bust facing. | ER
                Rev. **CIVITAS LONDON.** Long, cross pattée; in each angle, a rose.

---

[45] This mark has been variously described as an escallop or a flaming sun (cf. BNJ 48 (1978) p. 110).

[46] There appears to be a letter R in the centre of the quatrefoil on the reverse (cf. BNJ 48 (1978) pp. 110–1).

[47] R. C. Lockett Sale Lot 1360, where the rose is not clearly visible and may be two pellets.

HENRY IV

1399–1413

DENOMINATIONS—*HEAVY COINAGE.*

GOLD : Noble, Half-noble, Quarter-noble.

SILVER : Halfgroat, Penny, Halfpenny, Farthing.

LIGHT COINAGE.

GOLD : Noble, Half-noble, Quarter-noble.

SILVER : Groat, Halfgroat, Penny, Halfpenny, Farthing.

Obv. legend: HENRIC DI GRA REX ANGL Z FRANC DNS HIB Z AQ.

BUSTS (*HEAVY COINAGE*).

Early	Late	Early	Late
York Pence		Halfpence	

MARKS

| Annulet | Coronet | Crescent | Lis | Star |

| Trefoil | Do. (Slipped) |

NOTES

The coinage of this reign is divided into two sections by the reduction in the weights of the coins in 1412. The crescent, coronet, star, and pellet are used on the heavy coins, whilst the light are distinguished by the trefoil, annulet, and pellet.

Despite their rarity, examples of each denomination of the heavy coinage, with the exception of the groat, have survived. It is possible that none of these was struck, as altered dies of Richard II were used to strike light groats.

The true arrangement of the halfpence appears to be more complex than the generally accepted one, which has been used in the lists. They are examined by E. J. Harris in SNC 96 (1988) pp. 79–80, where seven styles of portrait are distinguished and illustrated. Owing to the rarity of the coins and the impossibility of deciding accurately by weight about small coins, students prefer to leave the question open and judge from individual examples. However, it would appear that heavy dies were used to strike light coins, and the annulets by the bust on the light halfpence are found in three positions. In the Lockett sale (Lot 1373), a halfpenny with annulets by the neck, and weighing 8·4 grains, was attributed to the heavy coinage.

A quick, though not infallible, distinction between the bust of this reign and those of subsequent Henries is the absence of sidelocks of hair by the crown. It must be remembered, however, that a number of dies of this reign, altered by the addition of a mullet or other symbol, were used by Henry V. There is also some muling between the two reigns in the silver coinage, especially the groats.

HEAVY COINAGE (1399–1412)

(Noble : 120 grains.   Penny : 18 grains).

GOLD

Noble

Standard Type "A" with H (sometimes over R) in centre of reverse cross. The French arms on the shield vary as follows: 1. Four lis. 2. Three lis—one above and two below. 3. Three lis—two above and one below.

LONDON.

1336	Type I. Crescent on rudder.	
	(a) Shield 1.	VR
	(b) Shield 2.	ER
1337/1	Type II. Lis on rudder. Broken annulet stops. Shield 3. Lis over head of lion in second quarter of reverse.	ER
1337/2	Type III. Pellet on rudder. Shield 3. Saltire at tail of lion in second quarter of reverse.	ER

CALAIS. Flat at stern.

1338	Type I. Coronet vertically to left of rudder. Shield 1.	ER
1339/1	Type II. Coronet horizontally on rudder.	
	(a) Shield 1.	ER
	(b) Shield 3.	ER
1339/2	Type III. Star on rudder. Shield 3.	ER

Half-noble

Standard Type "B" with H in centre of reverse cross.

LONDON.

1340	Probably no mark on rudder. Shield 1.	ER
1341	Perhaps crescent on rudder. Shield 2.	ER

CALAIS. Flag at stern.

1342	No mark on rudder. Shield 2.	ER

Quarter-noble

Standard Type "C" with pellet in centre of reverse cross.

LONDON. Crescent above shield.

1343	Shield 1.	VR
1344	Shield 2.	ER

CALAIS. Coronet initial mark on reverse.

1345	Shield 2.	ER

SILVER

Halfgroat

1346	Standard Type "F" with star on breast. Unbarred Ns in LONDON. Initial mark: Cross pattée.	ER

Penny		Standard Type " G ". Initial mark: Cross pattée.

LONDON.

1347	Obverse die of Richard II with name mutilated. Reverse die of Henry IV with extra pellet in two quarters.	ER
1348	Bust with long neck, star on breast, two pellets over central fleur of crown. Sometimes extra pellet in two quarters. Lombardic or Roman Ns in LONDON.	ER
1349	Bust with short neck. Sometimes extra pellets in two quarters. Lombardic Ns in LONDON.	ER

YORK. Quatrefoil in centre of reverse.

1350	Early style. Long neck. Square chin.	VR
1351	Late style. Oval face.	VR

Halfpenny   Standard Type " G ". LONDON only (Lombardic Ns).

1352	Early style. Small bust.	R
1353	Late style. Larger bust with rounded shoulders.	R

Farthing	1354	Standard Type " G ". Large face without bust. LONDON only (Lombardic Ns).	VR

LIGHT COINAGE (1412–1413)

(Noble : 108 grains. Penny : 15 grains).

GOLD

Noble	1355	Standard Type " A " with trefoil in one quarter of reverse. Trefoil or trefoil and annulet on ship's side. LONDON only.	VR
Half-noble	1356	Standard Type " B " with trefoil in one quarter of reverse. Trefoil and annulet on side of ship. LONDON only.	ER
Quarter-noble	1357	Standard Type " C " with lis above shield and in centre of reverse cross. Trefoils or trefoils and annulets at sides of shield. LONDON only.	VR

SILVER

Groat   Standard Type " F " with trefoil on breast and usually in reverse legend. LONDON only.

1358	Type I. Altered dies of Richard II. French title omitted. Annulet to right and pellet to left of crown.	ER
1359	Dies of Henry IV. Legend ends FRANC. Annulet to left and pellet to right of crown.	
	(a) Type II. Eight or ten arches in tressure.	ER
	(b) Type III. Normal tressure of nine arches usually slipped tressure at end of legend. One die reads FRANCIE.	ER

Halfgroat   Standard Type " F ". LONDON only.

1360	Type I. Pellet to left and annulet to right of crown.	ER
1361	Type III. Annulet to left and pellet to right of crown.	ER

Penny Standard Type " G ".

LONDON.

1362 Type I. Pellet to left and annulet to right of crown. Slipped ER trefoil on breast. Lombardic Ns in LONDON.

1363 Annulet to left and pellet to right of crown. Slipped trefoil on breast. Reversed or unbarred Roman Ns in LONDON.

    (a) Type II. Large bust with short neck and long hair. One VR die reads HENRIC DI GRA REX ANGL.

    (b) Type III. Small bust with short hair. Slipped trefoil VR before CIVI.

YORK. Quatrefoil in centre of reverse.

1364 Annulet on breast and after HENRIC. Annulet stops on R reverse.

DURHAM (DUNOLM).

1365 Trefoil on breast. R

Halfpenny Standard Type " G ". LONDON only.

1366 Struck from heavy dies. R

1367 Light dies. Whole or broken annulets beside crown, or neck. R One die has two pellets to right of neck.

Farthing 1368 Standard Type " G ". Small face without bust. Slipped trefoil ER after REX. Roman Ns in LONDON (? LOIDOI). LONDON only.

HENRY V

1413–1422

DENOMINATIONS—GOLD : Noble, Half-noble, Quarter-noble.

SILVER : Groat, Halfgroat, Penny, Halfpenny, Farthing.

BUSTS

1. Emaciated
Class A

2. Scowling
Class B

3. Frowning
Class C, etc.

4. New
(Halfgroats et infra)
Class G

MARKS

Cross pattée   Pierced cross
with central pellet

Broken   Lis   Mullet   Quatrefoil   Trefoil
annulet

LETTERING

Class A

Class B Early

Late

Class C onwards
(sometimes large
C, E, I, on early)

Obv. legend: HENRIC DI GRA REX ANGL Z FRANC DNS HYB.

NOTES

In his article on the privy marks of this reign, Brooke divided the coinage into nine classes. Subsequently he amended this in his " English Coins " to seven classes by combining Classes II and III into Class B, and IV and V into C. As this simpler classification has found favour amongst the majority of numismatists, it is used here, amended to conform with the most recent researches (cf. BNJ 30 (1960–1) pp. 136–49).

A selection of the lettering found on the first three classes is given above, as this forms an important feature in distinguishing certain coins. During the large Class C the lettering was used extensively for privy marking, and a variety of broken forms of the letters H, N, and P exist.

The majority of coins of this reign are distinguished and classified by marks in the field. Dies of Henry IV, which have been altered by the addition of symbols of Henry V, are used in the early issues, and muling between the reigns occurs. Classes A and B without the mullet added may have been struck during the reign of Henry IV.

GOLD

Noble

Standard Type " A " with quatrefoil over sail and in upper right quarter of reverse.

1369	Class A Short broad lettering.		ER
1370	Class B Ordinary lettering, sometimes with annulet on rudder.		VR
1371	Class C Mullet by sword arm, annulet on rudder, or subsequently broken annulet on ship's side.		S
1372	Class D Mullet and annulet by sword arm, trefoil by shield, broken annulet on ship's side.		S
1373	Class E Pellet at sword point, annulet or trefoil on ship's side, trefoil by shield, unbroken annulet and sometimes also mullet by sword arm.		R
1374	Class F No pellet at sword point, trefoil by shield, annulet or trefoil on ship's side. Mullet and sometimes also annulet by sword arm.		R
1375	Class G No marks in field, no quatrefoil on obverse or reverse. Annulet stops with mullet after first word.		ER

Half-noble

Standard Type " B .

1376	Class B Ordinary lettering, quatrefoil above sail. Known only from an obverse die muled with a reverse of Henry IV.		ER
1377	Class C *Early*. Nothing at sword arm, quatrefoil below sail, broken annulet on ship's side.		ER
	Later. Mullet above shield, no quatrefoil, broken annulet on on ship's side an in upper right quarter of reverse.		
1378	Class E Pellet in upper left, unbroken annulet in upper right quarter of reverse. Sometimes without trefoil in spandrels or without initial mark. Known only as mules with obverse of Class F.		VR
1379	Class F. Mullet above shield, usually trefoil between shield and prow, ropes 2/1, no annulet on ship's side. Muled with reverses of Class E.		VR
1380	Class G Style as No. 1375 above but with a quatrefoil above sail and Z is flanked by saltire stops on obverse. Annulet or mullet stop after first word on reverse.		VR

Quarter-noble		Standard Type " C " with lis above shield and in centre of reverse.	
	1381/1	Class A Short broad lettering. Quatrefoil and annulet at each side of shield, large trefoils on points of tressure. Stars at angle of central panel on reverse.	R
	1381/2	Class B Ordinary lettering (Small C, E and I). Quatrefoil and annulet beside shield, lis above. Trefoils at angles of central panel on reverse.	ER
	1382	Class C Marks in field as No. 1381 but lettering of Class C. Also with mullet below shield to right, no annulets beside shield, annulets on points of tressure. Trefoils at angles of central panel on reverse. Also with broken annulet to left and mullet to right of shield. Unbroken annulet also known.	S
	1383	Class F Trefoil to left, mullet to right of shield.	R
	1384	Class G No marks in field, mullet after first, and annulet after second word.	R

SILVER

Groat		Standard Type " F ".	
	1385	Class A " Emaciated " bust (no neck). Short broad lettering. Initial cross: Broad pattée with central pellet. Quatrefoil after **HENRIC** and **POSUI**. Fleurs over crown. (Sometimes muled with Henry IV reverse.)	VR
	1386	Class B " Scowling " bust (depressed corners to mouth). Ordinary lettering. Initial cross: Pierced with pellet in centre. Early and a few late coins have quatrefoil after **HENRIC**. Early coins have fleured cusps over crown. (Shares reverse dies with Class A.)	R
	1386/1	Old dies with mullet added to right breast. (a) Die of Henry IV. (b) Dies of Class B. One die has the mullet on the breast cusp.	ER ER
	1387	Class C " Frowning " bust. Usually a mullet on the right breast. (a) Type 1. Initial cross with pellet centre. Quatrefoil after **HENRIC**. (b) Type 2. Initial cross with sunk centre. No quatrefoil after **HENRIC**. (c) Legend ends **FRANIE**.[48]	N N VR
	1388	Class G Similar to No. 1387(c) but no mullet and legend ends **FRANC**.[48]	VR

Halfgroat		Standard Type " F ".	
	1389	Class A Similar to No. 1385 with annulet and pellet or nothing by crown.	ER

---

[48] Nos. 1387(c) and 1388 are primarily distinguished by the letter N which has no serif at the top of the upright in Class G (cf. BNJ 30 (1960–1) p. 145–N9).

1390	Class B Ordinary lettering. No marks. Found muled with Henry IV and Class C dies.	VR
1391	Class C Bust with tall neck with oval swelling, broken annulet to left of crown. Mullet on right shoulder, in centre of breast, or none.	
	(a) Initial cross with pellet centre. (A mule with a Richard II reverse is known.)	N
	(b) Initial cross with sunk centre. Shorter neck and spread shoulders. 1 die has a broken annulet on each side of crown.	N
1392	Class F Trefoil to right and annulet to left of crown, mullet on breast.	R
1393	Class G No marks. New neat bust with hollow neck and armpits. Found muled with Henry VI reverse.	S

Penny

Standard Type " G ".

LONDON.

1394	Class A Short broad lettering. " Emaciated " bust. Annulet to left and pellet to right of crown. Annulet before LON.	VR
1395	Old dies with mullet punched over pellet to right of crown.	ER
	(a) Die of Henry IV.	
	(b) Die of Class A.	
1396	Class C Ordinary lettering. Bust with a tall neck with an oval swelling. Mullet to left and broken annulet to right of crown.	N
1397	Class D Similar to Class C but whole annulet to right of crown.	N
1398	Class F Similar to Class C but trefoil to right of crown.	N
1399	Class G No marks. Bust as on No. 1393.	N

YORK (EBORACI).   Quatrefoil in centre of reverse.

1400	Class C Similar to No. 1396.	N
1401	Class D Similar to No. 1397.	N
1402	Class E Similar to No. 1397 with pellet above the mullet.	S
1403	Class F Similar to No. 1397 with trefoil above the mullet, or with mullet to left and trefoil to right of crown.[49]	N
1404	Class G Bust as on No. 1393 with mullet to left and trefoil to right of crown. Local dies exist with mullet to left and lis to right of crown and an annulet in one quarter of the reverse.	N

DURHAM (DUNOLM).

1405	Class C Similar to No. 1396.	N
1406	Class D Similar to No. 1397.	N
1407	Class G Bust as on No. 1393 with mullet to left and annulet to right of crown and an annulet in one quarter of the reverse.	S

Halfpenny

Standard Type " G ". LONDON only.

1408	Class A " Emaciated " bust. Annulets beside crown.	VR

---

[49] Most coins are from local dies of coarse work.

	1408/1	Altered obverse die of Henry IV with annulet to left and mullet over annulet to right of crown.	ER
	1409	Class c Ordinary bust with broken annulets by crown.	C
	1410	Class d Similar, but left annulet unbroken.	C
	1411	Class f Annulet to right and trefoil to left of crown (or vice versa).	N
	1412	Class g Bust as on No. 1393. Widely separated pellets on reverse. Usually muled with Henry VI dies.	VR
Farthing	1413	Standard Type " G ". Small face and neck, no special marks. Difficult to distinguish classes owing to small size. LONDON only.	VR

HENRY VI

1422–1461

DENOMINATIONS—**GOLD**: **Noble, Half-noble, Quarter-noble.**

SILVER: **Groat, Halfgroat, Penny, Halfpenny, Farthing.**

Obv. legend: HENRIC DI GRA REX ANGL Z FRANC DNS HYB.

INITIAL CROSSES

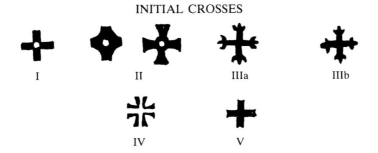

DISTINGUISHING MARKS

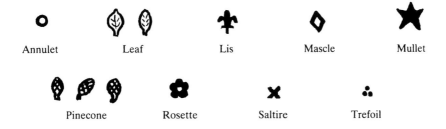

Annulet   Leaf   Lis   Mascle   Mullet

Pinecone   Rosette   Saltire   Trefoil

NOTES

The coinage of this reign divides into eleven classes named after the principal symbols, which are found either in the field of the coin or used as stops in the legend. There is considerable muling in the early issues especially between the Annulet and Rosette-Mascle issues. The various initial crosses are illustrated above and the Roman numbering in the lists refers to these.

I. ANNULET (1422–1427)

GOLD

Noble

Standard Type " A " with an annulet by sword-arm and in one spandrel on reverse. Initial mark: Lis.
Obv. stops: Trefoil with lis after HENRIC.
Rev. stops: Annulets with mullet after IHC.

1414	LONDON.		N
1415	CALAIS (Flat at stern). C or H in centre of reverse cross.		S
1416	YORK (Lis at stern).		S

Half-noble		Standard Type " B " with marks and stops as on No. 1414.	
	1417	LONDON.	N
	1418	CALAIS (Flag at stern). C or H in centre of reverse cross.	R
	1419	YORK (Lis at stern).	S

Quarter-noble

Standard Type " C " with lis in centre of reverse cross. Initial mark: Lis.
Obv. stops: Trefoils with lis after **HENRIC**.
Rev. stops: Annulets or mullet and annulet.

	1420	LONDON. Large initial mark. One lis above shield with trefoil, pellet, or nothing below.	N
	1421	CALAIS. Large initial mark with three lis about shield, or small initial mark with one lis above shield.	S
	1422	YORK. Large initial mark with two lis above shield.	S

SILVER

Groat[50]

Standard Type " F " with an annulet in two quarters of reverse. Old bust (wide forehead, stern look). Fleur on breast.

	1423	LONDON. Crosses I/I, II/II (sometimes without fleur on breast).	N
	1424	CALAIS. Annulets by bust. Crosses I/I, II/II (varieties have nothing on breast, no annulets on reverse).	C
	1425	YORK. Lis beside bust. Crosses II/II.	VR

Young bust (oval smiling face, prominent arched eyebrows). Nothing on breast.

	1426	LONDON. Crosses II/II, II/V (trefoil to left of crown).	N
	1427	CALAIS. Annulets by bust. Crosses II/II (varieties have no annulets on reverse, or a trefoil to left of crown).	C

Halfgroat

Standard Type " F " with an annulet in two quarters of reverse.

	1428	LONDON. Crosses I/None, II/None, V/None, V/V.	N
	1429	CALAIS. Annulets by bust. Crosses I/None, II/None, V/None, V/V (varieties have no annulets on reverse, one annulet under **CALI**, or a trefoil to left of crown).	C
	1430	YORK. Lis by bust. Crosses II/II.	ER

Penny

Standard Type " G " with annulet in two quarters of reverse. Initial cross on obverse only.

	1431	LONDON. Crosses I, II, V.	N
	1432	CALAIS. Annulets by neck. Crosses I, II, V. (Varieties have annulet under **CAL**, and trefoil to left of crown with or without annulet under **CAL**.)	N
	1433	YORK. Lis by bust. Cross II.	ER

---

[50] Details of the two portraits are given in BNJ 28 (1955–7) pp. 299–300.

Halfpenny		Standard Type " G " with annulet in two quarters of reverse. Initial cross on obverse only.	
	1434	LONDON. Crosses I, II, V.	S
	1435	CALAIS. Annulets by bust. Crosses I, II, V.	N
	1436	YORK. Lis by bust. Cross II.	ER
Farthing		Standard Type " G ". Initial cross (on obverse only): Pommée.	
	1437	LONDON.	VR
	1438	CALAIS. Annulets by neck.	ER

ROSETTE-MASCLE (1427–1430)

As the stops in this issue are very varied, they have been given in detail for each coin. The issue started with rosette stops only and the mascle was adopted as an additional mark later during the coinage.

GOLD

Noble		Standard Type " A " with lis by sword-arm and in second quarter of reverse.	
	1439	LONDON. Stops: Rosettes or rosettes and mascle.	VR
	1440	CALAIS (Flag at stern). Stops: Rosettes/Rosettes and mascle.	VR
Half-noble		Standard Type " B " with lis in second quarter of reverse. Initial mark (Rev.): Lis.	
	1441	LONDON. Stops: Rosettes and mascles.	VR
	1442	CALAIS (Flag at stern). Stops: Rosettes.	VR
Quarter-noble		Standard Type " C " with lis in centre of reverse cross. Initial mark: Lis.	
	1443	LONDON. With or without lis over shield. Stops: Rosettes and mascle/Rosettes or rosette and mascle.	VR
	1444	CALAIS. Lis above and rosettes at sides of shield. Stops: Rosettes.	VR

SILVER

Groat		Standard Type " F ".	
	1445	LONDON. Stops: Saltires, rosettes saltires and mascle, or rosettes and mascle/Rosettes saltire and mascle. Crosses: II/V, IIIa/V.	N
	1446	CALAIS. Stops: Saltires, rosettes, or both with or without mascle/Rosettes and saltires usually with mascle. Crosses II/V (sometimes with mascle in two spandrels) IIIa/V, IIIb/V.	C
Halfgroat		Standard Type " F ".	
	1447	LONDON. Stops: Saltires, or rosettes and mascle/Rosettes saltire and mascle. Crosses: V/V, IIIa/V, IIIb/V.	S

1448   CALAIS. Stops: Rosettes, saltires, or rosette and mascles/   C
Rosettes and saltires usually with mascle. Crosses: v/v
(sometimes with mascle in two spandrels), IIIa/v, IIIb/v.

Penny   Standard Type " G ". Initial cross on obverse only.

1449   LONDON. Stops: Saltires and mascle, or rosette and mascle/   R
Rosette and mascle. Cross IIIb.

1450   CALAIS. Stops: Saltires, or rosette and mascle/Saltires rosette   N
and mascle. Crosses: v, IIIa, IIIb.

1451   YORK (quatrefoil in centre of reverse). Cross IIIb.   N
(i)   Crosses by hair. Stops: Saltires and mascle/Mascle.
(ii)   Saltires by hair. Stops: Saltires and mascle/Mascle.
(iii)   Mullets by crown. Stops: Rosette and mascle, or mullet
and mascle/Mascle, rosette and mascle, or none.

1452   DURHAM (**DUNOLMI**). Star to left of crown. Stops: Saltires   R
and mascle/None. Cross v.

Halfpenny   Standard Type " G ". Initial cross on obverse only.

1453   LONDON. Stops: Saltires, saltires and mascle, rosette and   S
mascle, or mascles/Rosette, mascle, rosette and mascle, or
none. Crosses: v, IIIa, IIIb.

1454   CALAIS. Stops: Rosette and mascle/Saltire and rosette, or   N
rosette and mascle. Crosses: v, IIIa, IIIb.

Farthing   Standard Type " G ". Initial cross on obverse only.

1455   LONDON. Stops: Rosette after **LON**. Cross IIIb.   VR

1456   CALAIS. Stops: Rosette and mascle both sides. Cross pommée.   VR

PINECONE-MASCLE (1430–1434)

GOLD

Noble   1457   Standard Type " A " with lis in second or third quarter of   VR
reverse. Stops: Pinecones and mascles. Initial mark (Rev.):
Lis. LONDON only.

Half-noble   1458   Standard Type " B " Initial mark (reverse): Lis. Obverse   ER
stops: Rosettes and mascles. Reverse stops: Pinecones and
mascles. LONDON only.

N.B.—No true half-noble of this series is known, the above being a mule.

Quarter-noble   1459   Standard Type " C " with lis in centre of reverse cross and above   ER
shield on obverse. Initial mark: Lis. Stops: Pinecones and
mascles. LONDON only.

SILVER

Groat   Standard Type " F ". Stops: Pinecones and mascles with some
saltires on the reverse.

1460   LONDON. Crosses IIIa/v, IIIb/v, IIIb/None.   N

1461   CALAIS. Crosses IIIa/v, IIIb/v.   N

Halfgroat		Similar to groat.	
	1462	LONDON. Crosses IIIa/v, IIIb/v.	R
	1463	CALAIS. Crosses IIIb/v.	S

Penny Standard Type " G ". Stops: Pinecones and mascles, sometimes none on reverse.

	1464	LONDON. Cross IIIb/None.	S
	1465	CALAIS. Crosses IIIb/v, IIIb/None.	N
	1466	YORK. Cross IIIb/None.	N

        (i)   Mullets by crown (quatrefoil on reverse).
        (ii)   Rosette or mullet on breast (no quatrefoil on reverse).

	1467	DURHAM (**DUNOLMI**). Cross IIIb/None. Pinecone after **LMI** only stop on reverse.	R

Halfpenny Similar to penny. Initial mark on obverse only.

	1468	LONDON. Crosses IIIa, IIIb, v.	N
	1469	CALAIS. Cross IIIb.	N

Farthing Similar to penny. Initial mark on obverse only.

	1470	LONDON. Cross v.	R
	1471	CALAIS. Cross pommée.	VR

LEAF-MASCLE (1434–1435)

GOLD

Noble	1472	Standard Type " A " with leaf in waves. Obverse stops: Saltires with one mascle. Reverse stops: Saltires with one leaf and one mascle. LONDON only.	ER
Quarter-noble	1473	Standard Type " C " with lis above shield and in centre of reverse cross. Initial mark: Lis. Leaf below **R** of **GLORI** on reverse. Stops: Saltires and one mascle. LONDON only.	ER

SILVER

Groat Standard Type " F " with leaf in spandrel below bust. Stops: Saltire and one mascle.

	1474	LONDON. Crosses IV/v. (Usually found muled with a reverse of the previous or following issue.)	R
	1475	CALAIS. Crosses IV/v, v/v. (Usually with leaf below **MEUM**.)	N

Halfgroat Standard Type " F ".

	1476	LONDON. Crosses v/v. Obverse stops: Saltires and one mascle. No stops on reverse. Pellet under **TAS** and **DON**. (Probably a mule with Trefoil reverse.)	ER
	1477	CALAIS. Cross v/v. Leaf below bust. Obverse stops: Saltires or saltires and one mascle. Reverse stops: Saltires only or with a mascle and/or leaf.	ER

Penny		Standard Type " G " with leaf on breast. Initial mark on obverse only. Obverse stops: Mascle and saltires.	
	1478	LONDON. Crosses IV, V. No stops on reverse.	S
	1479	CALAIS. Cross V. Leaf below SIE. Reverse stops: Mascle and saltires.	N
Halfpenny		Standard Type " G " with leaf on bust. Initial mark on obverse only.	
	1480	LONDON. Cross V. Leaf below N of LON or S of TAS. Obverse stops: Saltires only or with one mascle. No stops on reverse.	N
	1481	CALAIS. Cross V. Leaf under SIE. Saltire stops on obverse. One mascle stop on reverse.	R

LEAF-TREFOIL (1435–1438)

GOLD

Noble	1482/1	Standard Type " A ". Stops: Leaves and trefoils. LONDON only.	ER
Half-noble	1482/2	Standard Type " B ". Stops: Leaves and trefoils. Reverse of Annulet issue. LONDON only.	ER
Quarter-noble	1483	Standard Type " C ". Stops: Leaves and trefoils. LONDON only.	ER

SILVER

Groat (Class A)		Standard Type " F " with leaf on breast. Stops: Saltires only or with leaves and/or trefoils.	
	1484	LONDON. Crosses IIIb/v, IIIb/IIIb, IIIb/None.	N
	1485	CALAIS. Crosses IIIb/IIIb.	ER
Groat (Class B)	1486	Standard Type " F ". Obverse stops: Leaves and saltires with one trefoil. Reverse stops: Saltires, leaves and trefoils. Crosses IIIb/v, IIIb/None. LONDON only.	N
Halfgroat (Class A)	1487	Standard Type " F " with leaf on breast. Obverse stops: Leaves and saltires. Reverse stops: Saltires. Cross v/v. LONDON only.	R
Halfgroat (Class B)		Standard Type " F ". Reverse stops: Saltires and trefoil usually with leaf. Crosses IIIb/v. LONDON only.	
	1488	Leaf on breast. Obverse stops: Saltires and trefoil.	R
	1489	No leaf on breast. Obverse stops: Leaves and saltires with or without trefoil.	VR
Penny		Standard Type " G " with leaf on breast.	
	1490/1	LONDON. Obverse stops: Saltires and trefoil. Reverse stops: Leaf and trefoil. Crosses IIIb/v, IIIb/None.	N
	1490/2	CALAIS. Obverse stops: Saltire and trefoil. Reverse stops: Trefoil. Crosses v/None.[51]	ER

---

[51] BNJ 46 (1976) p. 77.

	1491	DURHAM (**DUNOLM**). Rings in centre of reverse. Obverse stops: Saltires and leaf. No stops on reverse. Crosses IIIb/None.	S
Halfpenny		Standard Type " G " with or without leaf on breast.	
	1492	LONDON. Obverse stops: Saltires only or with leaf or trefoil. No stops on reverse. Crosses V/None.	N
	1493	CALAIS. Leaf on breast doubtful (Piedfort only). Obverse stops: Trefoil and saltires. Reverse stops: Trefoil. Crosses V/None.	ER
Farthing	1494	Standard Type " G " with leaf on breast. Obverse stops: Trefoil and saltire. No stops on reverse. Crosses V/None. LONDON only.	VR

TREFOIL (1438–1443)

GOLD

Noble	1495	Standard Type " A " with trefoil to left of ship. Obverse stops: Saltires. Reverse stops: Saltires, trefoils and pellet. LONDON only.	ER

SILVER

Groat (Class A)		Standard Type " F " with leaf on breast and trefoils by neck. Stops: Saltires and trefoils.	
	1496	LONDON. Sometimes a leaf before **LON**. Crosses IIIb/IIIb, IIIb/None, IIIb/V.	N
	1497	CALAIS. Crosses IIIb/IIIb.	R
Groat (Class B)	1498	Similar to groat, but fleurs in spandrels and obverse stops are saltires only. Sometimes extra pellet in two quarters. Crosses IIIb/IIIb, IIIb/None, IIIb/V. LONDON only.	N
Groat (Class C)	1499	Standard Type " F " with trefoils on cusps at shoulders and small leaf on cusp at breast. Obverse stops: Saltires and trefoils. Reverse stops: Saltires. Sometimes extra pellet in two quarters. Crosses IIIb/None. LONDON only.	N
Halfpenny	1500	Standard Type " G " with trefoils by neck and leaf on breast. Obverse stops: Saltires only or with a trefoil. No stops on reverse. Sometimes an extra pellet in two quarters. Crosses IIIb/None, V/None. LONDON only.	N

TREFOIL-PELLET (1443–1445)

SILVER

Groat	1501	Standard Type " F " with trefoils by neck, pellets by crown, and small leaf on breast. Obverse stops: Saltires and trefoils. Reverse stops: Saltires. Sometimes an extra pellet in two quarters. Crosses IIIb/None. LONDON only.	N

LEAF-PELLET (1445–1454)

GOLD

Noble 1502 Standard Type " A " with leaf, lis, and annulet below shield, and   ER
pellet before H in centre of reverse. Trefoil after first word,
annulet and saltire stops. LONDON only.

SILVER

Groat 1503 Standard Type " F " with leaf on breast and pellets by crown.   N
(Class A) Stops: Saltires. An extra pellet in two quarters of reverse.
ANGL. Crosses iiib/None. LONDON only.

Groat 1504 Similar to No. 1503, but ANGLI. Sometimes a trefoil in the   N
(Class B) obverse legend. LONDON only.

Groat 1505 Standard Type " F " with leaf on neck and pellets by crown.   N
(Class C) Obverse stops: Saltires. Reverse stops: Saltires or none. An
extra pellet in two quarters. Crosses iiib/None. LONDON only.

Groat 1506 Similar to No. 1505 but with four pellets in the obverse field, two   S
(Class D) by crown and two by hair. LONDON only.

Halfgroat 1507 Similar to No. 1503. LONDON only.   VR
(Class A)

Halfgroat 1508 Standard Type " F " usually with leaf on breast and pellets by   VR
(Class B) crown. Obverse stops: Saltires. No stops on reverse. Crosses
v/None. LONDON only.

Penny Standard Type " G " with leaf on breast (sometimes absent in
York pence) and pellets by crown (omitted from one London
die). Usually an extra pellet in two quarters except on Durham
coins. Crosses iiib/None.

1509 LONDON. Obverse stops: Saltires (one die has a trefoil).   N

1510 YORK (quatrefoil and pellet in centre of reverse). Two pellets   N
by crown (Class A); two pellets by crown and two by hair
(Class B—? local dies).

1511 DURHAM (rings in centre of reverse)—with or without trefoil in   S
obverse legend.

N.B.—Durham coins without rings are Henry VI/Edward IV mules (BNJ 58
(1988) pp. 84–9).

Halfpenny 1512 Standard Type " G " with leaf on breast and pellets by crown.   N
Usually an extra pellet in two quarters. Crosses iiib/None
(Class A), v/None (Class B). LONDON only.

Farthing 1513 Similar to No. 1512. Crosses v/None. LONDON only.   VR

UNMARKED (1445–1454)

SILVER

Groat 1514 Standard Type " F " without marks on obverse. Two, or rarely   R
four, extra pellets on reverse. Stops: Saltires. Crosses IIIb/v,
IIIb/None. LONDON only.

Halfgroat 1515 Standard Type " F " without marks on obverse. Two extra   ER
pellets on reverse. One saltire stop on reverse. Crosses IIIb/
None. LONDON only.

CROSS-PELLET (1454–1460)

SILVER

Groat 1516 Standard Type " F " with a saltire at each side of neck, pellets by   R
(Class A) crown, and leaf and fleur on breast. Two extra pellets on
reverse. Crosses IIIb/None. LONDON only.

Groat 1517 Standard Type " F " with saltire upon neck and pellets by crown.   N
(Class B) Usually two extra pellets on reverse. Usually a mullet after
HENRIC and/or POSUI and sometimes one after FRANC. Crosses
IIIb/None. LONDON only.

Groat 1518 Similar to No. 1517 but mascles on obverse instead of mullets   S
(Class C) after HENRIC (always), GRA (often), and FRANC (rarely). One
die has pellets by hair instead of crown. LONDON only.

Halfgroat 1519 Standard Type " F " with saltire on neck and pellets by crown.   ER
Two extra pellets on reverse. Mullet after HENRIC and MEUM.
Crosses v/None. LONDON only.

Penny Standard Type " G " with pellets by crown. Two extra pellets
on reverse. Crosses IIIb/None.

1520 LONDON. Saltire on neck. Obverse stops: Mascle(s) or mullet   R
and mascle.

1521 YORK (cross in quatrefoil in centre of reverse). Saltires beside   N
neck; leaf on breast (sometimes absent).

1522 DURHAM (rings in centre of reverse). Saltire and B by neck.   R
The three pellets in each quarter sometimes linked by lines.

Halfpenny 1523 Standard Type " G " with saltire at each side of neck. Usually   N
(Class A) two extra pellets on reverse. Crosses IIIb/None. LONDON only.

Halfpenny 1524 Standard Type " G " with saltire upon neck. Usually two extra   N
(Class B) pellets on reverse. Sometimes a mullet after HENRIC. Crosses
v/None. LONDON only.

Farthing 1525 Standard Type " G " with a saltire upon neck and pellets by   VR
crown. Two extra pellets on reverse. Crosses v/None. LONDON
only.

LIS-PELLET (1454–1460)

SILVER

Groat   1526   Standard Type " F " with lis on neck and pellets by crown. Two   s
extra pellets on reverse. Sometimes a mascle after HENRIC.
Crosses IIIb/None, IIIb/v, IIIb/Lis. LONDON only.

EDWARD IV

(First reign 1461–1470)

DENOMINATIONS—**GOLD : Noble, Ryal, Half-ryal, Quarter-ryal, Angel.**

SILVER : Groat, Halfgroat, Penny, Halfpenny, Farthing.

Obv. legend: EDWARD DI GRA REX ANGL Z FRANC DNS HIBERNIE.

INITIAL MARKS

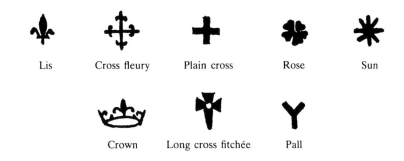

Lis	Cross fleury	Plain cross	Rose	Sun

Crown	Long cross fitchée	Pall

NOTES

The lists have been based on Messrs. C. E. Blunt and C. A. Whitton's comprehensive study of the coinage of this reign published in BNJ 25 (1945–8), and the Roman numerals indicate their type numbers. Although the coins bear initial marks, other details such as lettering, cusp ornaments and symbols by the bust play an important part in the division of the coinage into types. Details of these have been given where they are necessary for classification. It has also been found necessary to include a number of mules, which play an important part in the series.

In the case of the pence of York and Durham, where several symbols vary, the lists have been set out in tabular form for quick reference.

Types I–IV 1461–1464.
Type V (Gold) Mar. 1465–Jul. 1465.
Type V (Silver) Aug. 1464–Jul. 1465.
Type VI Jul. 1465–Jul. 1466.
Type VII Jul. 1466–Jul. 1467.

Type VIII Jul. 1467–Jul. 1468.
Type IX 1469 to March.
Type X 2 Mar. 1469–1470.
Type XI Mid 1470–3 Oct. 1470.

HEAVY COINAGE (1461–1464/5)

(Noble : 108 grains.   Penny : 15 grains)

GOLD

Noble	1527	Standard Type " A " with pellets by crown and lis below shield. ER Legend starts at top left. Initial mark: Lis. LONDON only.
Noble	1528	Standard Type " A " with quatrefoil below sword-arm. Initial ER mark (obv.): Rose. LONDON only.

SILVER

Groat Standard Type " F ". LONDON only.

1529	Class I Lis on neck and small pellet each side of crown. Cross fleury/lis, plain cross with plain cross, lis or no reverse mark.		s
1530	Class I Lis on breast. With or without pellets by crown. Plain cross/lis or plain cross.		s
1531	Class II Crescent on breast and quatrefoils by neck. I.m. Rose.		s
1532	Class III Small trefoil on breast and quatrefoils by neck. Eye in reverse legend. I.m. Rose. (One variety omits quatrefoils and trefoil; another omits the eye.)		s
1533	Class IV Annulet at each side of neck. Eye in reverse legend after **TAS**. I.m. Rose.		s

Halfgroat Standard Type " F ". LONDON only.

1534	Class I Lis on neck and small pellet at each side of crown. I.m. (Obverse): Cross fleury, plain cross.		ER
1535	Class II Similar to No. 1531.		ER
1536	Class III Quatrefoils by neck. Eye in reverse legend. I.m. Rose.		VR
1537	Class IV Annulets by neck. I.m. Rose.		VR

Penny Standard Type " G ".

LONDON.

1538	Class I Lis on neck. I.m. Plain cross.		VR
1539	Class II Quatrefoils by neck. I.m. Rose.		VR
1540	Class III Similar to No. 1539 with eye after **TAS**. I.m. Rose.		R
1541	Class IV Annulets by neck. I.m. Rose.		VR

YORK (quatrefoil in centre of reverse).

1542	Class III Quatrefoils by neck. I.m. Rose.		s

DURHAM **(DUNOLIN)** sometimes with pellet(s) beside or over crown. Local dies.

1543	Class IV I.m. Cross.		N
1544	Class IV Rose in centre of reverse, sometimes an extra pellet in one quarter. I.m. Cross.		N

Halfpenny Standard Type " G ". LONDON only.

1545	Class I Lis on neck, pellets by crown. I.m. Plain cross.		R
1546	Classes II and III Quatrefoils, saltires, or nothing by neck. I.m. Rose.		R
1547	Class IV Annulets by neck. I.m. Rose.		R

Farthing Standard Type " G ". LONDON only.

1548/1	Class I Lis on breast, pellets by crown. I.m. Plain cross.		ER
1548/2	Class III No marks. I.m. Rose.		ER

LIGHT COINAGE (1464/5–1470)

(Ryal : 120 grains.   Penny : 12 grains)

GOLD

Ryal

Obv. Design similar to Standard Type " A " but with a rose on the ship's side and a banner inscribed **E** at the stern.

Rev. Design similar to Standard Type " A " with a rose upon a radiate sun over the centre of the royal cross.

1549   LONDON.
Large fleurs in spandrels. v. Rose, None/rose. vi. Sun, None/ sun.* vii. None/crown.*
Small trefoils in spandrels. viiiA. None/crown. viiiB. Sun over crown. x. Long cross fitchée.   N

1550   BRISTOL (**B** in waves). I.m. on reverse only.   R
Large fleurs in spandrels. vi. Sun.† vii. Crown.
Small trefoils in spandrels. viii. Crown. x. Sun.

1551   COVENTRY (**C** in waves). vi. None/sun.†   VR

1552   NORWICH (**N** in waves). v. None/rose? vi. None/sun.   VR

1553   YORK (**E** in waves). I.m. on reverse only.   R
Large fleurs in spandrels. viA. Sun. viB. Sun and lis. vii. Lis.
Small trefoils in spandrels. viii. Lis. x? Sun/sun.

N.B.—Many continental copies of the London ryals exist, and these were mostly struck at a later date. They may be distinguished by their coarse work and large module (cf. BNJ 25 Part 2 (1947) p. 183).

Half-ryal   Similar to Ryal but reverse legend DOMINE NE IN FURORE
                                 TUO ARGUAS ME. Small trefoils in spandrels.

1554   LONDON. V. None/rose. VIA. Sun. VIB. None. VII. None/   S
        crown. VIIIA. None/crown (Lis in waves or pellet over shield).
        VIIIB. None/sun. VIIIC. Sun/crown. VIIID. None/sun and
        crown. IX. Rose/crown (Lis in waves). X. Long cross fitchée.

1555   BRISTOL (B in waves). I.m. on reverse. VIA. Sun.† VIB. None.   R
        VII. Crown.* VII/VIIID. Sun and crown.

1556   COVENTRY (C in waves). VI. None/Sun.†   VR

1557   NORWICH (N in waves). V. None/rose.   VR

1558   YORK (E in waves). I.m. on reverse. VI. Sun.† VII. Lis.*   R
        VIIIB. Sun over crown. IX. Rose and lis.

Quarter-ryal   Standard Type " C " with a rose upon a radiate sun over the
                                 centre of the reverse cross. Sometimes with lis and/or roses in
                                 legends. LONDON only.

1559   Tressure of eight arches. Rose over shield. V. Rose   ER
        (? forgery). VI/V. Sun/rose.

1560   Tressure of four arches. E over shield, rose and sun at sides. S
        VI. Sun. VII. Crown, Lis. VIII. Sun over crown, Sun/crown,
        Sun/crown and sun. IX? Crown/rose. XI. Long cross fitchée.

Angel   1561   Standard Type " D " with sun and rose at sides of ship's mast. ER
                         V. None/rose. VII. None crown.

SILVER

Groat   Standard Type " F ".   C

                LONDON.

		I. MARK	BY NECK	ON CUSPS	REMARKS
1562	Va	Rose	Annulets	Fleurs	Struck from heavy dies. Eye after **TAS**.
1563	Va	Rose/none or rose	,,	,,	New dies. Eye after **DON**, or **TAS**.
1564	Vb	Rose	Quatrefoils	,,	Struck from heavy dies. Eye after **TAS**.
1565	Vb	,,	,,	,,	New dies. Eye after **TAS** (one die omits). Fleur on breast.
1566	Vb	,,	—	,,	Ditto.
1567	Vc	,,	Quatrefoils	Fleurs or trefoils.	Extra pellet in one quarter. Fleur, rose, trefoil, or nothing on breast.[52]
1568	Vd	,,	,,	Fleurs	Extra pellet in one quarter. Fleur, or nothing on breast.[52]
1569	VI	Sun	,,	,,	Varieties omit fleurs on cusps or quatrefoils by neck.[53]

* Sometimes with two or three lis in the obverse legend.

† Sometimes with a rose in the reverse legend (before IBAT on ryals; after ME on half-ryals).

[52] The prime distinction between these two subclasses is the form of the lettering. It is small and neat on Vc changing to a rugged fount in Vd. The most distinctive is the letter P which has an exaggerated serif to the right of the base of the upright in Vd (cf. BNJ 25 (1945–8) p. 132).

[53] Reverses of this variety are also used with obverses with E over fleur or fleur over E over fleur on breast. I.m. Rose (cf. SNC 93 (1985) p. 117).

1570	VII	Crown/crown, or none.	,,	Fleurs or trefoils.	Variety omits quatrefoils by neck.
1571	VIII	Crown/sun or sun and crown/sun.	,,	Fleurs, trefoils or none.	Quatrefoil on breast.
1572	VIII/VII	Sun and crown/ crown.	,,	Fleurs	Quatrefoil on breast.
1573	IX/VIII	Rose and crown/sun.	,,	Trefoils	
1574	IX/VII	Rose and crown/ crown.	,,	,,	
1575	IX	Crown/rose	,,	,,	Quatrefoil on breast.
1576	Xa/IX	Long cross fitchée/ rose	Trefoils	,,	
1577	Xa	Long cross fitchée/ sun	Quatrefoils Saltires Trefoils	,,	
1578	Xb	,,	Nothing	,,	
1579	XI	Long cross fitchée	Trefoils Nothing	,,	

N.B.—Light coins struck from heavy dies may be distinguished from true heavy coins (apart from weight) by the fact that the dies are too large for the flans. The new dies of similar design are smaller with small neat lettering.

1580   BRISTOL (**B** on breast). Quatrefoils by bust. N
Fleurs on cusps. VI/V. Sun/rose. VIA. Sun (one die omits B).
VIB. Sun (no quatrefoils). VII. Crown.
Trefoils on cusps. VII. Crown. VIII. Crown/sun. X. Sun.

1581   COVENTRY (**C** on breast). Quatrefoils by bust. S
VI/V. Sun/rose. VI. Sun. Local dies. Rose (sometimes omit
C or quatrefoils).

1582   NORWICH (**N** on breast). Quatrefoils by bust. N
VI/V. Sun/rose. VI. Sun.

1583   YORK (**E** on breast). Quatrefoils by bust. N
Fleurs on cusps. VI. Sun.[54] VII. Lis/crown, Lis.
Trefoils on cusps. VIIIA. Sun. VIIIB. Lis (sometimes omit **E**).
X. Lis/sun (trefoils by bust). XI. Lis (trefoils by bust).

Halfgroat   Standard Type "F" with quatrefoils by bust unless shown otherwise in brackets after the initial mark.

1584   LONDON. S
va. Rose (from heavy dies). vd. Rose/none. VI/V. Sun/none.
VII. Crown (quatrefoils, saltires, or trefoils). VIII. Crown/sun
(quatrefoils, saltires, or trefoils by bust and on breast). IX?
Crown/rose. X. Long cross fitchée/sun (trefoils, saltires, or
nothing).

1585   BRISTOL. S
V/VI. Rose/sun (saltires). VI. Sun (saltires), Sun/none. VII.
Crown (saltires, quatrefoils, trefoils, or crosses), Crown/none.
VIII. Crown/Sun (no marks).

1586   COVENTRY. VI. Sun (crosses). ER

---

[54] An obverse of this variety is used with a London reverse of Vd, probably sent to York in error, as the same obverse die was also used with a York reverse.

1587   NORWICH. vi. Sun (saltires).   ER

1588   YORK.   S
vi. Sun. vii. Lis (quatrefoils or saltires). viii. Lis/none (E on breast). x. Lis (trefoils).

1589   CANTERBURY (Royal).   N
vi. Sun (nothing). vii. Crown (quatrefoils, trefoils, or saltires). viii. Crown/none (quatrefoils, trefoils, or saltires), Crown/sun (trefoils). ix. Rose (trefoils).

1590   CANTERBURY (Episcopal). Knot below bust and spur in one   C
quarter of reverse, except where stated.
Fleurs on cusps. va. Pall/none (nothing), Pall (nothing), Pall/rose (quatrefoils or nothing).
Trefoils on cusps. vb. Pall/none (nothing), Pall (quatrefoils or nothing), Pall/rose. via. Pall/none (saltires). vib. Pall/sun (quatrefoils or wedges).
No spur on reverse. vib/vii. Pall/none (quatrefoils or wedges).
No know below bust. vii/via. Pall/none. vii/vib. Pall (quatrefoils or nothing).
No spur or knot. vii. Pall/none.

Penny   Standard Type " G " with marks by bust as shown in brackets after the initial mark. I.m. on obverse only.

1591   LONDON.   S
va. Rose (annulets) struck from heavy dies. vi. Sun (quatrefoils). vii. Crown (quatrefoils, saltires, or trefoil and quatrefoil). viii. Crown (trefoils or quatrefoils with quatrefoil on breast). x. Long cross fitchée (trefoils or nothing).

1592   BRISTOL. I.m. Crown. vii. **BRISTOW** (crosses, quatrefoils, or   R
saltires). viii. **BRISTOLL** (quatrefoils or a trefoil).

YORK (Episcopal).   N

		TYPE	INITIAL MARK	BY BUST	CENTRE OF REVERSE
				SEDE VACANTE (1464–5)	
1593	{	V	Rose	Quatrefoils	Nothing
	{	VI	Sun	,,	,,
				ARCHBISHOP GEORGE NEVILLE	
1594	{	Local 1	Rose	G and key	Quatrefoil
	{	,, 2	Cross	,,	,,
1595	{	VI	Sun	,,	,,
	{	VII 1	Large lis	,,	,,
1596		VII 2	,,	No marks	,,
1597		VII 3	,,	Quatrefoils	,,
1598		VIII	,,	Trefoils	,,
1599	{	X 1	Small lis	G and key	,,
	{	X 2	Long cross fitchée	,,	,,

1600   CANTERBURY (Royal). VII. Crown (quatrefoils).   VR

1601   CANTERBURY (Episcopal). I.m. Pall.   S
VI. Knot on breast, spur in one quarter (quatrefoils, saltires or nothing). VII/VI. Spur in one quarter (quatrefoils or saltires). VII. No marks (crosses).

DURHAM (Bishop Lawrence Booth).

	TYPE	INITIAL MARK	BY BUST	REVERSE
1602	V	Rose	B and D	B in centre
1603	VI	Sun	Quatrefoil and B	,,
	VII 1	Crown	,,	No marks
1604	VII 2	,,	D and quatrefoil	,,
1605	VII 3	,,	Quatrefoils	,,
1606	VIII 1	,,	Trefoils	,,
1607	VIII 2	,,	Lis	,,

Halfpenny   Similar to penny.

1608   LONDON.   N
V. Rose (saltires). VI. Sun (saltires or trefoils). VII. Crown (saltires or trefoils). X. Long cross fitchée (trefoils or nothing).

1609   BRISTOL. I.m. Crown. VII. (crosses). VIII. (trefoils).   R

1610   YORK (Royal). I.m. Lis. VII. (saltires). VIII. (trefoils).   S

1611   CANTERBURY (Royal). I.m. Crown. VII. (saltires or millrinds).   S
VIII. (trefoils).

1612   CANTERBURY (Episcopal). VII? Pall (trefoils or nothing).   ER

Farthing   Similar to penny.

1612/1   LONDON. I.m. Crown. VII. (trefoils).[55]   ER

---

[55] Another farthing with no marks and reading **EDWARD DI GRA REX** (I.m. illegible) is possibly of the light coinage (cf. BNJ 29 (1960) p. 201).

HENRY VI

Restored (October 1470–April 1471)

DENOMINATIONS—**GOLD : Angel, Half-angel.**

SILVER : Groat, Halfgroat, Penny, Halfpenny.

Obv. legend: HENRIC DI GRA REX ANGL Z FRANC.

INITIAL MARKS

Cross pattée	Restoration cross	Short cross fitchée	Trefoil	Rose	Lis

GOLD

Angel Standard Type " D " with H and lis at sides of ship's mast. Stops: Pellets and trefoils, or saltires.

1613 LONDON. Restoration cross, None/cross pattée, None/lis, None. R

1614 BRISTOL. (**B** in waves). None/Restoration cross, None. VR

Half-angel Standard Type " E " with H and lis at side of ship's mast. Initial mark on reverse only.

1615 LONDON. Lis, cross pattée, Restoration cross. VR

1616 BRISTOL (**B** in waves). Restoration cross. ER

SILVER

Groat Standard Type " F ".

1617 LONDON. Restoration cross with Restoration cross, short cross S
fitchée, cross pattée or lis on reverse. Cross pattée with cross pattée, Restoration cross or lis on reverse.

1618 YORK (**E** on breast). Lis, Lis/sun. S

1619 BRISTOL. **BRISTOW** (**B** on breast). Restoration cross with R
Restoration cross, rose, or trefoil on reverse. Trefoil with trefoil, Restoration cross, short cross fitchée, or rose on reverse.

Halfgroat Standard Type " F " with trefoils over crown on some London coins.

1620 LONDON. Restoration cross (both sides, or obverse only). R

1621 YORK (**E** on breast). Lis. ER

Penny Standard Type " G ". Initial mark on obverse only.

1622 LONDON. Restoration cross, cross pattée, short cross fitchée. R

| 1622/1 | BRISTOL. Short cross fitchée. | ER |
| 1623 | YORK (**G** and key by bust; quatrefoil in centre of reverse). Lis. | S |

Halfpenny   Standard Type " G ".   Initial mark on obverse only.

| 1624 | LONDON. Short cross fitchée. | R |
| 1625 | BRISTOL. Uncertain cross. | R |

EDWARD IV

(Second reign, 1471–1483)

DENOMINATIONS—GOLD : Angel, Half-angel.

SILVER : Groat, Halfgroat, Penny, Halfpenny.

Obv. legend: EDWARD DI GRA REX ANGL Z FRANC.

INITIAL MARKS

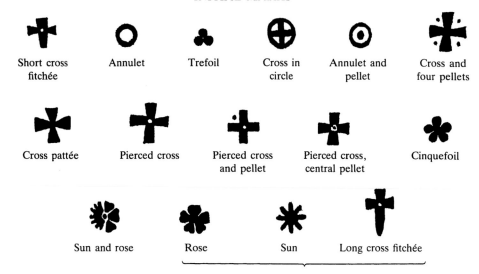

| Short cross fitchée | Annulet | Trefoil | Cross in circle | Annulet and pellet | Cross and four pellets |

| Cross pattée | Pierced cross | Pierced cross and pellet | Pierced cross, central pellet | Cinquefoil |

| Sun and rose | Rose | Sun | Long cross fitchée |

PROVINCIAL MINTS ONLY

NOTES

For many years the initial mark "sun and rose" has been listed in sale catalogues under Edward V, despite the attribution of this mark to Edward IV by Messrs. Blunt and Whitton. However, the consensus of opinion of numismatists is now in favour of the latter attribution, and the coins bearing this mark are listed under Edward IV (cf. BNJ 30 (1960–1) pp. 193–5), but the dies were probably still used for a short time in his son's reign.

Type XII April–Autumn 1471.
Type XIII Autumn 1471–23rd Feb. 1472.
Type XIV 23rd Feb. 1472–Mid 1473.
Types XV, XVI, XVII Mid 1473–3rd. Feb. 1477.

Types XVIII, XIX, XX 3rd Feb. 1477–Early 1480.
Type XXI Early 1480–12th Feb. 1483.
Type XXII 12th Feb. 1483–April 1483.

GOLD

Angel
Standard Type " D " with E and rose by ship's mast.

1626   LONDON.
XII. Short cross fitchée; XIV. Small annulet; XV. Pellet in annulet; XVI. Cross with pellet in each quarter; XVII. Pierced cross; XVIII. Cross with pellet in one quarter; XXI. Cinquefoil; XXII. Sun and rose.

| | 1627 | BRISTOL (**B** in waves). XIV. Small annulet. | ER |

Half-angel — Standard Type " E " with **E** and rose by ship's mast. LONDON only.

	1628	Obverse and reverse legends transposed. XII. Short cross fitchée/none.	ER
	1629	King's name and titles on both sides. XIV/XII. Small annulet/none.	ER
	1630	Normal legends. XIV. Small annulet; XVI. Cross in circle; XVIII. Cross with pellet in one quarter; XX/XVIII. Pierced cross with central pellet/cross with pellet in one quarter; XXI. Cinquefoil; XXII. Sun and rose.	S

SILVER

Groat — Standard Type " F ".

| | 1631 | LONDON. | C |

Trefoils on cusps. XII. Short cross fitchée. XIII. Large annulet/trefoil. XIV. Small annulet. XV. Pellet in annulet (sometimes roses by bust). XVI. Pierced cross with four pellets/ditto, cross or cross in circle; Plain cross/plain cross or cross in circle.
Fleurs on cusps. XVII. Pierced cross. XVIII. Pierced cross with one pellet. XIX. Pierced cross (pellets by bust and extra pellets in one or two quarters of reverse). XX. Pierced cross with central pellet. XXI. Cinquefoil (rose on breast). XXII. Sun and rose.

| | 1632 | BRISTOL (**B** on breast). | R |

XII. Rose. XIV. Sun/small annulet, small annulet/ditto or none, Sun.

| | 1633 | YORK (Royal). XII. Lis. | R |

Halfgroat — Standard Type " F ".

| | 1634 | LONDON. | N |

XII. Short cross fitchée/none. XIII. Annulet/rose. XIV. Annulet. XV. Annulet and pellet/rose. XVI. Cross in circle/ditto or none. XVIII. Pierced cross with one pellet. XXI. Cinquefoil. XXII. Sun and rose.

| | 1635 | BRISTOL (**B** on breast). XII. Rose/short cross fitchée. | ER |
| | 1636 | YORK (Royal). XII. Lis. | ER |

CANTERBURY (Royal).

	1637	**C** on breast. XVIII/XX. Rose.	N
	1638	**C** on breast and in centre of reverse. XVIII. Rose.	N
	1639	**C** on breast. Rose in centre of reverse. XX. Rose.	N
	1640	Nothing on breast. XXI. Long cross fitchée,[56] Cinquefoil?/cinquefoil.	S

[56] An obverse die with i.m. Lis is used with a Canterbury reverse i.m. Long cross fitchée.

Penny   Standard Type " G ". Initial mark on obverse only, except Class
                                   XVII which sometimes has mark on both sides.

        1641   LONDON.   N
                    XII. Short cross fitchée.   XIV. Annulet.   XV. Pellet in
                    annulet.   XVI. Cross in circle.   XVII. Pierced cross.   XVIII.
                    Cross and one pellet.   XXI. Cinquefoil.   XXII. Sun and rose.

        1642   BRISTOL.   XII. Rose.   ER

                    YORK (Episcopal).   N

	TYPE	INITIAL MARK	BY BUST	REVERSE	REMARKS
		ARCHBISHOP GEORGE NEVILLE			
1644	XII 1	Short cross fitchée over lis.	Quatrefoils	Quatrefoil	
1645	XII 2	Short cross fitchée.	G and key.	,,	
		SEDE VACANTE (1472–5)			
1646	XIV 1	,,	G and key.	Nothing	
	XIV 2	Small annulet.	Nothing	Quatrefoil	Rarely without quatrefoil.
1647	XVI 1	Cross in circle.	,,	,,	
	XVI 2	Rose	,,	,,	With or without rose on breast.
1648	XVI 3	,,	E and rose.	,,	
		ARCHBISHOP GEORGE NEVILLE			
1649	XVI 4	,,	G and rose.	,,	
1650	XVI 5	Rose over annulet.	G and key.	,,	
	XVI 6	Rose	,,	,,	
		SEDE VACANTE (1476)			
1651	—	Rose	G and key or nothing.	,,	Rose on breast.
		ARCHBISHOP LAWRENCE BOOTH			
1652	—	Rose	B and key.	,,	
	XXI 1	Cinquefoil	,,	,,	
		SEDE VACANTE (1480)			
1653	XXI 3	Rose	B and key.	Nothing	
		ARCHBISHOP THOMAS ROTHERHAM			
1654	XXI 4	Rose	T and key.	Quatrefoil	
1655	XXI 5	,,	,,	,,	Star on breast.
1656	XXI 6	,,	,,	,,	Star on breast and to right of crown.

        1657   CANTERBURY (Royal).   XIX. (With or without **C** on breast).   R
                    XXI. Long cross fitchée.

                    CANTERBURY (Episcopal).[57]

---

[57] A fragment with uncertain i.m. apparently has a pall to left of neck and possibly an annulet to right and
indicates the possibility of an archiepiscopal mint at this time (cf. BNJ 36 (1967) p. 212).

DURHAM (Deram or Dunolmie).

	TYPE	INITIAL MARK	BY BUST	REVERSE	REMARKS
			BISHOP LAWRENCE BOOTH		
1658	XII	Short cross fitchée.	Nothing	Nothing	
	XIII	Trefoil	,,	,,	
	XIII	,,	B and trefoil.	D in centre.	
1659	XIV	Rose	,,	,,	
	XVa	Pellet in annulet.	,,	,,	
1660	XVb	Rose	Lis	,,	
1661	Local	,,	Nothing	,,	Crosses over crown. Extra pellet in 1 or 4 quarters.
1662	Local	,,	,,	,,	Crosses over crown. **V** under **CIVI**.
	Local	Pansy	,,	,,	Similar
1663	Local	,,	Nothing, crosses or lis.	,,	Similar with **V** on breast and **B** to left of crown.
			SEDE VACANTE (1476)		
1664	Local	Rose	Nothing	D in centre.	
			BISHOP WILLIAM DUDLEY		
1665	Local	Rose	V to right.	D in centre.	
1666	Local	Cinquefoil	D and V.	,,	One omits **D** on reverse.

Halfpenny   Standard Type " G ". Initial mark on obverse only.

1667   LONDON.
XII. Short cross fitchée. XIV. Annulet. XV. Pellet in annulet. XVI. Cross and four pellets, Cross in circle. XVII. Pierced cross. XVIII. Cross and one pellet. XIX. Pierced cross with pellets by bust. XXI. Cinquefoil. XXII. Sun and rose.

1668   CANTERBURY (Royal).
XVIII. Rose (**C** on breast and in centre of reverse). XIX. Rose (**C** on breast). XXI. Long cross fitchée?

1699   DURHAM (**DERAM**). I.m. Rose, **V**, Lis or nothing by bust. **D**
in centre of reverse (omitted from one die used with an obverse with lis by neck).

EDWARD V

1483

DENOMINATIONS—**GOLD : Angel, Half-angel.**

SILVER : Groat, Halfgroat, Penny.

Obv. legend: EDWARD DI GRA REX ANGL Z FRANC.

INITIAL MARKS

Boar's head
(Obverse)

Sun and rose
(Reverse)

NOTES

Coins bearing the sun and rose as obverse initial mark, which were formerly attributed to this king, are listed under Edward IV, but the dies were probably still used for some time after the accession of Edward V.[58]

GOLD

Angel	1670	Standard Type " D " with E and rose beside ship's mast. Initial marks: Boar's head/sun and rose. LONDON only.	ER
Half-angel	1671	Standard Type " E " with E and rose beside ship's mast. Initial marks: Boar's head/sun and rose. LONDON only.	ER

SILVER

Groat	1672	Standard Type " F ". Initial marks: Boar's head/sun and rose. LONDON only.	ER
Halfgroat	1673	Standard Type " F ". Initial mark *(obv.)*: Boar's head.[59] LONDON only.	ER
Penny	1674	Standard Type " G ". Initial mark *(obv.)*: Boar's head. LONDON only.	ER

N.B.—A halfpenny with the same bust and lettering as late Edward IV halfpence has an indistinct initial mark which is possibly a boar's head.

---

[58] cf. BNJ 50 (1980) pp. 133–5.
[59] Possibly over sun and rose. A reverse die-link with Richard III reinforces the likelihood that the mark is a boar's head (cf. BNJ 22 (1934–7) p. 221 and pl. nos. 9 & 10).

RICHARD III

1483–1485

DENOMINATIONS—**GOLD** : Angel, Half-angel.

SILVER : Groat, Halfgroat, Penny, Halfpenny.

Obv. legend: RICARD DI GRA REX ANGL Z FRANC.

INITIAL MARKS

1	2	3	1	2	Lis
	Sun and rose (SR)		Boar's head (BH)		(Durham)

NOTES

During this reign the system of initial marks became very complex, and although only two marks are used, there are variations of each. For this reason the marks are given in detail in the lists. The pence and halfpence are usually so small and worn that accurate classification of the initial mark is impossible.

GOLD

Angel — Standard Type " D " with R and rose beside ship's mast. LONDON only.

1675 — With obverse reading **EDWARD** but R over E by mast on reverse. SR (1), BH (1)/SR (1). — ER

1676 — Obverse reading **RICARD**. R by mast is sometimes over E or rose. Large cross on reverse.
SR (1), BH (1)/SR (1), BH (1)/BH (2), BH (2), BH (2)/SR (2), SR (2)/ BH (2), SR (2). — R

1677 — Obverse reading **RICARD** or **RICAD**. Small cross on reverse. BH (2)/SR (2), SR (2)/BH (2), SR (2). — ER

Half-angel — 1678 — Standard Type " E " with R and rose beside ship's mast. LONDON only. BH (1). — ER

SILVER

Groat — Standard Type " F ".

LONDON.
1679 — Nothing below bust. SR (1), BH (1)/SR (1), BH (1), BH (1)/BH (2), BH (2), BH (2)/SR (2), SR (2), SR (2)/none, SR (3). — S

1680 — Pellet below bust. SR (2)/BH (2), SR (2), SR (2)/none. — S

1681 — YORK. Nothing below bust. SR (2)/none. — R

Halfgroat — Standard Type " F ". LONDON only.

1682 — Nothing below bust. SR (2), SR (2)/none. — VR

| | 1683 | Pellet below bust. BH (2)/none, SR (2). | VR |

Penny   Standard Type " G ".   Initial mark on obverse only.

| | 1684 | LONDON. BH. | VR |

YORK.   Quatrefoil in centre of reverse.

| | 1685 | No marks by bust. SR. | R |
| | 1686 | T and key by bust. SR, BH, Rose? | R |

DURHAM.   D in centre of reverse.

| | 1687 | S on breast. Lis. | S |

Halfpenny 1688 Standard Type " G ".   Initial mark on obverse. LONDON only. VR
BH, SR.

HENRY VII

1485–1509

DENOMINATIONS—**GOLD** : **Sovereign,**[60] **Ryal, Angel, Half-angel.**

SILVER : *Facing bust*—**Groat, Halfgroat, Penny, Halfpenny, Farthing.**

Profile—**Testoon, Groat, Halfgroat.**

Obv. legend: HENRICUS DEI GRACIA REX ANGLIE ET FRANC DNS IBAR.

INITIAL MARKS

TOWER

Halved sun and rose (1485–90)		Pansy (1490–1504)	
Halved lis and rose (1485–90)		Leopard's head (1490–1504)	
Lis upon sun and rose (1485–90)		Lis issuant from rose (1490–1504)	
Lis upon rose (1485–90)		Anchor (1490–1504)	
Lis (1485–90, 1504–9)		Greyhound's head (1500–7)	
Cross fitchée (1485–90)		Dragon (1504–7)	
Rose (1490–4, 1500–7)		Crosslet (1504–7)	
Cinquefoil (1490–1504)		Pheon (1507–9)	
Escallop (1490–1504)			

---

[60] It is possible that coins weighing twice the normal weight and struck from Sovereign dies of Type V were intended as Double Sovereigns (cf. BNJ 32 (1963) p. 153).

PROVINCIAL MINTS

Tun
  (Canterbury 1486–1504)   Cross
                                                          (Durham 1484–94)

Martlet
  (Canterbury and York   The lis mark was also used at
  1501–9)   Canterbury and York mints, and
                                                          the rose and lis upon sun and rose
                                                          at York.

CROWNS ON THE GROATS

Open   Two arches   Two arches   Single arch
                  unjewelled   jewelled

Profile   Profile
Tentative   Regular

NOTES

The London halfpenny with the initial mark cross fitchée, which was formerly attributed to this king, is now considered to belong to the "Restoration" coinage of Henry VI.

Some very small coins bearing the same types as the halfpence may be farthings, but opinions are divided as to whether any coins of this denomination exist for this reign.

There are considerable differences in the lettering on coins of Classes III and IV, but these have been omitted and readers are referred to recent papers on this reign (cf. BNJ 30 (1960–1) pp. 262–301 and 31 (1962) pp. 109–24). Reference should also be made to SCBI 32 where 971 coins of this reign are described and illustrated.

GOLD

Sovereign   *Obv.*   King enthroned holding orb and sceptre.
                       Rev.   IHS AUTEM TRANSIENS PER MEDIUM ILLORUM IBAT.
                                Royal shield in centre of Tudor rose.

            1689[61]   Type I. i.m. Cross fitchée (reverse). Throne with low ER back; lis in background. Small shield.

            1690[61]   Type II. i.m. Cinquefoil. No lis in background. Large ER shield crowned on rose on reverse.

---

[61] It has been suggested that Type II precedes Type I (cf. BNJ 33 (1964) pp. 118–34).

	1691	Type III. i.m. Dragon. High backed very ornamented throne.	ER
	1692/1	Type IV. i.m. Lis (obverse). Dragon (reverse). Throne with high canopy and broad seat.	VR
	1692/2	Type V. i.m. Lis (obverse). Crosslet, pheon (reverse). Narrower throne with portcullis at King's feet.	VR

Ryal
(c. 1489–90)

1693	*Obv.*	King standing in a ship, holding a sword and shield.	ER
	Rev.	IHC etc. Small shield of France in centre of a Tudor rose. Initial mark: Cross fitchée (reverse only).	

Angel

Standard Type " D " with H and rose at sides of ship's mast.

Old type. Angel has one foot on dragon.

	1694	Class I. Halved sun and rose, lis on rose, lis on sun and rose (altered obverse die of Richard III), rose (obverse only).	VR
	1695	Class II. None, cinquefoil (obverse or reverse mule).	R

New type. Angel has both feet on dragon.

	1696	Class III. Escallop, pansy, lis issuant from rose, anchor, none/anchor.	S
	1697	Class IV. Greyhound's head, crosslet.	S
	1698	Class V (large crook-shaped abbreviation after HENRIC). Crosslet, crosslet and pheon, pheon, pheon/none.	S

N.B.—Coins of (II) and (III) above sometimes have IHS TRANSIENS etc. as reverse legend.

Half-angel

Standard Type " E " with H and rose at sides of ship's mast.

Old type.

	1699	Class I. Lis on sun and rose (old dies altered).	ER

New type.

	1700	Class III. Pansy, anchor/pansy.	R
	1701	Class IV. None/greyhound's head, rose.	ER
	1702	Class V. Rose/crosslet, pheon.	R

SILVER

I. *Facing Bust Issue*

Groat

Standard Type " F ". LONDON only.

	1703	Class I. (Open crown without arches). Halved sun and rose, halved lis and rose, lis on rose (sometimes with rose on breast), lis on sun and rose, lis,* cross fitchée,* rose.* * I.m. usually on obverse only. Quatrefoils or saltires on neck.	R
	1704	Class II. (Crown with two plain arches). None (early coins have saltires by neck), cinquefoil. An extremely rare variety has a portcullis in the centre of the reverse: None/lis.	N
	1705	Class III. (Crown with jewelled arches). (a) Two jewelled arches—Bust 1 (as classes I and II)—cinquefoil.	R

(b)	Two jewelled arches—Bust 2 (hair curled at ends)— N escallop, pansy.
(c)	Only outer arch jewelled—Bust 3 (realistic hair, pupils to N eyes). Pansy, leopard's head, lis issuant from rose, anchor,* greyhound's head (two varieties),* greyhound's head/rose, crosslet.

* Also known with i.m. on reverse only.

1706 Class IV. (Single arched crown).
 (a) Single bar with 4 crockets (normal fleurs) as jewels. N
   Greyhound's head, greyhound's head/rose, crosslet.
 (b) Double bar with 6 uprights as jewels. N
   Crosslet, pheon.
 Very rare varieties with i.m. crosslet have a double bar with 4
 or 6 crockets.

Halfgroat   Standard Type " F ".

LONDON.
1707 Class I. (Open crown without arches; tressure unbroken). VR
 Lis on rose (obv. only).

1708 Class IIIa. (Double arched crown, outer arch jewelled). N
 Escallop, lis (lozenge panel in centre of reverse—sometimes
 with a lis on breast).

1709 Class IIIb. (Unarched crown; tressure broken; lozenge panel N
 in centre of reverse). Lis.

CANTERBURY.
Archbishop Morton (1486–1500). M in centre of reverse.
1710 Class I. (Open crown with arches). Tun. (obv. only). S

1711 Class II. (Double arched crown). None. N

King and Archbishop Morton jointly? (c. 1490–1500).
1712 Double arched crown. N
 Class IIIa. Trefoil stops. Lis, tun and lis/lis.
 Class IIIb. Rosette stops. Tun and lis/none, tun/lis, tun.
 Class IIIc. Saltire or no stops. Tun, tun and pansy/tun.

YORK.
Royal mint (c. 1495–1500?). I.m. lis. Usually lis on breast.
Pellet in lozenge panel in centre of reverse.

1713 Double arched crown. N

1714 Unarched crown with tressure broken above. N

Episcopal mint. Archbishop Savage (1501–1507)? I.m.
Martlet. Key at each side of bust. Double arched crown.
1715 No tressure on obverse. N

1716 Fleured tressure on obverse. N

Episcopal mint. Sede vacante (1507–1508)?
1717 Similar to No. 1716 but without keys by bust. N

Penny   Standard Type " G ".

LONDON.
1718 Lis and rose, none (crosses by bust).[62] ER

---

[62] There is a small cross in the place of the initial mark.

CANTERBURY.

1719   Archbishop Morton.   Open crown; M in centre of reverse.   ER
I.m. Tun/none.

1720   King and Archbishop jointly.   Arched crown.   I.m. Tun.   S

YORK.   Archbishop Rotherham (1480–1500).   Sometimes cross on breast.

1721   H in centre of reverse.   T and cross by bust.   I.m. uncertain.   N

1722   Quatrefoil in centre of reverse; extra pellets in two quarters.   N
T and trefoil or key by bust.   I.m. Lis over sun and rose.

DURHAM.   Bishop John Sherwood (1484–1494).

1723   S on breast and D in centre of reverse.   I.m. Cross.   S

Penny   *Obv.*   King enthroned holding orb and sceptre.
Rev.   Royal shield over long cross which divides the legend.

LONDON.

1724   Throne without pillars.   No initial mark.   R

1725   Single pillar.   None, lis, cinquefoil.   N

1726   Two single pillars.   None, pansy.   N

1726/1   Two double pillars.   None, crosslet, pheon.   N

YORK.   Archbishop Rotherham.   Keys below shield.   No initial mark.

1727   No pillars to throne.   No stops.   N

1728   One pillar to throne.   Trefoil or rosette stops.   N

1729   Two single pillars to throne.   No stops.   N

DURHAM.

1730   Bishop John Sherwood (1484–1494).   D S by shield.   One   N
pillar (crozier to right of king) or two single pillars to throne.

1731   Bishop Richard Fox (1494–1501).   D R or R D by shield and   N
mitre above.   One or two single pillars to throne.

Halfpenny   Standard Type " G ".

LONDON.

1732   Class I. (Open crown). Lis over rose, halved lis and rose, none   S
(trefoils by bust), rose (crosses or trefoils by bust).

1733   Class II. (Double arched crown).   None (crosses by bust),   N
cinquefoil.

1734   Class III. (Crown with lower single arch).   None, pansy.   N

1735   Class V. (Very small portrait).   None, lis, pheon.   N

CANTERBURY.

1736   Class I. (Open crown).   M in centre of reverse.   No initial   R
mark.   Archbishop Morton.

1736/1[63]   Class III. (Single arched crown).   M in centre of reverse.   ER
≡ before **HENRIC** (i.m. eye?). Archbishop Morton.

---

[63] cf. BNJ 30 (1960–1) pp. 191–2 and BNJ 31 (1962) p. 122.   The worn condition of the only known
specimen makes certain attribution difficult.

	1737	Class III. (Single arched crown). No mark on reverse. Lis, none. King and Archbishop.	R
		YORK. Archbishop Savage.	
	1738	Single arched crown and key below bust. Initial mark doubtful —martlet or rose?	R
Farthing	1739	Standard Type " G " with arched crown. (But see notes on p. 100). LONDON only.	VR

II. *Profile Issue*

Standard Type—*Obv.* Crowned bust to right.
Rev. POSUI DEUM ADIUTO(R)E MEU(M). Royal shield over cross fourchée which divides the legends.

Testoon		Initial mark: Lis. Weight: 144 grains. (Trial issue only?).	
	1740	HENRIC (US) DI GRA REX ANGLIE Z FR(AN).	ER
	1741	HENRIC SEPTIM DI GRA REX ANGL Z FR(A).	ER
	1742	HENRIC VII DI GRA REX ANGL Z FRA.	ER

Groat		LONDON only.	
		Tentative issue. Double band to crown.	
	1743	HENRIC VII DI GRA REX ANGL Z F. None, lis/none, lis, greyhound's head, crosslet.	R
	1744	HENRIC(US) DEI(DI) GRA REX ANGLI Z FRA. Lis, none, lis/greyhound's head.	R
	1745	HENRIC SEPTIM DI GRA REX ANGL Z FR. None/lis.	ER
	1746	Legend as 1743 with tressure of arches on obverse. Crosslet.	VR
		Regular issue. Triple band to crown.	
	1747	Legend as 1743. Crosslet, crosslet and pheon (only known muled either way with crosslet or pheon), pheon.	N

Halfgroat		Obverse legend HENRIC VII DI GRA REX AGL Z. Triple band to crown.	
		LONDON.	
	1748	No numeral after king's name. No initial mark.	VR
	1749	Normal obverse legend. Lis, pheon.	N
		CANTERBURY. King and Archbishop Warham jointly? (1507–1509).	
	1750	No mint signature. Martlet.	N
		YORK (no mint signature). Archbishop Bainbridge (from Dec. 1508).	
	1751/1	Two keys below shield. Martlet, rose.	N
	1751/2	No marks. Rose.[64]	VR
	1752/1[65]	X B by shield. Rose/martlet.	ER
	1752/2	X B by shield and two keys below. Rose?/martlet.	ER

[64] Formerly attributed to Canterbury mint, these coins are now transferred to York in view of a die-link with No. 1751/1. The omission of a mark on the reverse may be accidental (cf. SCBI 23, pp. xxxiv-v).

[65] BNJ 27 (1953) p. 218.

PATTERN—SILVER

Groat?[66] 1753 *Obv.* King enthroned with " LONDON " below. I.m. Cinquefoil. ER
        Rev. POSUI etc. Royal shield over long cross.

The following pieces although not English coins are inserted on account of their interesting connection with two pretenders to the English throne during the reign of Henry VII.

LAMBERT SIMNEL

Proclaimed Edward VI at Dublin in May, 1487, he claimed to be the Earl of Warwick. The revolt was quickly suppressed in Nottinghamshire and Simnel was captured. All his coins are of the Irish type (cf. NC (1941) pp. 133–5 and SNC 76 (1968) p. 118).

Groat   1754 *Obv.* REX ANGLIE FRANCIE. Shield with the arms of England   S
                    and France quartered by a long cross.
             Rev. ET REX HYBERNIE. Three crowns in pale on a cross.

             1755 *Obv.* EDWARDUS ANGLIE (lis) FRANCIE ⎱ Types as   S
                    Rev. ET (lis) REX HYBERNIE.   ⎰ No. 1754.

             1756 Similar in type to No. 1754 (legends uncertain) with reversed E ER
                    over H below lowest crown on reverse.

Penny   1757 *Obv.* REX AN --- F -- ⎱ Types as   ER
                    Rev. ET -- BERI -- ⎰ No. 1754.

PERKIN WARBECK

Claiming to be Richard, Duke of York, the brother of Edward V, he tried to invade England three times. He was finally captured near London and was executed in 1499. The following is probably a medallion or jetton (cf. BNJ 26 (1949–51) p. 215).

Groat   1758 *Obv.* DOMINIE SALVUM FAC REGEM. Crowned arms of VR
                    England with crowned lis to left and crowned rose to right,
                    all within a tressure of five arches. Initial mark: Lion.
             Rev. MANI TECKEL PHARES. 1494. Lis and lion with a crown
                    above, and a rose below, all within a tressure of five arches.

---

[66] Doubt has been cast on the authenticity of this coin (cf. Mints, Dies and Currency, pp. 161–4).

HENRY VIII

1509–1547

DENOMINATIONS—*FIRST COINAGE* (1509–1526)

GOLD : Sovereign, Ryal, Angel, Half-angel.

SILVER : Groat, Halfgroat, Penny, Halfpenny, Farthing.

SECOND COINAGE (1526–1544).

GOLD : Sovereign, Angel, Half-angel, George Noble, Half George Noble, Crown of the Rose, Crown of the Double Rose, Halfcrown.

SILVER : Groat, Halfgroat, Penny, Halfpenny, Farthing.

THIRD COINAGE (1544–1547).

GOLD : Sovereign, Half-sovereign, Angel, Half-angel, Quarter-angel, Crown, Halfcrown.

SILVER : Testoon, Groat, Halfgroat, Penny, Halfpenny.

Obv. legend.   HENRIC VIII DI GRA REX AGL Z FRA.
(Groats).   (First and second coinages).

HENRIC VIII (8) DI GRA AGL FRA Z HIB REX.
(1542 onwards).

INITIAL MARKS

TOWER	**Arrow** (1532–42)	
Pheon (1509–26; 1541–2)		
	Sunburst (1537–8)	
Castle (1509–26)		
	Annulet and pellet (1544–7)	
Castle with **H** (1509–26)		
	DURHAM	
Portcullis crowned (1509–26)	Spur rowel (1523–6)	
Rose (1526–9)	Star (1526–44)	radiant
Lis (1529–32; 1538–41; 1544–7)	Crescent (1526–9)	

Trefoil
(1526–9)

Lis (1509–26). See above.

BRISTOL

W.S. (1546–7)

CANTERBURY

Martlet
(1509–26)

Pomegranate
(1509–26)

Cross fitchée
(1509–26)

Cross patonce
(1526–32)

T
(1526–32)

Warham's (uncertain) mark
(1526–32)

Catherine wheel
(1533–44)

Rose (1509–26). See above.
Lis 1 (1509–26). See above.

YORK
Martlet (1509–14). See above.
Star (1514–26). See above.
Pansy
(1514–26)

Escallop
(1514–26)

Voided cross
(1514–30)

Acorn
(1526–30)

Key
(1530–44)

SOUTHWARK

Lombardic E (1544–7)

Roman E (1544–7)

S (1544–7)

NOTES
SECOND COINAGE—INITIAL MARKS: LIS

F2   F3   F4   M1   M2

The lis mark is used four times on the groats in the second coinage and, although the same puncheon is used on the first three occasions, the issues may be distinguished by the lettering in the following manner.

Lis (1)	1529–32	..	..	..	..	..	..	..	F2, M1
Lis (2)	1529–32	..	..	..	..	..	..	..	F3, M2
Lis (3)	1538–41	..	..	..	..	..	..	..	F4, M2

The fourth lis mark is from a new punch and is only found on groats bearing the title **HIB REX**. A true coin of this mark is known,[67] but most are muled either way with the pheon mark.

Similar differences of lettering are found on the halfgroats, but no method of dividing the lis mark on the pence and halfpence has yet been found. It is possible that the last lis issue may be distinguished in the latter by the Roman **N** which appears on the reverse of some.

The sequence of marks in the second coinage is discussed in BNJ 28 (1955–7) pp. 560–7.

THIRD COINAGE AND COINS OF EDWARD VI WITH THE NAME AND PORTRAIT OF HENRY VIII

BUSTS

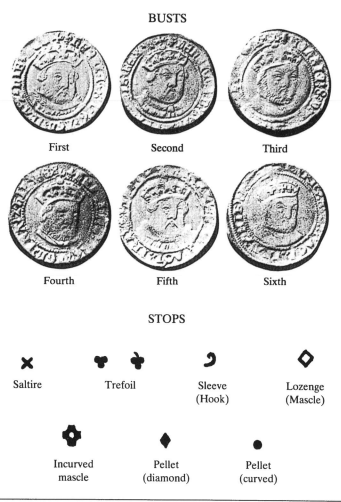

First	Second	Third
Fourth	Fifth	Sixth

STOPS

Saltire	Trefoil	Sleeve (Hook)	Lozenge (Mascle)

Incurved mascle	Pellet (diamond)	Pellet (curved)

---

[67] SNC 86 (1978) p. 361.

	STOPS	CROSS-ENDS	BUSTS (GROATS)
Henry VIII ..	Saltires, trefoils, or sleeves.	Annulets sometimes with letters, or open forks.	First, second, or third.
Both reigns ..	Lozenges.	Annulets with pellets.	Fourth.
Edward VI ..	Incurved mascles or pellets.	Crescents or half-roses.	Fifth or sixth.

The abbreviation mark after HENRIC is always a query shaped symbol on groats of Henry VIII, except those with sleeve stops when it is a comma. On groats of Edward VI it is nearly always a comma. The coins of Bristol mint do not conform exactly to the above, and often use a special form of Lombardic lettering.

FIRST COINAGE (1509-1526)

GOLD

Sovereign 1759/1 Types similar to No. 1692 with portcullis at feet. I.m. Portcullis. ER

Ryal[68] 1759/2 Types similar to No. 1549 but reads HENRIC VIII and has H on ER banner. I.m. Portcullis.

Angel 1760 Standard Type " D " with H and rose by mast. Pheon, castle, N castle and H, portcullis (one variety omits rose).

Half-angel 1761 Standard Type " E " with H and rose by mast. Castle, castle and S H, portcullis.

SILVER

Groat 1762 Types as No. 1747 with portrait of Henry VII but name of Henry N VIII. Pheon, castle, portcullis.

Halfgroat Similar to No. 1762.

LONDON.
1763 I.m. Portcullis. N

CANTERBURY. Archbishop William Warham.
Rev. POSUI DEUM etc.
1764 I.m. Rose. S

1765 W A above shield. Martlet. N

1766 W A beside shield. Cross fitchée. VR

Rev. CIVITAS CANTOR.
1767 W A beside shield. Lis, pomegranate. N

YORK.
Rev. POSUI DEUM etc.
1768 X B beside shield. Martlet. (Archbishop Christopher Bain- S bridge).

1769 Keys below shield. Martlet. (Archbishop Christopher Bain- N bridge).

---

[68] cf. BNJ 32 (1963) pp. 161-2.

	1770	Cardinal's hat and keys below shield. (Archbishop Thomas Wolsey). Martlet, radiant star.	N
	1771	*Rev.* CIVITAS EBORACI. Archbishop Thomas Wolsey. Marks as on No. 1770. Radiant star, star, pansy, escallop, cross voided.	N
	1772	Similar to No. 1771 with T W beside shield. Cross voided.	N

Penny Types as No. 1726.

		LONDON.	
	1773	I.m. Castle, portcullis.	N
		CANTERBURY. Archbishop William Warham.	
	1774	W A above shield. Martlet.	N
	1775	W A beside shield. Pomegranate.	N
		DURHAM.	
	1776	T D above shield. Lis. (Bishop Thomas Ruthall).	C
	1777	T D beside shield. Lis, radiant star. (Bishop Thomas Ruthall).	N
	1778	D W beside shield, hat below. (Bishop Thomas Wolsey). Spur rowel.	ER

Halfpenny Standard Type " G ".

		LONDON.	
	1779	I.m. Castle, portcullis.	N
		CANTERBURY. Archbishop William Warham.	
	1780	W A beside shield. Pomegranate.	R

Farthing	1781	*Obv.* HENRIC DI GRA REX. Portcullis. I.m. Portcullis.	ER
		Rev. CIVITAS LONDON. Rose on long cross.	

SECOND COINAGE (1526–1544)

GOLD

Sovereign		Similar to No. 1759.	
	1782	Sunburst, lis (3), lis (3)/arrow.	VR
Angel		Similar to No. 1760.	
	1783	Sunburst, lis (3).	VR
Half-angel	1784	Similar to No. 1761. I.m. Lis (3).	ER
George noble	1785/1	*Obv.* HENRIC D G R AGL Z FRANC DNS HIBERNIE. Ship with rose on mast with H K at sides. I.m. Rose.	VR
		Rev. TALI DICA SIGNO MES FLUCTUARI NEQUIT. St. George on horseback slaying the dragon.	

| | 1785/2[69] | *Obv.* | HENRIC D G R AGL Z FRANC DNS HYB. Ship with three cruciform masts; rose on centre one. | ER |
| | | *Rev.* | TALI DICATA SIGNO MEN FLUCTUARE NEQUIT. St. George on horseback brandishing a sword; dragon below. I.m. Rose. | |

Half George noble | 1786 | Similar to No. 1785/1. | | ER

Crown of the Rose | 1787 | *Obv.* Royal shield crowned. I.m. Rose. | ER
| | | *Rev.* HENRIC RUTILANS ROSA SINE SPINA. Rose on cross fleury with lion and crowned H in alternate angles, |
| | 1787/1 | Similar to No. 1787 but reverse reads DNS HIB RUTILANS ROSA SINE SPINA. | ER

Crown of the Double Rose | | *Obv.* HENRIC VIII RUTILANS ROSA SINE SPINA. Double rose crowned, with crowned initials at sides.
| | | *Rev.* DEI G R AGLIE FRANC DNS HIBERNIE. Royal shield crowned, with crowned initials at sides.

	1788	Initial H K (Henry and Katherine of Aragon 1526–33). Rose (initials on obverse only),[69] lis (12), arrow	S
	1789	Initials H A (Henry and Anne Boleyn 1533–6). Arrow.	VR
	1790	Initials H I (Henry and Jane Seymour 1536–7). Arrow.	R
	1791	Initials H R (Henricus Rex 1537–42). Arrow	S
	1792	As No. 1791 but HIBERIE REX. Pheon.	VR

Halfcrown | | *Obv.* RUTILANS ROSA SINE SPINA.
| | | *Rev.* HENRIC 8 DI GRA REX AGL Z FRA.

Types similar to Nos. 1788–92 but initials uncrowned.

	1793[69]	No initials in field. Rose.	VR
	1794	Initials H K. Rose (initials on obverse only), lis (12), arrow.	R
	1795	Initials H I. Arrow.	R
	1796	Initials H R with HIB REX. Pheon.	VR

SILVER

Groat | | *Obv.* Crowned portrait of Henry VIII right.
| | | *Rev.* Long cross fourchée over royal shield.

LONDON. Rev: POSUI etc.

| | 1797 | Omits Irish title. Rose, lis (12), arrow, sunburst, lis (3), pheon. | C |
| | 1798 | With title HIB REX. Pheon, lis (4). | VR |

N.B.—There is much muling between the above initial marks. The groats with the mark rose show three varieties of bust and sometimes have mixed Roman and Lombardic letters and a half-rose in the cross ends.

---

[69] Mixed Lombardic and Roman lettering.

YORK.
Rev. CIVITAS EBORACI. (Archbishop Thomas Wolsey).

1799   T W beside shield and hat below. Cross voided (one die   N
omits T W), acorn.

Halfgroat   Types as on Groat. I.m. sometimes on obverse only.

LONDON.
Rev. POSUI etc.

1800   Omits Irish title. Rose, lis (12), arrow, sunburst, lis (3).   S

1801   With title HIB REX. Pheon.   VR

CANTERBURY.
Rev. CIVITAS CANTOR.

1802   W A beside shield. Uncertain mark, ditto/rose, cross patonce,   C
T. (Archbishop William Warham).

1803   Nothing by shield. Uncertain mark. (Archbishop William   N
Warham).

1804   T C beside shield (Archbishop Thomas Cranmer). Catherine   N
wheel (sometimes Obverse only).

YORK.
Rev. CIVITAS EBORACI.

1805   T W beside shield and hat below (Archbishop Thomas Wolsey).   N
Cross voided.

1806   No marks (Sede Vacante? 1530–1). Key.   N

1807   E L or L E beside shield (Archbishop Edward Lee). Key.   C

Penny   H . D .G ROSA SIE SPIA. Types as No. 1726.

LONDON.

1808   I.m. Rose, lis, arrow, sunburst.   N

CANTERBURY.

1809   W A beside shield (Archbishop William Warham). Uncertain   R
mark, cross patonce, T.

1810   T C beside shield (Archbishop Thomas Cranmer). Catherine   R
wheel.

DURHAM.

1811   T W beside shield, hat below. (Bishop Thomas Wolsey).   C
Trefoil, crescent, star, cross with pellet in one angle.

1812   No marks (Sede Vacante? 1529–30). I.m. on obverse only.   N
Star, radiant star.

1813   C D beside shield (Bishop Cuthbert Tunstall). Star (both sides   C
or obverse only), radiant star (obverse only).

YORK.

1814   E L beside shield (Archbishop Edward Lee). Key.   VR

Halfpenny   H D G ROSA SIE SPIA. Standard Type " G ".

LONDON.

1815   I.m. Rose, lis, arrow, sunburst.   N

CANTERBURY.

1816   W A beside bust (Archbishop William Warham). T, cross   R
patonce?

1817   T C beside bust (Archbishop Thomas Cranmer). Catherine   R
wheel.

YORK.

1818   T W beside bust (Archbishop Thomas Wolsey). Cross voided?   R

1819   Key below bust (Sede Vacante? 1530–1). Cross voided.   R

1820   E L or L E beside bust (Archbishop Edward Lee). Key.   R

| **Farthing**[70] | 1821 | *Obv.* RUTILANS ROSA. Portullis. | ER |

Rev. DEO GRACIAS. Long cross with one pellet in each angle.

LONDON.
Rose, lis, sunburst.

Obv. Similar to No. 1821.
Rev. DEO GRACIAS. Rose on long cross.

| | 1822/1 | LONDON. Arrow. | ER |
| | 1822/2 | CANTERBURY. Catherine wheel. | ER |

THIRD COINAGE (1544–1547)

GOLD

Sovereign

Obv. Type similar to No. 1759 but with large bearded face and rose at feet.
Rev. IHESUS AUTEM TRANSIENS PER MEDIUM ILLORUM IBAT. Crowned shield with supporters (lion and dragon), H R in monogram below.
Lettering: Lombardic with some Roman.

	1823	TOWER. Large module (candlesticks on pillars of throne). Lis.	ER
	1824	Small module (birds on pillars of throne). Lis, Pellet in annulet/lis.	VR
	1825	SOUTHWARK. Similar to No. 1824. S, S/Є (Є below shield), Є /S.	VR
	1826	BRISTOL. Similar to No. 1824. WS/none.	VR

Half-sovereign

Types as No. 1824.

	1827	TOWER. Lis (Roman lettering), pellet in annulet (Roman, Lombardic, or mixed lettering).	S
	1828	SOUTHWARK. S (Roman, Lombardic, or mixed lettering—sometimes Є below shield), Є (Lombardic lettering with Є below shield).	S
	1829	BRISTOL. WS (Lombardic lettering), WS/none (Lombardic lettering).	VR

| **Angel** | 1830 | Standard Type " D " with H and rose by mast; annulet by angel's head and on ship. I.m. Lis. Varieties omit annulet by angel's head or on ship. | S |

| **Half-angel** | 1831 | Standard Type " E " with H and rose by mast; one or three annulets on ship. I.m. Lis. | R |

Quarter-angel

Obv. HENRICUS VIII DI GRA AGL.
Rev. FRANCIE ET HIBERNIE REX.
Types as Standard Type " D " with H and rose by mast. I.m. Lis.

| | 1832 | Early style. Angel in armour. | R |
| | 1833 | Late style. Angel wears tunic. | R |

---

[70] cf. SNC 95 (1987) p. 218.

Crown		Similar to No. 1792; often omits RUTILANS from obverse legend. Lombardic lettering.	

              TOWER.

1834   Pellet in annulet.   Sometimes with annulet against the inner   S
circle.

              SOUTHWARK.

1835   S, Є , E/S, E/Є .   S

              BRISTOL.

1836   WS, none/WS. (One die has RH beside shield).   N

Halfcrown   Similar to No. 1796.   Lombardic or Roman lettering.

              TOWER.

1837   Pellet in annulet.   Sometimes with annulet on inner circle.   R

              SOUTHWARK.

1838   S.   R

              BRISTOL.

1839   WS/none.   R

      Obv.   HENRIC 8 ROSA SINE SPIN.
      Rev.   DEI GRA AGL FRA Z HIB REX.
              SOUTHWARK.

1840   Є .   R

SILVER

Testoon[71]   *Obv.*   Crowned bearded bust facing.[72]
              Rev.   Crowned rose with crowned H and R at sides.

              LONDON.

1841   (POSUI etc.). Lis, pellet in annulet,[73] none/pellet in annulet.[73]   R

              SOUTHWARK.

1842   (CIVITAS LONDON). S, S/E (over Є), Є , Є /E.   R

              BRISTOL.

1843   None/WS.   R

Groat   *Obv.*   Crowned bearded bust facing.
            Rev.   Long cross over royal shield.

              TOWER.

1844   (POSUI etc). Busts 1, 2 and 3. Lombardic lettering. I.m. Lis.   N

              SOUTHWARK.

1845   (CIVITAS LONDON). Busts 1, 2, 3 and 4. Lombardic, Roman, N
or mixed lettering. In forks, S in all or Є in upper and lower
and S in sides. I.m. None, lis.

              BRISTOL.

1846   Bust 2 and 3. Lombardic or Bristol lettering. In forks, no N
mark, annulets, lis, or trefoils. I.m. None/WS.

---

[71] A fine series of testoons is illustrated in BNJ 24 (1941–4) facing p. 116.

[72] There is some variation in the portrait, lettering and stops. A study appears in SNC 83 (1975) pp. 283–6; 334–6.

[73] Coins with lozenge stops may have been struck under Edward VI.

CANTERBURY.

1847   Bust 1 (var). and 2. Roman or mixed lettering. Spur from   N
shield to inner circle. I.m. None.

YORK.

1848   Bust 1 (var)., 2 and 3. Lombardic, Roman or mixed lettering.   N
Spur from shield to inner circle. I.m. None.

Halfgroat   Types as groat. All bust No. 1.

TOWER.

1849   (**POSUI** etc). Lombardic lettering. Annulet in forks. I.m.   S
Lis, none.

SOUTHWARK.

1850   (**CIVITAS LONDON**). Mixed lettering. In forks, S in all or   S
Є in upper and lower and S in sides. I.m. None.

BRISTOL.

1851   Lombardic or Bristol lettering. In forks, no mark, lis, trefoils,   N
or quatrefoils. I.m. None/**WS**.

CANTERBURY.

1852   Lombardic or mixed lettering. Stops: Saltires, trefoils, sleeves   N
or none. Sometimes with spur on reverse. I.m. None.

YORK.

1853   Lombardic or mixed lettering. Spur from shield to inner circle.   N
I.m. None.

Penny   *Obv.*   H D G ROSA SINE SPINA. Facing bust.
             Rev.   Long cross over royal shield.

TOWER.

1854   (**CIVITAS LONDON**). Lis (Lombardic lettering), none (Lom-   N
bardic or mixed lettering, sometimes Roman on reverse).

SOUTHWARK.

1855   (**CIVITAS LONDON**). S (chiefly Roman lettering), Є (Lom-   N
bardic or mixed lettering).

BRISTOL.

1856   Bust 1 (Lombardic lettering), Bristol bust (Bristol lettering).   N
I.m. None.

CANTERBURY.

1857   Lombardic lettering. Stops: Saltires, trefoils, or sleeves. Some-   N
times spur on reverse. I.m. None.

YORK.

1858   Lombardic or chiefly Roman lettering. Stops: Saltires, trefoils,   N
sleeves or none. Sometimes spur on reverse. I.m. None.

Halfpenny   *Obv.*   Similar to penny.
             Rev.   Long cross with three pellets in each angle.

TOWER.

1859   Lombardic lettering. Pellet in annulet in centre of reverse. I.m.   N
Lis, None.

BRISTOL.

1860   Bristol lettering. I.m. None?   R

CANTERBURY.

1861   Lombardic or mixed lettering.   Some read H 8.   I.m. None.   S

YORK.

1862   Mixed lettering.   Trefoil stops.   I.m. None.   S

EDWARD VI

1547–1553

DENOMINATIONS—*COINAGE IN NAME OF HENRY VIII.*

GOLD : Sovereign, Half-sovereign, Crown, Halfcrown.

SILVER :[74] Groat, Halfgroat, Penny, Halfpenny.

COINAGE IN OWN NAME.

FIRST PERIOD (April 1547–January 1549).

GOLD : Half-sovereign, Crown, Halfcrown.

SILVER : Shilling, Groat, Halfgroat, Penny, Halfpenny.

SECOND PERIOD (January 1549–April 1550).

GOLD : Sovereign, Half-sovereign, Quarter-sovereign, Half-quarter-sovereign.

SILVER : Shilling.

THIRD PERIOD (1550–1553).

GOLD : Sovereign of 30s., Sovereign of 20s., Half-sovereign, Crown, Halfcrown, Angel, Half-angel.

SILVER : Crown, Halfcrown, Shilling, Sixpence, Threepence, Penny, Halfpenny, Farthing.

Obv. legend: EDWARD VI D G ANGLIE FRANCIE Z HIBERNIE REX.

INITIAL MARKS

TOWER		TOWER	
Lis (1547–8, 1550–1)	🌸	Pheon (1549)	↓
Arrow (1547–9)	↓	Trefoil (1549)	♣
K (1547–9)	K	Six (1549–50)	σ
Grapple (1549)	⌘	Swan (1549–50)	🦢

---

[74] Testoons with lozenge stops may belong to this series (cf. No. 1841).

Rose
(1549–51)

Y
(1549–51)

Crowned
leopard's
head[75]
(1550)

Lion
(1550–1)

Martlet
(1550–1)

Ostrich head
(1551)

Tun
(1551–3)

Escallop
(1551–3)

DURHAM HOUSE
Bow
(1548–9)

BRISTOL
W.S.
(1547–9)

T.C.
(1549)

CANTERBURY
t
(1549–50)

T
(1549–50)
Rose (1549). See above.
Lis (1549). See above.

YORK
Lis
(1547–8). See above.

SOUTHWARK
E
(1547–9)

Pierced mullet
(1552–3)

COINAGE IN THE NAME OF HENRY VIII (1547–1551)[76]

GOLD

Sovereign   Similar to No. 1824. Roman lettering.

1863	TOWER.	Lis.	VR
1864	BRISTOL.	W S.	VR

---

[75] cf. BNJ 50 (1980) pp. 135–6.
[76] For notes see Henry VIII, pp. 108–9.

Half-sovereign

Similar to No. 1827 but with youthful portrait. Roman lettering.

1865   TOWER. Arrow, arrow/none, none/K or none (K below shield),   R
grapple (both sides or either or absent—grapple below shield),
lis, martlet.

1866   SOUTHWARK. Ꝫ (Roman lettering, with Ꝫ below shield), E,   R
none/E (usually with E below shield).

Crown

Similar to Henry VIII No. 1834 but RUTILANS not omitted.
Roman lettering.

1867   TOWER. Arrow, arrow/none (a variety has transposed legends),   S
none/K, grapple, martlet.

1868   SOUTHWARK. E (transposed legends), E/none, none/E.   VR

Halfcrown

Similar to Henry VIII No. 1837. Roman lettering.

1869   TOWER. Arrow, none/arrow, K/none, grapple/none, martlet.   S

1870   SOUTHWARK. E, none/E, E/none.   R

SILVER

Groat

Types as on Nos. 1844–8.

1871   TOWER (**POSUI** etc.). Busts 4, 5, and 6. Roman or rarely   N
Lombardic lettering.
Lis, arrow, K, none/K, K/none, none/grapple, martlet, none.

1872   SOUTHWARK (**CIVITAS LONDON**). Busts 4, 5, and 6. Roman   N
lettering. Crescents or roses in forks. I.m. None, none/E.

1873   DURHAM HOUSE (*Rev.* **REDDE CUIQUE QUOD SUUM EST**).   R
Bust 6. Roman lettering. I.m. Bow.

1874   BRISTOL. Busts 2 and 3. Bristol lettering. I.m. None/T C.   S

1875   CANTERBURY. Busts 5 and 6. Roman lettering. I.m. None,   N
rose.

1876   YORK. Busts 4, 5 and 6. Roman lettering. I.m. Lis, none.   N

Halfgroat

Types as on Nos. 1849–53. All Bust No. 1 except late York.

1877   TOWER (**POSUI** etc.). Roman lettering. Open forks. I.m.   N
Arrow, none/arrow, none/K, grapple.

1878   SOUTHWARK (**CIVITAS LONDON**). Roman lettering. I.m. E,   N
none/E, none.

1879   DURHAM HOUSE (*Rev.* **REDD CUIQ QD SUUM EST**). Roman   VR
lettering. I.m. None/bow.

1880   BRISTOL. Bristol lettering. I.m. None/T C.   R

1881   CANTERBURY. Lombardic or mixed lettering with lozenge   N
stops. Roman lettering with round pellet or lozenge stops.
I.m. None, t/none, none/t.

1882   YORK. Busts 1 and 6. Roman lettering. I.m. None.   N

Penny		Types as on Nos. 1854–8. All facing bust unless stated.	
	1883	TOWER **(CIVITAS LONDON)**. Roman lettering, occasionally a Lombardic H. I.m. Arrow, none/K, grapple/none, none/ grapple, none (sometimes with threequarters bust).	N
	1884	SOUTHWARK **(CIVITAS LONDON)**. I.m. E.	ER
	1885	DURHAM HOUSE (*Rev.* **RED CUIQ Q S EST**). I.m. None/bow?	VR
	1886	BRISTOL. Roman lettering. I.m. None.	N
	1887	CANTERBURY. Facing or threequarters bust. Lombardic with lozenge stops or Roman lettering. I.m. None.	N
	1888	YORK. Facing or threequarters bust. Roman lettering. Stops: Lozenges, pellets, or none. I.m. None.	N
Halfpenny		Types as on Nos. 1859–62.	
	1889	TOWER. Roman lettering. I.m. None.	S
	1890	CANTERBURY. Roman lettering. Some read **H 8**. I.m. None.	S
	1891	YORK. Roman or mixed lettering. Stops: Lozenges or pellets. I.m. None.	S

COINAGE IN OWN NAME

FIRST PERIOD (April 1547–January 1549)[77]

GOLD

Half-sovereign		Types similar to Nos. 1865–6 but obverse legend **EDWARD 6**, etc.	
	1892	TOWER. Arrow.	VR
	1893	SOUTHWARK. E (sometimes with E or E below shield).	R
Crown	1894	*Obv.* **RUTILANS ROSA SINE SPINE**. Crowned rose with crowned E R at sides.	ER
		Rev. **EDWARD 6** etc. Crowned shield with crowned E R at sides. I.m. Arrow.	
Halfcrown	1895	Similar to No. 1894 but initials uncrowned.	ER

SILVER

Shilling[78]	1896	*Obv.* Crowned bust right.	R
		Rev. **TIMOR DOMINI FONS VITE. MDXLVIII**. Oval shield crowned and garnished, with E R at sides. I.m. Bow (Durham House).	

---

[77] Nearly all the coins of this period were struck before those bearing the name of Henry and from a historical and artistic point the two issues form one coinage. For ease of reference they have been listed separately.

[78] The only recorded specimens of this coin are of brass alloy (cf. BNJ 31 (1962) pp. 128–9).

Groat		*Obv.* Crowned bust right.	
		Rev. Royal shield on long cross.	
	1897	TOWER (**POSUI** etc.). Arrow.[79]	R
	1898	SOUTHWARK (**CIVITAS LONDON**)—**E**, none.	R
Halfgroat		Similar to groat.	
	1899	TOWER (**POSUI** etc.). Arrow.	R
	1900	SOUTHWARK (**CIVITAS LONDON**). Arrow, **E**.	R
	1901	CANTERBURY (name spelt **EDOARD**). None.	R
Penny		Types similar to groat, but obverse legend **E D G ROSA** etc.	
	1902	SOUTHWARK. (**CIVITAS LONDON**). Arrow, **E**.	R
	1903	BRISTOL. None.	R

Halfpenny 1904 *Obv.* **E D G ROSA SIN SPIN.** Crowned bust right. I.m. VR
Uncertain.
Rev. **CIVITAS LONDON.** Long cross with three pellets in
each angle.

Halfpenny 1905 Similar to No. 1903. BRISTOL only. No initial mark. VR

SECOND PERIOD (January 1549–April 1550)

GOLD

Sovereign 1906 *Obv.* King seated on throne holding a sword. VR
Rev. **IHS AUTEM TRANSIENS PER MEDIUM ILLORUM IBAT.**
Crowned shield with supporters. **ER** on scroll below.
Arrow, **Y**.

Half-sovereign *Obv.* Legends as under. Uncrowned bust right.
Rev. **EDWARD VI** etc. Crowned oval garnished shield with
E R at sides.

	1907	**TIMOR DOMINI FONS VITE MDXLIX.** Arrow.	ER
	1908	**SCUTUM FIDEI PROTEGET EUM.** Arrow, **6, Y**.	R
	1909	Similar to No. 1908 with or without **MDXLVIII** after obverse legend. Bow (Durham House).	ER
	1910	**LUCERNA PEDIBUS MEIS VERBUM TUUM.** Bow (Durham House).	ER

Half-sovereign *Obv.* **EDWARD VI** etc. Crowned bust right.
Rev. **SCUTUM FIDEI PROTEGET EUM.** Type as Nos. 1907–10.

	1911	LONDON. Arrow, swan, grapple, **Y**, martlet.	R
	1912	DURHAM HOUSE. Bow (usually with **EDWARD VI** etc. on both sides).	ER

---

[79] A variety reads **EDOARD**.

Quarter-sovereign	1913	Similar to No. 1908. Arrow, **6**, **Y**.	VR
Quarter-sovereign	1914	Similar to No. 1911. Arrow, swan, grapple, **Y**.	VR
Half-quarter-sovereign	1915	Similar to No. 1908. Arrow, **Y**.	VR
Half-quarter-sovereign	1916	Similar to No. 1911. Arrow (legends sometimes transposed), arrow/swan, **Y**, grapple (legends transposed).	VR

SILVER

Shilling[80]		Types and legends as No. 1896 except for date.	
		MDXLIX. Legends transposed.	
	1918/1	LONDON. Arrow, none.	R
	1918/2	SOUTHWARK. **Y**, **EY**/**Y**.	R
	1918/3	CANTERBURY. None/rose.	VR
		MDXLIX. Normal legends.	
	1917/1	LONDON. Arrow, arrow over **G**, grapple (one die omits **ER** beside shield), grapple over **G**, pheon, swan, swan over **Y**/swan.	S
	1917/2	SOUTHWARK. **Y**, **Y** over **G**, **Y**/**Y** over grapple.	S
	1920	BRISTOL. **TC** over **G**/**TC**.	R
	1921	CANTERBURY. **t**, **t** over **G**, **T**.	R
		MDL. Normal legends.	
	1919/1	LONDON. Pheon/swan, swan (two varieties), martlet, crowned leopard's head.	R
	1919/2	SOUTHWARK. **Y**.	R
		Shillings of DURHAM HOUSE mint (i.m. Bow).	
	1922	**MDXLIX.** Normal legends.	R
	1923	**MDXLIX.** Legends transposed.	VR
	1924	No date. *Rev.* INIMICOS EIUS INDUAM CONFUSIONE.	VR
	1925	Similar to No. 1924 but legends transposed.	R

THIRD PERIOD (1550–1553)

GOLD

Sovereign of 30s.	1926	*Obv.* King on throne holding orb and sceptre; portcullis at feet. *Rev.* IHESUS AUTEM TRANSIENS PER MEDIUM ILLORUM IBAT. Royal shield on full blown rose. Ostrich head, tun.	ER

---

[80] Mules are frequent and there is some variation in the portraits (cf. BNJ 55 (1985) pp. 134–43).

Sovereign of 20s.	1927	*Obv.*	Half length figure right, crowned and carrying orb and sceptre.	VR
		Rev.	Similar to No. 1906. Y, tun.	
Half-sovereign	1928	*Obv.*	Similar to No. 1927.	R
		Rev.	IHS AUTEM etc. Crowned square shield with E R at sides. Y, tun.	
Crown	1929		Similar to No. 1928 but SCUTUM etc. on reverse. Y, tun.	VR
Halfcrown	1930		Similar to No. 1929. Y, tun.	VR
Angel	1931		Standard Type " D " with E and rose beside mast. Ostrich head, tun.	ER
Half-angel	1932		Standard Type " D " with E and rose beside mast. Reverse legend as on Angel in Roman letters. I.m. Ostrich head.	ER

FINE SILVER

Crown[81]	1933	*Obv.*	King on horseback right with date below horse.	S
		Rev.	POSUI etc. Long cross fourchée over royal shield. 1551. Y, tun. 1552. Tun. 1553. Tun.	
Halfcrown			Similar to No. 1933.	
	1934		Walking horse with plume on head. 1551. Y.	S
	1935		Galloping horse without plume. 1551. Tun; 1552. Tun.	S
	1936		Walking horse without plume. 1553. Tun.	VR
Shilling	1937	*Obv.*	Crowned bust facing with rose to left and XII to right.	C
		Rev.	Similar to No. 1933. Y, tun.	
Sixpence			Similar to No. 1937 but VI instead of XII.	
	1938		LONDON (POSUI etc.). Y, tun.	N
	1939		YORK. Mullet.	S
Threepence			Similar to No. 1937 but III instead of XII.	
	1940		LONDON. (POSUI etc.). Tun.	N
	1941		YORK. Mullet.	S
Penny	1942	*Obv.*	E D G ROSA SINE SPI. King enthroned holding orb and sceptre.	ER
		Rev.	CIVITAS LONDON. Long cross fourchée over royal shield. I.m. Tun.	

N.B.—Modern forgeries of this type exist.

---

[81] A classification of the Crown dies was published in the sale catalogue of the H. M. Lingford collection (Glendinning 24.10.50) p. 8.

BASE SILVER

Shilling[82] Types and legends as No. 1896 except for date. LONDON only.

MDL.

1943/1	LONDON. Lion, rose over lion.		R
1943/2	SOUTHWARK. Lis/Y.		VR

MDLI.

1944/1	LONDON. Rose, lion, lion/rose over lion.		R
1944/2	SOUTHWARK. Y/lis, lis.		R

Penny *Obv.* E D G ROSA SINE SPINA. Double rose.
Rev. Long cross fourchée over royal shield.

1945	LONDON. Escallop.		N
1946	YORK. Mullet.		N

Halfpenny 1947 Similar to No. 1945 but single rose on obverse. ER

Farthing 1948 *Obv.* E D G ROSA SINE SPI. Portcullis. ER
Rev. CIVITAS LONDON. Long cross pattée with three pellets in each angle.

PATTERNS

GOLD

Angel 1949 *Obv.* St. Michael, holding shield and spear, slaying the dragon. ER
Rev. Three masted ship with shield on side. Weight: 472$\frac{3}{4}$ grains. I.m. Rose.

Half-sovereign 1950 *Obv.* SCUTUM etc. Uncrowned bust right. I.m. Rose. ER
Rev. EDWARD VI etc. Rose on stalk crowned and with E R at sides.

Crown 1951 Similar to No. 1950. Legends sometimes transposed. ER

Halfcrown 1952 Similar to No. 1950 but initial mark a cross. ER

SILVER

Shilling 1953 Similar to No. 1896 but dated MDXLVII and weight 482 grains. ER
I.m. Rose. (One specimen weighs 88 grains).

Shilling 1954 *Obv.* TIMOR DOMIN FONS VITAE MDXL7. Crowned bust ER
right. I.m. Rose.
Rev. POSUI etc. Long cross over royal shield. I.m. Arrow.

---

[82] See n. 80.

Shilling 1955 *Obv.* **EDWARD VI** etc. King in armour on galloping horse ER right.

Rev. **TIMOR DOMINI FONS VITE MDLI.** Crowned square shield with **E R** at sides.

I.m. Ostrich head.

N.B.—A number of shillings of types Nos. 1917–25 and 1943–4 are found countermarked with a portcullis or a greyhound's head. This was done to reduce their value at the beginning of Elizabeth I's reign and they will be found listed under that reign (Nos. 1989 and 1990).

MARY

1553–1554

DENOMINATIONS—GOLD : Sovereign, Ryal, Angel, Half-angel.

SILVER : Groat, Halfgroat, Penny.

Obv. legend: MARIA D G ANG FRA Z HIB REGINA.

PRIVY MARKS

(In legends, usually after first or second word)

Pomegranate		Halved rose and castle.	

GOLD

Sovereign	1956	*Obv.*	Queen enthroned, portcullis at feet. Date in Roman figures at end of legend.	VR
		Rev.	A DNO FACTU EST ISTUD Z EST MIRA IN OCUL NRIS. Royal shield on Tudor rose. Pomegranate. 1553, 1554, undated. Halved rose and castle, 1553, undated.	
Ryal	1957	*Obv.*	Queen holding shield and sword, standing in ship with rose on side and flag at stern. MDLIII, at end of legend.	ER
		Rev.	A DNO etc. Floriated cross with a lis at end of each limb and rose on sun in centre; in each angle, a lion passant, guardant, with a crown above; all within a tressure of eight arches.	
Angel	1958		Types as Standard Type " D " with M and rose beside mast. Reverse legend: A DNO etc. Pomegranate. Halved rose and castle.	R
Half-angel	1959		Similar to No. 1958. Privy mark: Pomegranate.	ER

SILVER

Groat	1960	*Obv.*	Crowned bust left.	N
		Rev.	VERITAS TEMPORIS FILIA. Long cross fourchée over royal shield. Privy mark: Pomegranate.	

N.B.—Groats reading POSUI etc. are modern forgeries.

Halfgroat	1961		Similar to No. 1960	VR
Penny		*Obv.*	M D G ROSA SINE SPINA. Crowned bust left.	
		Rev.	Similar to No. 1960. Legends as follows:	
	1962		VERITAS TEMP FILIA.	VR
	1963		CIVITAS LONDON.	VR

Base penny[83]   1964   *Obv.*   M D G ROSA SINE SPINA. Rose.   VR
                      Rev.   CIVITAS LONDON. Type as No. 1960.

N.B.—Mr. Schneider has drawn attention to the strange and unique type
of stop appearing at the end of the reverse legend on the angels and
half-angels thus: ℛ It has never been explained and apparently is not
commented on in existing literature. It has been suggested that this is a
contraction of " et cetera " (SNC 69 (1961) p. 185).

---

[83] The existence of this coin is dubious as it was probably recorded from an Emery forgery (cf. BNJ 40 (1971) p. 166, No. 77). No indenture for its issue exists.

PHILIP AND MARY

1554–1558

DENOMINATIONS—**GOLD : Angel, Half-angel.**

SILVER : Shilling, Sixpence, Groat, Halfgroat, Penny.

Obv. legend: PHILIP Z MARIA D G REX Z REGINA. (Fuller titles on large silver—see below)

INITIAL MARKS

Lis   Halved rose and castle.

GOLD

Angel	1965	Types as Standard Type " D " with P and M beside mast. Reverse legend: A DNO etc. I.m. Lis.	VR
Half-angel	1966	Similar to No. 1965.	ER

SILVER

Shilling

Obv. Busts of Philip and Mary facing each other; above, a large crown, which usually divides the date.

Rev. POSUIMUS DEUM ADIUTOREM NOSTRUM. Oval garnished shield with arms of Spain and England; above, a crown, which divides the mark of value XII, when this is shewn.

1967	Full titles. PHILIP ET MARIA D G R ANG FR NEAP PR. HISP. 1554, undated, undated and without XII.	S
1968	English titles. PHILIP ET MARIA D G REX ET REGINA ANGL. 1554, 1554 without XII, 1555,[84] 1555 without XII, undated.	S
1969	English titles with date below bust. 1554, 1555.	VR

N.B.—Coins of No. 1969 dated 1554 have been extensively forged in modern times, and forgeries dated 1557 also occur.

Sixpence

Similar to Shilling but mark of value is VI.

1970	Full titles. 1554, undated.	S
1971	English titles. 1555, 1557 (i.m. Lis).	S
1972	English titles with date below bust. 1554, 1557.	ER

N.B.—Specimens exist dated 1555 with a beaded inner circle on the obverse.

---

[84] One die has X only as mark of value.

Groat	1973	*Obv.*	Crowned bust of Mary left.	N
		Rev.	POSUIMUS DEUM ADIUTO NOS. Cross fourchée over royal shield. I.m. Lis.	
Halfgroat	1974		Similar to No. 1973.	VR
Penny	1975		Similar to No. 1963 but obverse legend P Z M D G ROSA SINE SPINE. I.m. Lis.	R
Base penny	1976		Similar to No. 1964 but obverse legend P Z M D G ROSA SINE SPINE. I.m. Halved rose and castle.	N

PATTERN (SILVER)

Halfcrown	1977	*Obv.*	PHILIPPUS D G R ANG FR NEAP PR HISP. Bust of Philip in armour right; above, a crown; below, 1554.	ER
		Rev.	MARIA D G R ANG FR NEAP PR HISP. Bust of Mary left: above, a crown; below, 1554.	

ELIZABETH I

1558–1603

HAMMERED ISSUES

FIRST COINAGE (1558–1561).

DENOMINATIONS—**GOLD : Sovereign of 30s., Angel, Half-angel, Quarter-angel, Halfpound, Crown, Halfcrown.**

SILVER : Shilling, Groat, Halfgroat, Penny, Countermarked testoons of Edward VI.

SECOND COINAGE (1561–1582).

GOLD : Angel, Half-angel, Quarter-angel, Halfpound, Crown, Halfcrown.

SILVER : Sixpence, Threepence, Halfgroat, Three-halfpence, Penny, Three-farthings.

THIRD COINAGE (1583–1603).

GOLD : Sovereign of 30s., Ryal, Angel, Half-angel, Quarter-angel, Pound, Halfpound, Crown, Halfcrown.

SILVER : Crown, Halfcrown, Shilling, Sixpence, Halfgroat, Penny, Halfpenny.

MILLED ISSUE.

GOLD : Halfpound, Crown, Halfcrown.

SILVER : Shilling, Sixpence, Groat, Threepence, Halfgroat, Three-farthings.

Obv. legend: **ELIZABETH D G ANG FRA ET HIB REGINA.** (see lists for details).

INITIAL MARKS

HAMMERED

Lis (1558–60)		Rose 1565–65/6	
Cross crosslet (1560–1)		Portcullis (1565/6–66/7)	
Martlet (1560–1)		Lion (1566/7–67)	
Pheon (1561–5)		Coronet (1567–70)	

Castle (1570–2)		Tun (1591/2–94)	
Ermine (1572–3)		Woolpack (1594–95/6)	
Acorn (1573–4)		Key (1595/6–97/8)	
Eglantine (1574–8)		Anchor (1597/8–1600)	
Plain cross (1578–80)		Cypher (1600–1)	
Long cross (1580–1)		One (1601–2)	
Sword (1581–82/3)		Two (1602–3)	
Bell (1582/3–83)		MILLED	
A (1583–84/5)		Star (1560–66/7)	
Escallop (1584/5–87)		Lis (1566/7–70). See above. Castle (over lis) (1570–1). See above.	
Crescent (1587–89/90)		MILLED PATTERNS	
		Lis (1560). See above.	
		Mullet (1560, 1574–5)	
Hand (1589/90–91/2)		Pierced mullet (1570)	

N.B.—The above dates do not necessarily correspond with those on the coins.

NOTES

It has been usual in the past to catalogue the hammered coinage of this reign as one series, with the distinction made between the early and late styles of bust on the gold coins.[85]   One of the main obstacles to the classification into issues has been the fact that the various coinages of gold and silver do not in the main coincide in date.

However, the silver has been divided into seven issues,[86] but these have been reduced in the lists to three main coinages.   For ease of reference, the gold has been divided in the same manner, although the real pattern is more complicated than is apparent from this.[87]   The first issue in this metal coincides with that in silver, but the later coinages were struck as follows:

ANGEL GOLD	Sovereign of 30s.	..	..	..	1584–1595/6
	Ryal ..	..	..	..	..	1583–1592
	Angel and divisions		..	..	1566–1600
CROWN GOLD	Early bust	..	..	..	..	1565–1571
	Later bust	..	..	..	..	1593–1602

It will be appreciated from the above that the angel and its divisions form a continuous issue without change of type, although divided in the lists into second and third coinages.   Similarly the silver penny was struck throughout the reign without change of type, while the type of the halfgroat does not change until the third issue.

An unusual feature worthy of mention is that the ship on some of the angels is sailing to the left instead of the right as in all previous and subsequent reigns.

Hammered coins normally have a beaded inner circle except for the early lis issues with the wire-line circle,[88] and the cross crosslet halfgroat, which may be a pattern.   The letter Z is used for ET in the hammered coinage only on very early coins (1558–60).

The base testoons of Edward VI countermarked in 1560–61, to denote their reduced values, have been listed at the end of the first coinage.

HAMMERED COINAGE

FIRST ISSUE (1558–1561)

GOLD

Sovereign of 30s.	1978	*Obv.*	ELIZABETH D G ANG FRA ET (or Z) HIB REGINA. VR Queen enthroned holding orb and sceptre, with portcullis at feet.
		Rev.	A DNO FACTU EST ISTUD ET (or Z) EST MIRA IN OCUL NRIS. Square shield on Tudor rose. Lis (beaded inner circles), cross crosslet.

---

[85] Nine master portraits used on forty nine punches have been distinguished and are described and illustrated together with the punches used for patterns in BNJ 58 (1988) pp. 90–5.

[86] I. D. Brown, " Some Notes on the coinage of Elizabeth I ". BNJ 28 (1957) p. 568.

[87] The gold, which cannot be co-ordinated with the silver, divides into five issues (cf. SNC 91 (1983) pp. 221–3) or three main issues (SNC 92 (1984) pp. 116–8).   Details of the classification of the silver also is given in the later paper.

[88] It has been suggested that the beaded inner circle on coins with the lis mark was introduced to distinguish those struck after 31st July 1560 (SNC 80 (1972) pp. 59–60).

| **Angel** | 1979 | *Obv.* | ELIZABETH D G ANG FRA ET (or Z) HIB REGI(NA). Similar to Standard Type " D ". | R |

Obv. ELIZABETH D G ANG FRA ET (or Z) HIB REGI(NA). Similar to Standard Type " D ".

Rev. A DNO FACTUM EST ISTUD ET (or Z) EST MIRABILE. Similar to Standard Type " D " with E and rose beside mast.
Lis (wire-line or beaded inner circles), cross crosslet.

Half-angel   1980   Similar to No. 1979. Lis (wire-line or beaded inner circles), cross crosslet.   R

Quarter-angel   1981   *Obv.* ELIZABETH D G ANG FRANCIE. Type as No. 1979. VR
I.m. Lis?
Rev. ET HIBERNIE REGINA FIDEI. Type as No. 1979.
I.m. Lis?

Halfpound   1982   *Obv.* ELIZABETH D G ANG FRA ET (or Z) HI REGINA.   N
Crowned bust left in plain dress.
Rev. SCUTUM FIDEI PROTEGET EAM.   Crowned   square shield with ER at sides.
Lis (wire-line inner circles), cross crosslet.

Crown   1983   Similar to No. 1982. Lis (wire-line inner circles), cross crosslet.   S

Halfcrown   1984   Similar to No. 1982. Lis (wire-line inner circles), cross crosslet.   R

SILVER

Shilling   1985   *Obv.* ELIZABETH D G ANG FRA ET (or Z) HIB REGINA.   N
Crowned bust left.
Rev. POSUI DEU ADIUTOREM MEU. Square shield on long cross fourchée dividing the legend.
Lis (wire-line or beaded inner circle), cross crosslet, martlet.

Groat   1986   Similar to No. 1985. Lis (wire-line or beaded inner circle), cross crosslet, martlet.   N

Halfgroat   1987   Similar to No. 1985. Lis (wire-line inner circle), cross crosslet, martlet.   N

N.B.—A variety (probably unique) with i.m. cross crosslet, omits inner circles.

Penny   1988   *Obv.* E D G ROSA SINE SPINA. Type as No. 1985.   N
Rev. CIVITAS LONDON. Type as No. 1985.
Lis (wire-line inner circle), cross crosslet, martlet.

N.B.—A variety with the lis initial mark (probably unique) has the date 1558 in the obverse legend.

Countermarked testoons of Edward VI (1560–61)[89]

Four pence Halfpenny   1989   Shillings of Edward VI Nos. 1917–25. Countermarked with a VR
portcullis before the face.
1549. Bow (undated), arrow, grapple, pheon, swan, Y, TC, t.

---

[89] SNC 70 (1962) No. 1, pp. 1–3.

N.B.—Forged countermarks on genuine coins exist. These may be easily distinguished by the chains, which are represented by lines with a flaw in the left one on the genuine mark. The forged marks have a row of six annulets as chains. It was also used to fabricate a number of " oddities " on fine shillings, Mary groats, etc. (cf. SNC 69 (1961) p. 136).

Two pence 1990   Shillings of Edward VI No. 1943–4, or with i.m. harp, marked   VR
Farthing   with a greyhound on the king's shoulder.
                         1550. Lion, rose, swan (Greyhound mark used in error).
                         1551. Lis, rose.
                         1552. Harp.

N.B.—A shilling dated 1549 (i.m. doubtful) and one dated 1550 (i.m. Swan) exist with this mark. They should in fact bear the portcullis mark.

SECOND ISSUE (1561–1582)

GOLD

Angel   1991/1 Similar to No. 1979. Coronet, ermine, acorn, eglantine, plain   R
                         cross, long cross, sword.

                 1991/2 Variety has ship to left. Eglantine.   ER

Half-angel   1992/1 Similar to No. 1980. Coronet, ermine, acorn, eglantine, plain   R
                         cross, sword.

                 1992/2 Variety has ship to left. Sword.   ER

Quarter-angel 1993 Similar to No. 1981. Coronet, ermine, acorn, eglantine, plain   R
                         cross, long cross, sword.

Halfpound   1994   Similar to No. 1982. Rose, portcullis, lion, coronet, castle.   N

Crown   1995   Similar to No. 1982. Rose, portcullis, lion, coronet, castle.   S

Halfcrown   1996   Similar to No. 1982. Rose, portcullis, lion, coronet, castle.   R

N.B.—The pound of this issue (i.m. rose) has been included in the patterns.

SILVER

Sixpence   1997   Similar to No. 1985, with a rose behind the head and the date   N
                         above the shield.
                         Pheon. 1561, 1562, 1563, 1564, 1565.
                         Rose. 1565.
                         Portcullis. 1566.
                         Lion. 1566, 1567, undated.
                         Coronet. Undated, 1567, 1568, 1569, 1570.
                         Castle. 1569, 1570, 1571.
                         Ermine. 1571, 1572, 1573, undated.
                         Acorn. 1573, 1574.
                         Eglantine. 1573, 1574, 1575, 1576, 1577.
                         Plain cross. 1578, 1579.
                         Long cross. 1580, 1581.
                         Sword. 1582.
                         Bell. 1582, 1583.

Threepence	1998	Similar to No. 1997.	N
		Pheon. 1561, 1562, 1563, 1564, 1565.	
		Rose. 1565.	
		Portcullis. 1566.	
		Lion. 1566, 1567.	
		Coronet. 1567, 1568, 1569, 1570. (One obverse die omits rose behind head. Used with 1568 die).	
		Castle. 1570, 1571.	
		Ermine. 1572, 1573.	
		Acorn. 1573, 1574.	
		Eglantine. 1573, 1574, 1575, 1576, 1577.	
		Plain cross. 1578, 1579.	
		Long cross. 1580, 1581.	
		Sword. 1582.	

Halfgroat   1999   Similar to No. 1985.   Portcullis, lion, coronet, castle.   N
(1561–72)

Three-   2000   *Obv.*   **E D G ROSA SINE SPINA**.   Crowned bust left with rose   S
halfpence   behind.

                            Rev.   **CIVITAS LONDON**.   Square shield with date above, on long cross fourchée dividing the legend.

                            Pheon. 1561, 1562, 1564.
                            Rose. 1565.
                            Portcullis. 1566.
                            Lion. 1567.
                            Coronet. 1567, 1568, 1569.
                            Castle. 1570.
                            Ermine. 1572.
                            Acorn. 1572, 1573, 1574.
                            Eglantine. 1573, 1574, 1575, 1576, 1577.
                            Plain cross. 1578, 1579.
                            Long cross. 1581.
                            Sword. 1582.

Penny   2001   Similar to No. 1988.   Rose, portcullis, lion, coronet, castle,   N
                            eglantine, plain cross, long cross, sword.

Three-   2002   Similar to No. 2000.   R
farthings   Pheon. 1561, 1562.
                            Coronet. 1567, 1568.
                            Ermine. 1572, 1573.
                            Acorn. 1573.
                            Eglantine. 1573, 1574, 1575, 1576, 1577.
                            Plain cross. 1578, 1579.
                            Long cross. 1581.
                            Sword. 1582.

THIRD ISSUE (1583–1603)

GOLD

Sovereign   2003   Similar to No. 1978, with minor differences.   A, escallop,   R
of 30s.   crescent, hand, tun.

Ryal	2004	*Obv.* ELIZAB D G ANG FR ET HIB REGINA. Queen holding orb and sceptre, standing facing in a ship with rose on side and flag with E thereon at stern. *Rev.* IHS AUT TRANSIENS PER MEDIU ILLORUM IBAT. Royal cross with rose over sun in centre. Lombardic lettering on both sides. A, escallop, crescent, hand.	VR

N.B.—A number of Dutch imitations of these coins exist. The most obvious difference is in the obverse legend which varies from that on the English coins.

Angel	2005	Similar to No. 1979. Bell, A, escallop, crescent, hand, tun, key, anchor, cypher, one, two.	S
Half-angel	2006	Similar to No. 1979. Bell, A, escallop, crescent, hand, key, anchor.	R
Quarter-angel	2007	Similar to No. 1981. Bell, A, escallop, crescent, hand, tun, woolpack (? doubtful), key, anchor.	R
Pound	2008	*Obv.* ELIZABETH D G ANG FRA ET HIB REGINA. Crowned bust left with long hair and richly ornamented dress. *Rev.* SCUTUM FIDEI PROTEGET EAM. Crowned square-shield with E R at sides. Tun and lion/tun, tun, woolpack, key, anchor, cypher, one, two.	S
Halfpound	2009	Similar to No. 2008. Some read ELIZAB. Tun, woolpack, key, anchor, cypher, one, two.	S
Crown	2010	Similar to No. 2008 but ELIZAB D G ANG FRA ET HIB REGI. Tun, woolpack, key, cypher, one, two.	S
Halfcrown	2011	Similar to No. 2010. Tun, woolpack, key, cypher, one, two.	S

SILVER

Crown[90] **(1601–3)**	2012	*Obv.* ELIZABETH D G ANG FRA ET HIBER REGINA. Crowned bust left holding sceptre and orb. *Rev.* POSUI DEUM ADIUTOREM MEUM. Square garnished shield over long cross fourchée dividing the legend. One, two.	R
Halfcrown **(1601–3)**	2013	Similar to No. 2012. One, two.	R
Shilling	2014	Similar to No. 1985, but obverse legend ELIZAB D G ANG FR ET HIB REGI. Bell, A, escallop, crescent, hand, tun, woolpack, key, anchor, cypher, one, two.	N

---

[90] cf. SNC 79 (Jun 1971) pp. 238–9, for a note on the crown dies.

Sixpence	2015	Similar to No. 1997, but obverse legend ELIZAB D G ANG FR ET HIB REGI.	N

          Bell. 1582, 1583.
          A. 1582, 1583, 1584.
          Escallop. 1584, 1585, 1586.
          Crescent. 1587, 1588, 1589.
          Hand. 1590, 1591, 1592.
          Tun. 1592, 1593, 1594, 1595.
          Woolpack. 1594, 1595.
          Key. 1595, 1596, 1597, 1598.
          Anchor. 1598, 1599, 1600.
          Cypher. 1600.
          One. 1601, 1602.
          Two. 1602.

Halfgroat 2016   *Obv.* E D G ROSA SINE SPINA. Crowned bust left with two   N
               pellets behind.
          Rev. CIVITAS LONDON. Square shield on cross fourchée.
               Bell (sometimes omits pellets), A, escallop, crescent,
               hand, tun, woolpack, key, anchor, cypher, one, two.

Penny 2017   Similar to No. 1988. Bell, A, escallop, crescent, hand, tun,   N
          woolpack, key, anchor, cypher, one, two.

Halfpenny 2018   *Obv.* No legend. Portcullis with i.m. above.   N
          Rev. No legend. Cross and pellets.
               No mark, bell, A, escallop, crescent, hand, tun, wool-
               pack, key, anchor, cypher, one, two.

MILLED[91]

Portraits on the milled coinage.

A (1560–1).   Small-faced bust with ornate dress.
B (1561–2).   Small bust with very plain dress.
C (1562).   Tall or upright bust with ornate dress.
D (1562–4).   Large broad bust with elaborate dress.
E (1564–6).   Similar to D but with low ruff exposing the ear.
F (1567–8).   Small plain bust with low ruff and exposed ear.
G (1570–1).   Large crude bust breaking the legend. Reversed Ns.

GOLD

Obv. ELIZABETH D G ANG FRA ET HIB REGINA. Crowned
       bust left.
Rev. SCUTUM FIDEI PROTEGET EAM. Crowned square
       shield with E R at sides.

Halfpound 2019/1   Bust A. Star.[92]   ER

             2019/2   Bust C. Star.   ER

---

[91] cf. BNJ 53 (1983) pp. 108–32.
[92] Possibly a pattern struck in 1561.

| | 2019/3 | Bust D. Star. Plain Z (1562–3) or curly Z (1564). | VR |
| | 2019/4 | Bust E. Lis (grained edge). | R |

Crown | | Similar to halfpound. |
	2020/1	Bust A. Star.[92]	ER
	2020/2	Bust D. Star. Curly Z (1564).	ER
	2020/3	Bust E. Lis (1567–8).	ER

Halfcrown | | Similar to halfpound. |
| | 2021/1 | Bust D. Star. Curly Z (1564). | ER |
| | 2021/2 | Bust E. Lis (1567–8). | ER |

SILVER

Obverse similar to gold. Reverse. **POSUI DEUM ADIUTOREM MEUM.** Square shield on long cross fourchée.

Shilling | 2022 | Bust A with plain dress. Star. Large size (32 mm). | R |
| | 2023 | Bust A with decorated dress. Three sizes (Large—32 mm; intermediate—30 mm; small—29 mm). | S |

Sixpence | | Similar to shilling but rose behind head and date above shield. |
	2024	Bust A. Star. 1561.	N
	2025/1	Bust B. Large rose. Star. 1561.	S
	2025/2	Bust B. Medium rose. Star. 1562.	N
	2026	Bust C. Medium rose. Star. 1562.	N
	2027	Bust D. Small rose. Star. 1562.	N
	2028	Bust D. Small rose. Reverse cross is pattée. Star. 1562, 1563, 1564.	N
	2029	Bust E. Reverse cross is pattée. Star. 1564, 1566.	N
	2030	Bust F (HI REGI(NA)). Lis. 1567, 1568.	N
	2031	Bust G (AN F & HI REGINA). Lis. 1570, Castle over lis. 1571.	N

Groat | 2032 | Similar to shilling. Bust A. Star. | VR |

Threepence | | Similar to sixpence. I.m. Star. |
	2033	Bust A. 1561.	R
	2034	Bust C. 1562.	R
	2035	Bust D. 1562.	R
	2036	Bust D. Reverse cross pattée. 1563, 1564.	R

Halfgroat | 2037 | Similar to shilling. Bust A. I.m. Star. | R |

Three-farthings | 2038 | *Obv.* E D G ROSA SINE SPINA. Bust D with rose behind. *Rev.* CIVITAS LONDON. Square shield on long cross pattée with 1563 above. I.m. Star (both sides). | ER |

PATTERNS

GOLD

Pound (1565) 2039   *Obv.* ELIZABETH D G ANG FRA ET HIB REGINA. Crowned ER
                                  bust left with plain dress.
                          Rev. IHS AUTEM, etc. Crowned square shield with E R at
                                  sides.
                                  Initial mark: Rose.

Halfpound 2040   Similar to No. 1982, but small module and without inner circles. ER
                                Initial mark: Tun.

SILVER

Halfcrown 2041   Types as Nos. 2022–3, but bust in high relief and obverse legend ER
(1560)   ends REGI. Weight: 211 grains. I.m. Lis. Probably a piedfort
                                pattern shilling.

Shilling 2042   Similar to No. 2023, small module. I.m. Mullet. (1560).   VR

Shilling 2043   Similar to No. 1985, but without inner circles. I.m. Martlet. ER
                                (1561).

Shilling   Similar to No. 2124, but very ornate bust. I.m. Key.

         2044   **REGI.** Plain shield.   VR

         2045   **REGINA.** Ornately garnished shield.   VR

Sixpence 2046   Similar to No. 2039, but of different style. I.m. Pierced mullet. VR
                                1570.

Sixpence 2047   *Obv.* ELIZABETH D^E G^R AN^G F^R & HI^B REGINA. Very ER
                                    elaborate bust left with rose behind. Crown reaches top
                                    of coin.
                          Rev. POSUI DEU^M ADIUTOREM MEU^M.   Broad   flat   cross
                                  over square shield with date above.
                                  Mullet. 1574, 1575.

Threepence 2048   Similar to No. 2047. I.m. Mullet. 1575.   ER

Halfgroat 2049   Similar to No. 2016, but with lis behind the head. I.m. Bell. ER

    N.B.—The following coins mentioned in the earlier list may also be
       patterns.

            Threepence. No. 1998, without rose behind head. I.m.
               Coronet. 1568.
            Halfgroat. No. 1987, without inner circles. I.m. Cross crosslet.
            Halfgroat. No. 2016, without pellets behind head. I.m. Bell.

COPPER

Penny (Gold, 2050   *Obv.* UNUM A DEO DUOBUS SUSTINEO.   Crowned   bust VR
silver, copper   facing.
or tin)   *Rev.* AFFLICTORUM CONSERVATRIX.   1601.   Crowned
                                    monogram of Elizabeth.

    N.B.—This may be a pattern groat or medalet.

Penny (Silver or copper)	2051	*Obv.* THE PLEDGE OF. Crowned bust facing. *Rev.* A PENNY. 1601. Crowned monogram of Elizabeth.	VR
Halfpenny (Silver or copper)	2052	Similar to No. 2051, but reverse legend A HALFPENNY. 1601.	VR
Halfpenny (Silver or copper)	2053	*Obv.* THE PLEDGE OF. Crowned monogram of Elizabeth. *Rev.* A HALFPENNY. Crowned rose.	VR
Farthing (Silver)	2054	*Obv.* No legend. Crowned monogram of Elizabeth. *Rev.* No legend. Portcullis with 1601 above.	VR
Penny (Silver, copper or tin)	2055	*Obv.* ROSA SINE SPINA. Crowned rose. *Rev.* PRO LEGE REGE ET GREGE. Shield of St. George.	VR
Halfpenny	2056	Similar to No. 2055.	VR
Farthing	2057	Similar to No. 2055.	VR
Halfpenny[93] (Silver)	2058	*Obv.* E D G ROSA SINE SPINA. Crowned rose with E R at sides. *Rev.* TURRIS LONDINENSIS. Shield of St. George.	ER
Halfpenny (Billon)	2059	*Obv.* ELIZAB D G, etc. Crowned bust right. *Rev.* A HALFPENNY PECE. Crowned shield.	ER
Farthing (Silver)	2060	*Obv.* No legend. Crowned E R with bell below. *Rev.* No legend. Rose.	ER

LEAD OR PEWTER TOKENS

There exist a number of lead or pewter pieces which have in the past been described as patterns or tokens. It is more probable however that they were political medalets or counters, as some would appear to relate to Mary, Queen of Scots, and the workmanship on most is rather crude. They are normally found in London, and were struck about 1574. A selection of the types relating specifically to Elizabeth is given below (cf. Medallic Illustrations, Pl. VIII, 6–16).

	2061	*Obv.* Double headed eagle. No legend. *Rev.* Crowned portcullis with chains. No legend.	VR
	2062	*Obv.* As No. 2061. *Rev.* GOD SAVE THE QUENE. Crowned rose with E R at sides.	VR
	2063	*Obv.* As No. 2061. *Rev.* BEATI REGINA. Crowned rose.	VR
	2064	*Obv.* Lion rampant left with E R at sides. No legend. *Rev.* Crowned portcullis with chains. No legend.	VR

---

[93] Reputedly struck by Elizabeth when she visited the Tower on 10th July 1561 (cf. Medallic Illustrations. Pl. VII, 3).

JAMES I

1603–1625

DENOMINATIONS—*FIRST COINAGE* (1603–1604).

> **GOLD : Sovereign, Half-sovereign, Crown, Halfcrown.**

SECOND COINAGE (1604–1619).

> **GOLD : Rose-ryal, Spur-ryal, Angel, Half-angel, Unite, Double-crown, Britain crown, Thistle crown, Half-crown.**

THIRD COINAGE (1619–1625).

> **GOLD : Rose-ryal, Spur-ryal, Angel, Laurel, Half-laurel, Quarter-laurel.**

ALL COINAGES.

> **SILVER : Crown, Halfcrown, Shilling, Sixpence, Halfgroat, Penny, Halfpenny.**

> **COPPER : Farthing.**

Obv. legend: IACOBUS D G ANG SCO FRAN ET HIBER REX.
(First coinage).

IACOBUS D G MAG BRIT FRAN ET HIB REX.
(Second and Third coinages).

INITIAL MARKS

Thistle (1603–4, 1621–3)		Grapes (1607)	
Lis (1604–5, 1623–4)		Coronet (1607–9)	
Rose (1605–6, 1620–1)		Key (1609–10)	
Escallop (1606–7)		Bell (1610–11)	

Mullet (1611–2)	★	Book (1616–7)	📖
Tower (1612–3)	♜	Crescent (1617–8)	☽
Trefoil (1613, 1624)	♣	Plain cross (1618–9)	✚
Cinquefoil (1613–5)	✿	Saltire (1619)	✖
Tun (1615–6)	▥	Spur rowel (1619–20)	✷

BUSTS

Silver; Shillings & Sixpences

FIRST
Square beard.
Rounded bust.

SECOND
Pointed beard,
resting on chest.

THIRD
Square beard,
which projects.

FOURTH
Hair brushed forward.
Armour plain.

FIFTH
Hair longer and
brushed back.

SIXTH
Hair longer still
and very curly.

The busts shown above are those found on the shillings and sixpences and on the smaller gold of the first two coinages. The portrait on the sovereigns and unites of these coinages is a half-length bust which displays the same differences.

THIRD COINAGE GOLD

FIRST   SECOND   THIRD

FOURTH   FIFTH

The above division shows the main varieties of "laurel" busts, but a number of minor varieties exists, the main difference being in the ties of the wreath.

HALFGROATS ET INFRA

Early   Late

Second and third coinage issues of halfgroats and pence which bear the same initial mark may easily be distinguished by the smaller outer petals of the obverse rose. The two styles are illustrated above, and the change appears to take place during the issue of coins bearing no initial mark.

NOTES

FIRST COINAGE.   Obverse legend reads **ANG SCO FRA (N)**.
Distinctive reverse legends.
Sovereigns: First bust: Plain armour.
                 Second bust: Decorated armour.

SECOND COINAGE.   Obv. legend reads **MAG BRI**.
Rev. legends changed.

THIRD COINAGE.   **Gold:** Laureated busts.
Silver: Similar to second coinage but with sixth bust.

N.B.—The silver crown and halfcrown of the first coinage may be easily distinguished from the Scottish coins of a similar size and type by the crowned rose on the housings and the fact that Scottish coins employ & for **ET** on the obverse.

FIRST COINAGE (1603–1604)

GOLD

Sovereign		*Obv.* Crowned half-length bust to right with sceptre over right shoulder and orb in left hand.	
		Rev. EXURGAT DEUS DISSIPENTUR INIMICI. Square shield crowned and garnished, with I R at sides.	
	2065	First bust. Thistle.	R
	2066	Second bust. Thistle, lis.	R
Half-sovereign	2067	*Obv.* Crowned bust right. I.m. Thistle.	ER
		Rev. Similar to sovereign but shield ungarnished. I.m. Thistle.	
Crown	2068	Similar to No. 2067 but shield extends to the bottom of the coin and I R is beside the crown. Rev. legend: TUEATUR UNITA DEUS.	ER
		Thistle, Lis/thistle.	
Halfcrown	2069	Similar to No. 2068.	VR
		Thistle, lis.	

N.B.—The quarter-angel of this coinage is included in the patterns.

SILVER

Crown	2070	*Obv.* King crowned and in armour with a sword over his right shoulder, on horseback right.	VR
		Rev. EXURGAT DEUS DISSIPENTUR INIMICI. Square garnished shield.	
		Thistle, lis.	
Halfcrown	2071	Similar to No. 2070.	VR
		Thistle, lis.	
Shilling		*Obv.* Crowned bust right; behind, XII.	
		Rev. EXURGAT DEUS DISSIPENTUR INIMICI. Square shield.	
	2072	First bust—Thistle.	S
	2073	Second bust—Thistle, lis.	N
Sixpence		Similar to shilling but VI on obverse and date over shield on reverse.	
	2074	First bust. 1603, Thistle.	S
	2075	Second bust. 1603, Thistle. 1604, Thistle, lis.	N
Halfgroat	2076	*Obv.* I D G ROSA SINE SPINA. First bust right: behind, II.	N
		Rev. No legend. Square shield with initial mark above.	
		Thistle, lis.	
Penny	2077	Similar to No. 2076 but I behind head.	N
		Thistle, lis.	
Halfpenny	2078	*Obv.* No legend. Portcullis with initial mark above.	N
		Rev. No legend. Cross and pellets.	
		Thistle, lis.	

SECOND COINAGE (1604–1619)

GOLD

Rose ryal	2079	*Obv.* King enthroned holding orb and sceptre; portcullis at feet.	R
		Rev. A DNO FACTUM EST ISTUD ET EST MIRAB IN OCULIS NRIS. Square shield on Tudor rose. Rose, escallop, grapes, coronet, key, mullet, tower, trefoil, cinquefoil, tun, book.	
Spur ryal	2080	*Obv.* King holding sword and shield standing in ship with rose on side.	VR
		Rev. A DNO FACTUM EST ISTUD ET EST MIRABILE. Rose on spur rowel in centre of royal cross. Rose, escallop, coronet, mullet, tower, trefoil, cinquefoil, book.	
Angel	2081	*Obv.* St. Michael slaying the dragon.	R
		Rev. A DNO FACTUM EST ISTUD. Ship bearing a shield; I and rose beside mast. Rose, escallop, grapes, coronet, bell, mullet, tower, trefoil, cinquefoil, tun, book, crescent, plain cross, saltire.	
Half-angel	2082	Similar to No. 2081. Tower, trefoil, cinquefoil, tun, book, plain cross, saltire.	ER
Unite		Similar to No. 2066 but rev. legend FACIAM EOS IN GENTEM UNAM.	
	2083	Second bust. Lis, rose.	N
	2084	Fourth bust. Rose, escallop, grapes, coronet, key, bell, mullet, tower, trefoil, cinquefoil.	N
	2085	Fifth bust. Cinquefoil, tun, book, crescent, plain cross, saltire.	N
Double crown		*Obv.* Crowned bust right.	
		Rev. HENRICUS ROSAS REGNA IACOBUS. Square shield crowned with I R at sides.	
	2086	Third bust. Lis, rose.	N
	2087	Fourth bust. Rose, escallop, grapes, coronet, key, bell.	N
	2088	Fifth bust. Mullet, tower, trefoil, cinquefoil, tun, book, crescent.	N
	2089	Fifth bust (variety). Plain cross, saltire.	N
Britain crown		Similar to double crown but I R beside crown on rev.	
	2090	First bust. Lis, rose, escallop, grapes, coronet.	N
	2091	Third bust. Key, bell, mullet, tower, trefoil, cinquefoil.	N
	2092	Fifth bust. Cinquefoil, tun, book, crescent, plain cross, saltire.	N
Half-crown		Similar to crown but rev. legend TUEATUR UNITA DEUS.	
	2093	First bust. Lis, rose, escallop, grapes, coronet, key (over coronet).	N

| | 2094 | Third bust. Key, bell, mullet, tower, trefoil. | N |
| | 2095 | Fifth bust. Cinquefoil, tun, book, crescent, plain cross. | N |

Thistle crown 2096 *Obv.* Crowned rose and two leaves with I R (occasionally omitted) at sides. S
                   Rev. **TUEATUR UNITA DEUS.** Crowned thistle and two leaves with I R at sides.
Lis, rose, escallop, grapes, coronet, key, bell, mullet, tower, trefoil, cinquefoil, tun, book, crescent, plain cross.

SILVER

Crown 2097[94] Types as No. 2070 with rev. legend **QUAE DEUS CONIUNXIT NEMO SEPARET.** VR
Lis, rose, escallop, grapes.

Halfcrown 2098 Similar to No. 2097. VR
Lis, rose, escallop, tun.

Shilling Types as No. 2072 with rev. legend **QUAE DEUS CONIUNXIT NEMO SEPARET.**

	2099	Third bust. Lis, rose.	N
	2100	Fourth bust. Rose, escallop, grapes, coronet.	N
	2101[95]	Fifth bust. Coronet, key, bell, mullet, tower, trefoil, cinquefoil, tun, book, plain cross.	N

Sixpence Similar to No. 2099 but VI behind bust and date over shield on rev.

| | 2102 | Third bust. 1604, Lis; 1605, Lis, rose. | S |
| | 2103 | Fourth bust. 1605, Rose; 1606, Rose, escallop; 1607, Escallop, grapes, coronet; 1608, Coronet; 1609, Coronet, key; 1610, Key, bell, mullet; 1611, Mullet, tower; 1612, Tower; 1613, Trefoil; 1614, Cinquefoil; 1615, Cinquefoil, tun; 1618, plain cross. | N |

Halfgroat *Obv.* I D G ROSA SINE SPINA. Rose with crown above.
                  Rev. **TUEATUR UNITA DEUS.** Thistle with crown above.

	2104[96]	Large crowns. Lis, rose, escallop, grapes, coronet.	C
	2105/1[97]	Small crowns. Coronet, key, bell, mullet, tower, trefoil, cinquefoil, tun, book, plain cross.	C
	2105/2	**TUEATUR UNITA DEUS** on both sides. Mullet (obv.).	ER

Penny 2106/1 Similar to halfgroat without crowns over the rose and thistle. C
Lis, rose, escallop, grapes, coronet, key, bell, mullet, tower, trefoil, cinquefoil, plain cross, none.

         2106/2 **TUEATUR UNITA DEUS** on both sides. Mullet. ER

---

[94] The crown dies are studied in a note in SNC 79 (1971) pp. 238–9.
[95] A variety has a single arched crown (i.m. Coronet).
[96] A variety omits the inner circles. Lis.
[97] A mule 2104/2105 exists. I.m. uncertain (probably coronet).

Halfpenny	2107	*Obv.*	Rose. No legends.	N
		Rev.	Thistle with i.m. above. No legends.	
			Lis, rose, escallop, grapes, coronet, key, bell, mullet, cinquefoil.	

THIRD COINAGE (1619–1625)

GOLD

Rose ryal	2108	*Obv.*	King enthroned holding orb and sceptre with portcullis at feet; pattern of roses and lis in the field.	R
		Rev.	A DNO FACTUM EST ISTUD ET EST MIRA INOC NRIS. Shield on cross fleury with XXX above, encircled by a band with lis, lions, and crowns.	
			Spur rowel, rose, thistle, lis, trefoil.	

Spur ryal	2109	*Obv.*	Crowned lion supporting royal shield and holding sceptre; X V at sides of shield.	VR
		Rev.	Similar to No. 2080.	
			Spur rowel, rose, thistle, trefoil.	

Angel	2110	*Obv.*	St. Michael slaying the dragon.	VR
		Rev.	A DOMINO FACTUM EST ISTUD. Three masted ship with royal arms on mainsail.	
			Spur rowel, rose, thistle, lis, trefoil.	

Laurel		*Obv.*	Laureated bust in armour left with XX behind.	
		Rev.	FACIAM EOS IN GENTEM UNAM. Long cross fleury over crowned square shield.	
	2111		First bust. Spur rowel.	R
	2112		Second bust. Spur rowel, rose.	S
	2113		Third bust. Rose, thistle.	N
	2114		Fourth bust. Lis, trefoil.	N
	2115		Fifth bust. Trefoil.	ER

Half-laurel			Types as laurel but X behind head and reverse legend HENRICUS ROSAS REGNA IACOBUS.	
	2116		First bust. Spur rowel.	R
	2117		Fourth bust. Spur rowel, rose, thistle, lis, trefoil.	N

Quarter-laurel			Similar to half-laurel but V behind head. Reverse inner circle sometimes omitted.	
	2118		Second bust. Spur rowel, rose, thistle, lis.	N
	2119		Fourth bust. Lis, trefoil.	N

SILVER

Crown			Similar to No. 2097.	
	2120		Without plumes. Rose, thistle, lis, trefoil.	R
	2121		Plumes over shield. Thistle, lis, trefoil.	R

Halfcrown		Similar to No. 2097.	
	2122	Without plumes. Rose, thistle, lis, trefoil.	R
	2123	Plumes over shield. Thistle, lis, trefoil.	R
Shilling		Similar to No. 2099 but with sixth bust.	
	2124	Without plumes. Spur rowel, rose, thistle, lis, trefoil.	N
	2125	Plumes over shield. Thistle, lis, trefoil.	S
Sixpence		Similar to No. 2102 but with sixth bust.	
	2126	1621, Rose, thistle; 1622, Thistle; 1623, Thistle, lis; 1624, Lis, trefoil.	N
Halfgroat		Similar to No. 2105 without stops on reverse.	
	2127	Spur rowel, none, rose, thistle, lis, trefoil, trefoil and lis.	C
Penny		Similar to No. 2106 without stops on reverse.	
	2128	Spur rowel, none, lis, trefoil.	C
Halfpenny	2129	Similar to No. 2107 but no initial mark.	N

COPPER

ROYAL FARTHING TOKENS

INITIAL MARKS

Although some of the copper tokens bear similar marks to the silver and gold coins, there is probably no connection. A selection of the marks is given below, but those which are shown elsewhere or are simple enough to be described, are omitted.

Cross pattée fourchée		Grapes	
Dagger		Lion passant	
Eagle's head erased		Lion rampant	
Ermine		Millrind	
Flower		Stirrup	

Fret Woolpack

A.

GENERAL TYPE   *Obv.*   IACO D G MAG BR (IT). Two lis-headed sceptres in saltire through a single-arched crown.

Rev.   FRA ET HIB REX. A harp surmounted by a single-arched crown.

Type 1   *Harrington* (19 May 1613–28 June 1614?).
IACO between sceptre-heads. Fret before rev. legend.
Diam: 12.25 mm. Average weight: 5 grains.

2130   (a) Letter or other mark below the crown between the   R
sceptres. Usually a mullet between D . G.

A, B, C, D, F, S, ermine, millrind, pellet, ⸫ℒ .

2131   (b) No marks, but central jewel of crown varies as shown   R
below. Sometimes a mullet between D .G.
Central jewel: Normal, trefoil, crescent, mullet.

Type 2   *Harrington* (19 May 1613–28 June 1614?).

2132   IACO between sceptre-heads. I.m. before rev. legend. Diam: S
15 mm. Average weight: 9 grains.
Cinquefoil, saltire, lis, martlet, mullet, trefoil.

Type 3   *Lennox* " rounds " (1614–25).
IACO close to right sceptre-head. Sub-classes (a) to (c) have five jewels on the circlets of the crowns.

2133   (a) I.m. on reverse only. Bell.   R

2134   (b) I.m. on both sides. Flower, fusil (solid lozenge).   C

2135   (c) I.m. on obverse only. Annulet, ball, coronet, crescent,   C
cross fleury fitchée, cross pattée fourchée, dagger, eagle's head, fusil, grapes, key, lion passant, mascle, quatrefoil, rose (double), star, star (pierced), thistlehead, trefoil, triangle (pellet below), tun, woolpack.

2136   (d) Larger crown on obv. and rev.; nine jewels on circlets.   C
I.m. on obverse only. A, dagger, fusil, lion rampant, lis three, mascle, stirrup, trefoil, triangle, tun.

Type 4   *Lennox* " ovals " (1622–25).

2137   Legend reads from bottom left upwards. Initial mark on both   S
sides: Cross pattée.

PATTERNS

GOLD

Quarter-angel   2138   *Obv.*   St. Michael slaying the dragon. I.m. Lis.   ER
Rev.   TUEATUR UNITA DEUS. Square shield.

N.B.—This is probably a pattern for the obverse only, as a halfcrown die die was used to strike the reverse.

COPPER

Halfpenny?	2139	*Obv.*	BEATI PACIFICI (small tun between each word). Crown with a small tun below.	VR
		Rev.	HOC OPUS DEI (small tun between each word). Thistle and rose dimidiated.	
?	2140		Uniface. Two roses and thistles with stems intertwined, a crown above.	VR
?	2141		Uniface. Rose and thistle with stems intertwined, a crown above. Two sizes: $1\frac{1}{8}$ in. and $\frac{3}{4}$ in.	VR

N.B.—Nos. 2139–41 are probably medalets.

Farthing (Silver)	2142	*Obv.*	I R crowned with small rose to left, thistlehead to right, and flower below.	VR
		Rev.	Crowned portcullis.	

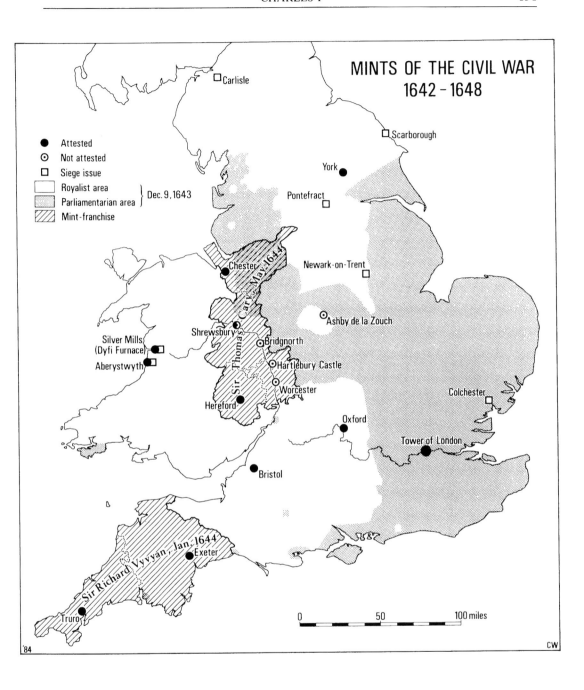

MINTS OF THE CIVIL WAR
1642 - 1648

- ● Attested
- ⊙ Not attested
- □ Siege issue
- Royalist area
- Parliamentarian area ⎱ Dec. 9, 1643
- Mint-franchise ⎰

Carlisle

Scarborough

York ●

Pontefract □

Chester ● Newark-on-Trent □

Sir Thomas Cary, May 1644

⊙ Ashby de la Zouch

Shrewsbury ● Bridgnorth ⊙

Silver Mills (Dyfi Furnace) □

Aberystwyth □ Hartlebury Castle ⊙

Worcester ⊙

Hereford ●

Colchester □

Oxford ⊙

Tower of London ●

Bristol ●

Sir Richard Vyvyan, Jan. 1644

Exeter ●

Truro ●

0   50   100 miles

'84   CW

CHARLES I

1625–1649

TOWER MINT

DENOMINATIONS—**GOLD : Angel, Unite, Double-crown, Britain crown.**

SILVER : Crown, Halfcrown, Shilling, Sixpence, Halfgroat, Penny, Halfpenny.

COPPER : Farthing tokens.

Obv. legend: CAROLUS D G MAG BRI FR ET HIB REX.

INITIAL MARKS

Lis (1625)		Rose (1631–2)	
Cross calvary (1625–6)		Harp (1632–3)	
Blackamoor's head (1626–7)		Portcullis (1633–4)	
Castle (1627–8)		Bell (1634–5)	
Anchor (1628–9)		Crown (1635–6)	
Heart (1629–30)		Tun (1636–8)	
Plume (1630–1)		Anchor (1638–9). See above.	

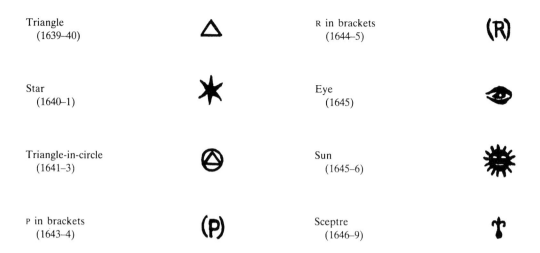

Triangle (1639–40)	△	R in brackets (1644–5)	(R)
Star (1640–1)	✶	Eye (1645)	👁
Triangle-in-circle (1641–3)	⊜	Sun (1645–6)	☀
P in brackets (1643–4)	(P)	Sceptre (1646–9)	♱

N.B.—The king left London during the currency of the initial mark "triangle-in-circle". Some coins bearing this mark and all coins with the subsequent marks were struck by Parliament during his absence. In accordance with usual practice, pellets have been shown as the initial mark where they occur alone. It is unlikely that they were intended as such, and more probably served as space fillers.

BUSTS

Group A   Group B   Group C   Group D

Double-crown   Shilling

Group E   Group F

Unite   Shillings (a) & (b).   Sixpence
           Group G

The above is a selection of the main types of portrait on the Tower coins. Where the characteristics are similar for all denominations, only one portrait is given. In groups E and G however, different busts are used on the gold and silver, and examples of these are shown. For further variations, readers are referred to the specialised articles which are listed in the bibliography or SCBI 33 where most varieties are illustrated.

EQUESTRIAN PORTRAITS

Group I
Plume on head and crupper.
Sword raised.

Group II
Plume on head only.
Sword on shoulder.
Cross on housings.

Group III
(Early halfcrowns)
Lace collar vice ruff.
No comparisons on horse.
Sword upright.

Group III
(Late halfcrowns)
Cloak at shoulder.

Group IV
Horse foreshortened.
Tail between legs.
Mane in front of chest.

Group V
Tall horse with
upright head.
Tail flowing back.

N.B.—Line drawings of the portraits, shields and many other important details of the Tower coinage of this reign were published in BNJ 54 (1984) pp. 164–209.

GOLD

Angel

    Obv. St. Michael slaying the dragon.
    Rev. AMOR POPULI PRAESIDIUM REGIS. Three masted ship with royal arms on the mainsail.

2143	No mark of value. Lis, cross calvary.	VR
2144	X to right of angel. Blackamoor's head, castle, anchor, heart.	R
2145	X to left of angel. Blackamoor's head, heart, rose, harp, portcullis, bell, crown, tun, anchor, triangle, triangle-in-circle.	R

Unites

    Obv. Crowned bust left with XX behind.
    Rev. FLORENT CONCORDIA REGNA. Crowned shield.

Group A   First bust. Square shield plainly or elaborately garnished.

2146	(a)	Bust with high double-arched crown. Lis, cross calvary.	N
2147	(b)	Bust with flatter single-arched crown. Lis, cross calvary.	N

Group B   Second Bust. Square shield lightly garnished.

2148	(a)	Short bust with straight and small crown. Cross calvary, blackamoor's head, castle, anchor, heart.	N
2149	(b)	Longer bust with wider and larger crown. Anchor (sometimes below bust), heart, plume.[98]	N

Group C   Third bust, shorter with heavier armour. Garnished oval shield with C R at sides (omitted on one experimental coin).

2150	(a)	Large head with large wide crown. Plume,[99] rose.	S
2151	(b)	Narrower head with smaller, higher crown. Plume, rose.	R

Group D   Fourth bust with longer hair, lovelock on left shoulder, lace collar. Garter ribbon on breast. Garnished oval shield with crowned C R at sides.

2152	(a)	Large head with large, high, jewelled crown. Harp, portcullis.	S
2153	(b)	Smaller, flatter and unjewelled crown. Some slight variation in the portrait. Portcullis, bell, crown, tun, anchor, triangle, star, (P).	N

Group F   Sixth bust with different portrait and armour, lace of stellate pattern, and wider crown. Shield as Group D except for i.m. anchor which have Briot's reverse and are probably experimental.

2154	(a)	Earlier bust modelled after Briot's silver. Anchor, triangle, star, triangle-in-circle.	S
2155	(b)	Later portrait with straight profile. Triangle-in-circle, (P), (R).	R

[98] Some coins with this mark have a new garniture to the shield.
[99] Very rare transitional coins with this mark have the crown of Group B.

Group G		Seventh bust of cruder design with larger nose and small collar of different lace.	
	2156	(a) Reverse as Group D. Eye.	ER
	2157	(b) Late reverse with smaller rounder shield. Sun, sceptre.	VR

Double-crowns		Similar to Unites but with X behind head and reverse legend CULTORES SUI DEUS PROTEGIT.	
Group A		First bust. Square shield plainly garnished.	
	2158	(a) Bust with small, very high, double-arched crown. Lis.	VR
	2159	(b) Bust with larger, wider, and flatter double-arched crown. Lis, cross calvary.	N
Group B		Second bust. Square shield lightly garnished.	
	2160	(a) Very small head and crown. Cross calvary, blackamoor's head.	VR
	2161	(b) Larger bust with short truncation. Cross calvary, blackamoor's head, castle, anchor.	N
	2162	(c) Elongated portrait with long truncation. Anchor.	ER
	2163	(d) Shorter, larger, and broader bust. Heart, plume.	S
	2164	(e) Smaller bust with shorter truncation. Heart, plume.	N
Group C		Third bust. Garnished oval shield with C R at sides.	
	2165	(a) Bust with broad flat crown. Plume, rose.	VR
	2166	(b) Bust with smaller rounder crown. Plume, rose.	R
Group D		Fourth bust. Garnished oval shield with crowned C R at sides.	
	2167	(a) Large head with high wide crown. Harp.	ER
	2168	(b) Smaller head with flatter crown. Harp, portcullis, tun (over portcullis).	N
	2169	(c) Head and crown further reduced in size. Bell, crown, tun, anchor.	N
	2170	(d) Similar to (a) but crown flatter and arches unjewelled. Crown.	ER
Group Da	2171	Similar to No. 2169 with irons slightly re-cut. I.m. Eye.	ER
Group E		Fifth bust as on silver coins of Aberystwyth. Reverse as Group D.	
	2172	(a) Early bust. Anchor.	ER
	2173	(b) Later bust. Anchor, triangle.	R
Group Ea		Fifth bust as No. 2173 from slightly re-cut irons.	
	2174	(a) Reverse as Group D. Sun.	ER
	2175	(b) Late reverse with crude simplified garnishing. Sun, sceptre.	VR

Group F			Sixth bust similar to No. 2154.	
	2176	(a)	Briot's reverse (rectangular shield). Anchor.	ER
	2177	(b)	Normal reverse as Group D. Triangle, star, triangle-in-circle, (P), (R).	R
Group G	2178		Seventh bust similar to No. 2156/7. Reverse as Group D. I.m. sun.	ER

Crowns   Similar to Double-crowns but V behind bust.

Group A			First bust with small round crown.	
	2179	(a)	Rectangular shield on reverse. Lis.	N
	2180	(b)	Longer, narrower, shield. Lis, cross calvary.	N

Group B			Second bust. Square shield slightly garnished.	
	2181	(a)	Large bust with short truncation. Cross calvary, blackamoor's head, castle.	N
	2182	(b)	Longer narrower bust with more prominent truncation. Anchor, heart,[100] plume.	N

Group C			Third bust. Garnished oval shield with C R at sides.	
	2183	(a)	True coins of Group C. Plume.	ER
	2184	(b)	Mules of Group B/C. Plume, rose (over plume on obverse).	S

Group D			Fourth bust. Garnished oval shield with crowned C R at sides.	
	2185	(a)	Standard design. Harp, portcullis, bell, crown, tun, anchor, triangle, star, triangle-in-circle, (P), (R), eye, sun (both over (R)).	N
	2186[101]	(b)	Arches of king's crown unjewelled. Eye.	ER
	2187	(c)	Same portraits as No. 2186. Smaller shield on reverse, more plainly and crudely decorated. Eye, sun, sceptre.	VR

Group E	2188	Fifth bust, as on Aberystwyth silver coins. Reverse as on Group D (early). I.m. Anchor.	VR
Group F	2189	Sixth bust, similar to No. 2154. Reverse as Group D (early). I.m. Anchor.	ER

SILVER

Crowns	*Obv.*	King on horseback left.
	Rev.	CHRISTO AUSPICE REGNO. Shield.

Group I		First horseman. Square garnished shield on reverse.	
	2190	Long cross fourchée over shield. Lis, cross calvary.	R
	2191	No cross. Plume above shield. Lis, cross calvary, castle (over cross calvary).	VR

---

[100] Initial mark omitted from the reverse on one coin.
[101] This coin is a mule 2187/2185 with the reverse initial mark over (R). The counter mule (2185/2187) also exists with initial mark sun (over eye, probably over (R) on obverse).

Group II		Second horseman.	
	2192	Oval garnished shield with C R divided by plume above. Plume, rose.	R
	2193	Oval garnished shield on cross fourchée with C R above. Harp.	R
	2194	Similar to No. 2193 but C R divided by plume. Harp.	R
Group III		Third horseman. Round garnished shield on reverse.	
	2195	No plume on reverse. Bell, crown, tun, anchor, triangle, star (very rarely star in circle).	R
	2196	Plume above shield. Portcullis, crown, tun.	R
	2197	Briot horseman with groundline. Lozenge stops on obverse. Triangle-in-circle.	ER
Group IV		Fourth horseman. Reverse as Group III.	
	2198	(P), (R), eye, sun.	R
Group V	2199	Fifth horseman. Reverse as Group III. I.m. Sun.	R
Halfcrowns		Types similar to Crown.	
Group I		First horseman. Square shield on reverse.	
	2200	Rose on housings and ground line. Long cross fourchée over shield. Lis.	R
	2201	No rose or ground-line. Long cross fourchée over shield. Lis (one die has ground-line), cross calvary (over lis), blackamoor's head (over cross calvary over lis) with vertical anchor to right on obverse.	R
	2202	Obverse as No. 2201; no cross fourchée on reverse.[102] Cross calvary, blackamoor's head, castle.	R
	2203	As No. 2202 with plume above shield.[102] Lis, cross calvary, blackamoor's head, castle, anchor.	R
Group II		Second horseman.	
	2204	Rose on housings. Reverse as No. 2203 but with plain garniture. Heart, plume.	ER
	2205	Broad cross on housings. Oval garnished shield with C R above.[103] Plume, rose.	S
	2206	Plume between C R above shield. Plume, rose.	R
	2207	C R at sides of shield. Harp, portcullis.	S
	2208	As No. 2207, with plume above shield. Harp.	R
Group III		Third horseman. Round garnished shield on reverse.	
	2209	Early horseman. King wears long scarf about his waist and the horse is large. Bell, crown, tun.	N

[102] The shield sometimes has a plain garniture similar to that on James I unites.
[103] A variety has a rose (overstruck by the lis garniture) between the initials.

	2210	Similar to No. 2209, with plume over shield. Portcullis, bell, crown, tun.	R
	2211	Later horseman. King wears cloak flying from shoulders and the horse's head is turned towards the viewer. Tun, anchor, triangle, star, triangle-in-circle.	N
	2212	Similar to No. 2211, with rough ground beneath horse. Triangle, star (over triangle on obverse).	S
	2213	Similar to No. 2211, but rough workmanship. (P), (R), eye, sun.	N
Group IV	2214	Fourth horseman. Reverse as Group III. Star, triangle-in-circle, (P).	N
Group V	2215	Fifth horseman. Reverse as Group III. Sun, sceptre.	R

Shilling[104]

Obv. Crowned bust left with **XII** behind.
Rev. **CHRISTO AUSPICE REGNO.** Shield.

Group A   First bust. Plain square shield.

	2216	Shield over long cross fourchée. Lis, cross calvary.	N
	2217	No cross. Plume above shield. Lis, cross calvary.	VR

Group B   Second bust. Bust reaches lower edge of coin on later marks. Plain square shield.

	2218	Reverse as No. 2216. Cross calvary, blackamoor's head, castle.	S
	2219	Reverse as No. 2216, with plume above. Blackamoor's head.	ER
	2220	Reverse as No. 2217. Cross calvary, blackamoor's head, castle, anchor, heart, plume.	R

N.B.— Light weight shillings ($81\frac{33}{47}$ grs.) exist of Nos. 2216 and 2218, with i.m. cross calvary.

Group C   Third bust. Garnished oval shield with **C R** above.

	2221	No plume on reverse. Plume, rose.	N
	2222	Plume above shield. Plume, rose.	R

Group D[105]   Fourth bust. Crown usually reaches to edge of coin on those with i.m. Harp.

	2223	Inner circles. Garnished oval shield with **C R** at sides. Harp, portcullis.[106]	N
	2224	Similar to No. 2223, with plume above shield. Harp.	VR
	2225	No inner circles. Round garnished shield. Bell, crown, tun.	N
	2226	Similar to No. 2225, with plume above shield. Bell, crown, tun.	R

---

[104] There is some variation in the portrait in most groups (cf. BNJ 47 (1977) pp. 102–13).

[105] Sharp, in BNJ 47 (1977) p. 106, assigns coins without inner circles (N. 2225–6) to a new Group E and his subsequent lettering does not concord with that used in this book, viz. S. Group F = N. Group E, G = F and H = G.

[106] One reverse die omits the inner circle.

Group E		Fifth (Aberystwyth) bust. Single-arched crown except No. 2228. Square shield usually over cross pattée moline on reverse.	
	2227	Large bust similar to No. 2328. Small or large XII. Tun, anchor (over tun on obverse).	S
	2228	Smaller busts of similar style with double-arched crown. Small XII. Tun. Large XII. Anchor.	S
	2229	Similar to No. 2228, but with single-arched crown. Large XII. Tun, anchor, triangle (over anchor).[107]	N
	2230/1	Similar to No. 2227 with more rounded shoulder. Anchor, triangle.[107]	S
	2230/2	Briot style bust similar to No. 2231 but wearing armour and small single-arched crown. Triangle.[107]	R
	2230/3	Bust of No. 2229 recut with shoulder armour showing rivets. Triangle-in-circle.	VR
Group F		Sixth (Briot style) bust. Widespread double-arched crown. Collar with large stellate lace border. Reverse similar to Group E, but cross ends are usually larger and plain moline.	
	2231	Early bust of good style. Triangle, star, triangle-in-circle, (P), (R).	N
	2232	Later bust of crude workmanship. Eye, sun.	N
Group G		Seventh bust. Reverse as Group F.	
	2233	Long, narrow bust. Sun, sceptre.	S
	2234	Short and older bust. Sceptre.	S
Sixpences		Similar to shillings, but VI behind bust.	
Group A	2235	First bust. Square shield on cross fourchée with date above. 1625, lis, cross calvary. 1626, cross calvary.	S
Group B		Second bust.[108] Square shield with date above.	
	2236	Shield on cross fourchée. 1625, Cross calvary. 1626, cross calvary, blackamoor's head. 1627, blackamoor's head, castle. 1628, castle, anchor. 1629, anchor, heart.	S
	2237	No cross fourchée. 1630, heart, plume.	R
Group C		Third bust. Oval garnished shield with C R above.	
	2238	No plume on reverse. Plume, rose.	N
	2239	Plume above shield. Plume, rose.	R

N.B.—A specimen (probably unique) exists with this obverse and the reverse of a half unite. I.m. Rose (over plume)/Rose.

---

[107] Reverse cross normally plain moline.
[108] There is some variation in the portrait.

Group D		Fourth bust.[108]	
	2240	Inner circles. Garnished oval shield with C R at sides. Harp, portcullis.	N
	2241	No inner circles. Garnished round shield. Bell, crown, tun.	N
Group E		Fifth (Aberystwyth) bust. Square shield over cross pattée moline on reverse.	
	2242	Double-arched crown. Upright bust with short beard and short pointed lace collar. Small VI. Tun.	R
	2243	Similar to No. 2242, but with large VI. Tun.	S
	2244[109]	Similar to No. 2242. Anchor, triangle?	N
	2245	Single-arched crown. Head[110] slightly narrower, well thrown back and with longer beard. Lace collar more upcurved. Anchor, triangle.	R
Group F	2246	Sixth bust as on No. 2232. Reverse similar to Group E, but cross ends are larger and plain moline. Triangle, star, triangle-in-circle, (P), (R), eye, sun.	N
Group G	2247	Late Aberystwyth bust. Head similar in style to No. 2245, but longer, round-shouldered bust with armour clearly marked. Reverse similar to Group F. (R), eye, sun, sceptre.	N
	2247/1	Squat bust of crude style. Sun (over eye).	VR

Halfgroats

Without bust

Group A		*Obv.* C D G ROSA SINE SPINA. Crowned rose.	
		Rev. IUS THRONUM FIRMAT. Crowned rose.	
	2248	Inner circles. Lis, cross calvary, blackamoor's head.	N
	2249	No inner circles. Blackamoor's head, castle (i.c. on reverse), anchor, heart, plume.	N

With bust

Group B		Second bust with mark of value II behind. Oval garnished shield on reverse. King's name CARO(LUS). Reverse has IUSTITIA in full.	
	2250	Nothing above shield. Plume, rose.	N
	2251	Plume above shield. Plume, rose (over plume).	S

N.B.—An extremely rare mule Group B/A, with i.m. Plume, may be a trial piece.

Group C		Third bust. King's name CAROLUS.	
	2252	Nothing above shield. Plume, rose.	S
	2253	Plume above shield. Plume.	R

---

[109] Previously thought to have a different portrait to No. 2242, subsequent research has identified it as the same (SNC 89 (1981) pp. 239–40).

[110] Larger on some coins with triangle initial mark.

Group D		Fourth bust.	
	2254	Oval garnished shield with C R at sides. No inner circles. Rose (over plume), harp, crown.	C
	2255	Similar to No. 2254, but with inner circle on one or both sides. Harp, portcullis.	N
	2256	Oval garnished shield, no inner circles or inner circle on obverse only. Harp, portcullis.	S
	2257	Rounder shield with new garniture. No inner circles. Bell, crown, tun,[111] anchor, triangle (over anchor).	C
	2258	Similar to No. 2257, with inner circles on both sides. Triangle, star, triangle-in-circle, (P), (R), eye, sun, sceptre.	C
Group E	2259	Fifth (Aberystwyth) bust. Small flat single arched crown and round pointed lace collar. No inner circles or on reverse only. I.m. Anchor to right.	R

N.B.—One die has a very small bust from a penny puncheon.

| Group G | 2260 | Seventh bust. Older and shorter with heavy moustache and pointed beard. Large single arched crown. Inner circles. Eye, sun, sceptre. | N |

Pence
Without bust

Group A		Similar to Group A halfgroats, but roses are uncrowned.	
	2261	Inner circles. One or two pellets.	N
	2262	No inner circles. Lis,[112] blackamoor's head/two pellets (i.c. on reverse), one or two pellets.	N

With bust

Group B		Second bust. Similar to Group B halfgroats, but with I behind head.	
	2263	Inner circles. Plume.	S
	2264	No inner circles. Plume.	S
Group C		Third bust.	
	2265	Inner circles. Plume, rose.	N
	2266	No inner circles. Plume, rose.	N
Group D		Fourth bust.	
	2267	C R at sides of oval garnished shield. No inner circles. Harp, one or two pellets.	C
	2268	As No. 2267, without C R. Harp, portcullis, two pellets.	N
	2269	As No. 2268. Inner circle on one side. Harp.	S

---

[111] Some specimens have the shield inverted.
[112] A variety has an inner circle on the reverse.

	2270	Rounder shield with new garniture. No inner circles. Bell, triangle, one or two pellets, two pellets/anchor (reverse from halfgroat die).	C
	2271	Shield as No. 2270. Inner circle on one or both sides. Triangle, two pellets.	S
Group E	2272	Fifth (Aberystwyth) bust as on No. 2259. Inner circle on obverse only, or none. I.m. One or two pellets, none.	N
Group G	2273	Seventh bust, as on No. 2260. Inner circle on obverse only. I.m. One or two pellets.	N
Halfpenny	2274	*Obv.* Rose. No initial mark or legend. *Rev.* Rose. No initial mark or legend.	C

COPPER

ROYAL FARTHING TOKENS

INITIAL MARKS

As during the reign of James I, a number of the copper tokens bear similar initial marks to the silver. However, a large number of the other marks are used, and a selection of these, on similar lines to those given for the previous reign, is appended. A number of i.m.s. previously listed for this reign have proved to be either mis-strikes or on contemporary forgeries.

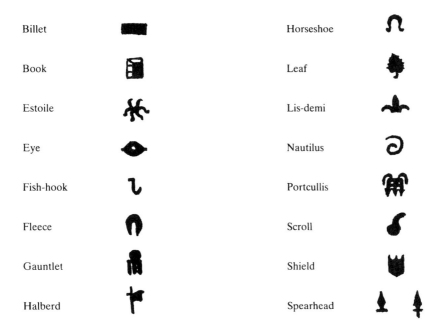

Billet	Horseshoe
Book	Leaf
Estoile	Lis-demi
Eye	Nautilus
Fish-hook	Portcullis
Fleece	Scroll
Gauntlet	Shield
Halberd	Spearhead

N.B.—By kind permission of the author, the above illustrations have been taken from C. W. Peek's " English Copper, Tin and Bronze Coins ", (etc.).

Type 1		*Richmond* " rounds " (1625–34).	

Obv.   CARO D G MAG BRIT (see below).   Crown with two sceptres in saltire.

Rev.   FRA ET HIB REX.   Crowned harp.   No initial mark. Single arched crowns.   No inner circles.

2275   (a)   CARO over IACO—BRI or BRIT.   Colon stops.   Coronet,   c
crescent with mullet, dagger, mascle.

2276   (b)   CARA—BRIT.   Colon stops.   ER
Annulet, coronet, cross pattée fourchée, dagger, fusil, key, mascle, trefoil?, tun.

2277   (c)   CARO—BRI.   Colon stops.   c
A, annulet, bell, book, cinquefoil, crescent, cross (pellet in each angle), cross calvary, cross pattée, cross pattée fitchée, cross patonce, cross patonce saltire, cross saltire, dagger, ermine, estoile, estoile pierced, eye, fish-hook, fleece, fusil, fusils two, gauntlet, halberd, harp, heart, horseshoe, leaf, lion passant, lis, lis demi, lis three, martlet, mascle, nautilus, rose (single), shield, spearhead, tower, trefoil, woolpack.

2278   (d)   CARO—BRI.   Apostrophe stops.   c
Crescent, lion rampant, rose (double), trefoil.

N.B.—Variations occur in the number of jewels on the circlets and the style of the harp on coins of class (d) bearing i.m. rose.

Type 2   *Transitional* (c. 1634).

2279   Similar to No. 2278 but with double-arched crowns.   No inner   R
circles.
Harp, quatrefoil.

Type 3   *Maltravers* " rounds " (1634–36).

Obv.   CAROLUS D G MAG BRIT.   Crown with two sceptres in saltire.

Rev.   FRAN ET HIB REX.   Crowned harp.
Double arched crowns.   Inner circles.

2280   (a)   I.m. on obv. only.   s
Bell, rose (double), woolpack.

2281   (b)   Same i.m. on both sides.   c
Bell, cross pattée, lis, martlet, rose (double), woolpack.

2282   (c)   Different i.m. on each side.   c
Bell/cross pattée fitchée, cross pattée fitchée/bell, harp/ bell, harp/billet, lis/portcullis, martlet/bell, woolpack/ portcullis, woolpack/rose (double).

Type 4   *Richmond* " ovals " (1625–34).

Similar to Type 1 but legend starts at bottom left on both sides.

2283   (a)   CARO over IACO.   MA or MAG, BR, BRI or BRIT.   Cross   c
pattée (sometimes obv. only).

2284   (b)   CARO D G MAG BRI.   Colon or rose stops.   c
Lis demi (obv. only), martlet (rev. only), mill-rind (rev. only), crescent, scroll, 9.

	2285	(c)	**CARO D G MAG BRI.** Apostrophe stops. Rose double (sometimes obv. only).	C

Type 5

Maltravers " ovals " (1634–36).

	2286		Similar to Type 3 but without inner circles and legend starts at bottom left on both sides. I.m. Lis.	C

Rose (Type 1)

> *Obv.* **CAROLUS D G MAG BRIT.** Double arched crown with two sceptres in saltire through it.
> *Rev.* **FRAN ET HIB REX.** Double rose surmounted by double arched crown.

	2287	(a)	Sceptres within inner circle. Lis (both sides or one only), lis/martlet, martlet/lis.	VR
	2288	(b)	Sceptres just cut inner circle. Lis (both sides or obv. only).	R
	2289	(c)	Sceptres reach nearly to edge of coin. Lis (both sides or one only), lis/cross pattée.	S
	2290	(d)	Similar to (c) but reading **BRI.** Lis, mullet (both sides or obv. only), cross pattée/lis, cross pattée/none.	S

N.B.—In class (d) the i.m. lis is found muled both ways with mullet. There is also some muling between Types 1 (d) and 2.

Rose (Type 2)

2291	*Obv.* **CAROLUS** (or **CAROLU**) **D G MAG** (or **MA**) **BRI.** Single arched crown with two sceptres in saltire through it.	C

> *Rev.* **FRAN** (**FRA** or **FR**) **ET HIB** (or **HI**) **REX.** Single rose surmounted by single arched crown.
> Lis, crescent (sometimes obv. only), mullet.

N.B.—Mules exist between crescent and lis (both ways) and crescent/mullet. Examples exist in silver with i.m. Lis or crescent.

Rose (Type 3)

> *Obv.* **CAROLU D G MAG** (or **MA**) **BRI** (or **BR**). Single arched crown with two sceptres in saltire below. I.m. Mullet.
> *Rev.* **FRA** (or **FR**) **ET HIB REX.** Single rose surmounted by single arched crown. I.m. Mullet.

	2292	(a)	Sceptre handles each ornamented with two large bosses.	S
	2293	(b)	Plain sceptre handles, sometimes twisted.	S

NICHOLAS BRIOT'S COINAGE

A. First milled issue (1631–32).

DENOMINATIONS—**GOLD : Unite, Double-crown, Crown.**

SILVER : Crown, Halfcrown, Shilling, Sixpence, Halfgroat, Penny.

INITIAL MARKS

Anemone & B **B.** ⬤   Daisy & B
(Position of B varies) **B.** ✿

GOLD

Unite	2294	*Obv.*	CAROLUS D G MAGN BRITANN FRAN ET HIBER REX. Crowned bust left draped and wearing falling lace collar; behind, XX.	R
		Rev.	FLORENT CONCORDIA REGNA. Crowned square garnished shield with crowned C R at sides. B to right or left of crown. Anemone & B/B to left of crown, Daisy & B/B to right or left of crown.	

Double-crown
Similar to No. 2294 but X behind head and rev. legend CULTORES SUI DEUS PROTEGIT. B always left of rev. crown.

	2295	King's crown jewelled—Anemone & B, Daisy & B.	R
	2296	King's crown unjewelled—Daisy & B, B without flower.	VR

Crown 2297 Similar to No. 2295 but V behind head. B always right of rev. crown. I.m. B without flower.   ER

(N.B.—These crowns may well be patterns).

SILVER

Crown	2298	*Obv.*	CAROLUS D G MAGN BRITAN FRAN ET HIBER REX. Equestrian figure of king similar to Tower type V but of finer workmanship.	R
		Rev.	CHRISTO AUSPICE REGNO. Crowned oval garnished shield with crowned C R at sides. Daisy & B/B.	
Halfcrown	2299		Similar to No. 2298. I.m. Daisy & B/B.	R
Shilling	2300		Types as Tower Group E but with Briot's bust and obv. legend and of finer work. B without flower (Rev. legend starts bottom left). Daisy & B/B.	S

| Sixpence | 2301 | Similar to No. 2300 but **VI** behind bust. I.m. Daisy & **B/B**. | N |

| Halfgroat | 2302 | *Obv.* Briot's bust with **II** behind and **B** below truncation. | N |
| | | *Rev.* **IUSTITIA THRONUM FIRMAT.** Square shield over long cross fourchée. | |

| Penny | 2303 | Similar to No. 2302 but with **I** behind head. | N |

B. Second milled issue (1638–39).

DENOMINATIONS—**SILVER : Halfcrown, Shilling, Sixpence.**

INITIAL MARK

Anchor (usually with B)   ⚓

| Halfcrown | 2304 | Similar to No. 2299 but smaller lettering and obv. legend reads **BRITANN FR.** I.m. Anchor and B (flukes to left on obverse). | R |

| Shilling | 2305 | Similar to No. 2300 but with normal Tower obv. legend and second Briot bust which has a large lace collar of stellate pattern. I.m. Anchor and B, anchor. | S |

| Sixpence | 2306 | Similar to No. 2305 but **VI** behind bust. I.m. Anchor (sometimes with mullet on obv.). | N |

C. Hammered issue (1638–39).

DENOMINATIONS—**SILVER : Halfcrown, Shilling.**

INITIAL MARKS

Anchor   ⚓   Triangle (over anchor)   ⚓

Halfcrown	2307	*Obv.* Tower legend. Briot's horseman with groundline.	VR
		Rev. **CHRISTO** etc. Square garnished shield.
		Anchor, triangle over anchor.

N.B.—A mule exists struck from the triangle over anchor obv. die and a normal Tower Group III die with i.m. Triangle.

Shilling	2308	*Obv.* Similar to No. 2305.	VR
		Rev. **CHRISTO** etc. Square shield on short cross fleury.
		Anchor, triangle over anchor, triangle.

N.B.—Mules exist both ways of Briot's shilling dies i.m. Triangle over anchor combined with Tower Group F dies i.m. Triangle. True Briot rev. dies may be distinguished by the lozenge stops and the ornate harp in the coat of arms.

NOTE. As no documentary evidence exists for a gold coinage by Briot at this period, the few surviving coins in that metal which tally basically with his hammered silver coinage must be regarded as Tower trial pieces and are recorded under Tower Group F. A hammered crown exists with a Briot style obverse (cf. No. 2197).

A. Thomas Bushell's Mints (1637–45).

ABERYSTWYTH MINT (1638–42).[113]

DENOMINATIONS—SILVER : Halfcrown, Shilling, Sixpence, Groat, Threepence, Halfgroat, Penny, Halfpenny.

INITIAL MARK

Book

Halfcrown		*Obv.* Equestrian figure with plume behind king. I.m. Book.
		Rev. CHRISTO etc. Oval garnished shield with large plume above. I.m. Book.
	2325	Horseman as Tower No. 2211. Small plume without bands. FRA ET HI.	R
	2326	Horseman as Tower No. 2212. Plume with bands.	R
	2327	Similar to No. 2325 but horse more spirited and legend FRAN ET HIB.	R
Shilling		*Obv.* Bust left wearing flat single arched crown, with XII behind and plume in front. I.m. Book.
		Rev. Similar to Halfcrown.
	2328	Well proportioned bust with large square lace collar. Plume without bands, small XII.MAG.BR. No inner circles.	S
	2329	Obverse as No. 2328. Reverse with inner circle.	S
	2330	Small head and crown, rounded lace collar. Large plume with bands, large XII.MA.BR. Inner circles.	R
	2331	Large bust as on No. 2328. Large plume with bands, large XII.MA.BR. Inner circles.	R
	2332	"Briot" bust resembling No. 2231 but smaller square lace collar. Plume without bands. MAG.BRIT. Inner circles.	VR
Sixpence		Similar to Shilling but VI behind bust.
	2333	Similar to No. 2328.	S
	2334	Bust similar to No. 2330. Plume without bands, large VI. Inner circle on obverse only.	R
	2335	Similar to No. 2334 with inner circle on both sides. Known with early and late reverse. The latter may be distinguished by the smaller square-shaped plume above the shield.	S
	2336	Bust as on No. 2247. Crown cuts inner circle.	VR

---

[113] There is evidence that this mint was also active in 1645/6, but no coins can be specifically attributed to this period. It is probable that old dies were used.

Groat		Similar to Shilling but IIII behind bust. With inner circles.	
	2337	Large bust similar in design to No. 2330. Plume above reverse shield with or without bands.	C
	2338	As No. 2337 but small bust.	C
	2339	Bust as on No. 2247. Plume with bands above reverse shield.	R
Threepence		Similar to Shilling but III behind head. Inner circles.	
	2340	Small bust similar to No. 2338. M . B . FR. Plume above reverse shield with or without bands.	C
	2341	Similar bust to No. 2340 but with small square plume in front. MAG . B . F. Reverse plume without bands.	R
Halfgroat		*Obv.* Bust left with II behind. I.m. Book.	
		Rev. IUSTITIA THRONUM FIRMAT. Large plume. I.m. Book.	
	2342[114]	Bust similar to No. 2328. No inner circles.	N
	2343	Bust similar to No. 2259 (round lace collar). Inner circles.	N
	2344	"Briot" type bust (square lace collar). Inner circles.	N
Penny		Similar to Halfgroat but with I behind head.	
	2345	As No. 2342. CARO.	S
	2346	As No. 2343. CARO.	S
	2347	Bust similar to No. 2328. CAROLUS. Inner circles.	S
	2348	Bust as on No. 2247. CAROLUS. Inner circles.	R
Halfpenny	2349	*Obv.* Rose. No legends or i.m.	S
		Rev. Plume. No legends or i.m.	

NOTES.   No. 2324 has been reattributed to Chester mint (cf. p. 188). Obverse or reverse dies of this mint are also used at Shrewsbury, Oxford and Bristol.

ABERYSTWYTH—DOVEY FURNACE (1648–9).[115]

DENOMINATIONS—SILVER : Halfcrown, Shilling, Sixpence, Groat, Threepence, Halfgroat, Penny.

INITIAL MARK

Crown

Halfcrown	2351	*Obv.* Briot style horseman, but no groundline and with plume behind king. I.m. Crown.	ER
		Rev. Similar to Aberystwyth Halfcrown but i.m. Crown.	

---

[114] The reverse of this type is found muled with a Tower obverse i.m. Pellet.

[115] A temporary mint was authorised at the silver mills near the river Dyfi in 1647 as Aberystwyth Castle had been damaged. A small amount was coined there in that year probably from old dies. The mint was reactivated for a short period in 1648/9 and the following coins were struck then.

Shilling	2352	*Obv.*	Bust left with XII behind and small plume in front. I.m	ER
			Crown.	
		Rev.	Similar to Aberystwyth Shilling but i.m. Crown.	

| **Sixpence** | 2353 | Similar to No. 2352 but with VI behind head. | ER |

| **Groat** | 2354 | Similar to No. 2352 but with IIII behind head. | R |

| **Threepence** | 2355 | Similar to No. 2352 but with III behind head. | R |

| **Halfgroat** | 2356 | Similar to Aberystwyth Halfgroat with inner circles and i.m. | ER |
| | | Crown. | |

| **Penny** | 2357 | Similar to No. 2356 but with I behind head. | ER |

SHREWSBURY MINT (1642).[116]

DENOMINATIONS—**GOLD : Triple Unite.**

SILVER : Pound, Halfpound, Crown, Halfcrown, Shilling.

MINT MARK

Plume (without bands)

Except in the case of the Shillings, a number of pellets usually takes the place of the initial mark. The Shrewsbury plume, by which the coins of this mint are distinguished, will be found on the obverse behind the king and/or on the reverse above the " Declaration ".

GOLD

Triple Unite	2360	*Obv.*	Crowned half-length figure of the king to left, holding a	ER
			sword in the right hand and an olive branch in the left;	
			behind, a plume. I.m. Two pellets.	
		Rev.	EXURGAT DEUS DISSIPENTUR INIMICI surrounding	
			RELIG PROT LEG ANG LIBER PAR in two wavy lines,	
			with III and three plumes above, and 1642 below.	

SILVER

Pound		*Obv.*	Equestrian figure with plume behind.	
		Rev.	Legend and type as No. 2360 but with "Declaration"	
			between two straight lines and XX instead of III.	
	2361	Horseman as Tower Type III with nothing beneath horse.	VR
		Three plumes around XX.	
	2362	Shrewsbury horseman with pile of arms beneath horse. Three	VR
		plumes around XX.	
	2363	Similar to No. 2362 but with cannon and arms beneath horse.	ER
		Single plume over XX.	

---

[116] It is possible that coins of the " SA " mint were struck here in 1644.

Halfpound		Similar to Pound but X on reverse.	
	2364	Similar to No. 2361.	R
	2365	Similar to No. 2361 but only two plumes on reverse.	VR
	2366	Shrewsbury horseman with groundline. Three plumes on reverse.	R
	2367	Similar to No. 2366 but with arms beneath horse.	R
	2368	Similar to No. 2367 but without plume in obverse field.	S

N.B.—The Halfpounds and some of the Pounds are of the same diameter as the Crowns, being struck on thicker flans.

Crown		Similar to Pound but V on reverse.	
	2369	Aberystwyth horseman with groundline.	ER
	2370	Similar to No. 2366.	R

Halfcrown		Types and legends similar to Pound but no mark of value.	
	2371	Aberystwyth obverse die i.m. Book. Single plume on reverse.	ER
	2372	Aberystwyth horseman with fat plume behind. Three plumes on reverse.	R
		Shrewsbury horseman without groundline.	
	2373	*Reverses.* Single plume above " Declaration ".	VR
	2374	Single plume dividing value 2. 6.	ER
		Shrewsbury horseman with groundline.	
	2375	*Reverses.* Single plume above " Declaration ".	VR
	2376	Single plume dividing value 2. 6.	ER
	2377	Three thin plumes.	R
	2378	Shrewsbury horseman with groundline, no plume in obverse field, and i.m. Plume without coronet or bands. Three plumes on reverse.	R

Shilling		*Obv.* Crowned bust left with XII behind.	
		Rev. Legend and type similar to Pound without mark of value.	
	2379	Aberystwyth obverse die (plume before face). I.m. Book.	VR
	2380	Shrewsbury obverse die. I.m. Plume without coronet or bands.	ER

OXFORD MINT (1642–46).

DENOMINATIONS—**GOLD : Triple Unite, Unite, Half-unite.**

SILVER : Pound, Halfpound, Crown, Halfcrown, Shiling, Sixpence, Groat, Threepence, Halfgroat, Penny.

MINT MARK

Plume (with bands)

As in the case of Shrewsbury, the coins of this mint often have a number of pellets instead of an initial mark, and the distinctive Oxford plume is found in the field.

GOLD

Triple Unite

Types and legends similar to No. 2360 except that the " Declaration " is in three lines and the dates vary. I.m. (*Obv.*). Plume.

" Declaration " between wavy lines.

2381   Tall narrow bust. 1642.   VR

Reverse legend and " Declaration " on continuous scroll.

2382   Tall narrow bust. 1642, 1643.   VR

2383   Well proportioned bust with scarf. 1643.   VR

2384   Bust as No. 2383 without scarf. 1643, 1643 (OXON below).   VR

2385   Small module. 1644 (OX or OXON below).   ER

Unite

Obv.   Bust similar to No. 2360 with XX behind.
Rev.   EXURGAT etc. "Declaration" across field with three plumes above (except 2392) and date below.

"Declaration" in two wavy lines.

2386   Tall narrow bust, i.m. One or two pellets or none. 1642.   R

Reverse legend and " Declaration " (in three lines) on continuous scroll.

2387   Tall narrow bust; no i.m. 1642, 1643.   R

2388   Tall well proportioned bust, i.m. Pellet. 1643.   R

2389   Shorter and wider bust (four minor varieties), i.m. Plume. 1643, 1644 (OX below), 1645.   R

2390   Tall bust extending to lower edge of coin; obverse legend starts at bottom left. 1643.   VR

" Declaration " in three lines between two straight lines.

2391   Bust as No. 2389. 1644 (OX below).   ER

" Declaration " in three lines on scroll; single plume above.

2392   Bust similar to No. 2389; i.m. Plume, rosette, or pellet. 1645 (OX below), 1646 (OX below).   VR

Half-unite

Obv.   Crowned bust left with X behind.
Rev.   EXURGAT etc. "Declaration" in three lines across the field with three plumes above and date below.

" Declaration " in three straight lines.

2393   No initial mark. 1642.   ER

" Declaration " and legend on scroll.

2394   I.m. Plume. 1642, 1643.   ER

2395   Bust extends to bottom of coin and obverse legend starts at bottom left. 1643, 1644 (OX below).   R

SILVER

Pound

Obv. King on horseback left trampling on arms; behind, a plume. I.m. Plume.

Rev. EXURGAT etc. "Declaration" in two lines across field between two straight lines; above, XX and three plumes; below, date. Except No. 2402.

2396   Large artistic horseman. Fine workmanship attributed to Rawlins. Three Shrewsbury plumes on reverse. 1642.   VR

2397   Similar to 2396, but with three Oxford plumes on reverse. 1643.   VR

2398   Smaller horse with arms and cannon. 1642, 1643.   R

2399   Similar to No. 2398, without cannon. 1642.   R

2400   Obverse exergue is chequered, otherwise as No. 2399. 1642.   VR

2401   Briot's horse. 1643.   ER

2402   Obverse as No. 2396. Reverse: "Declaration" within cartouche with large single plume above and 1644 OX below.   ER

Halfpound   Types and legends similar to Pound, but X above "Declaration".

2403   Oxford plume behind king and as obverse i.m. Three Shrewsbury plumes on reverse. 1642.   R

2404   Obverse as No. 2403. Three Oxford plumes on reverse. 1642, 1643.   R

N.B.—The Halfpounds and some of the Pounds are of the same diameter as the Crowns, being struck on thicker flans.

Crown

Obv. Equestrian figure of the king left—details below.

Rev. Similar to Pound, but mark of value V (on one die of 1643 a line divides the Declaration).

2405   Shrewsbury horse and plume in field, groundline. No i.m. 1642, 1643.   R

2406   Oxford horse and plume in field, grass below horse. I.m. Plume. 1643.   VR

2407   Rawlin's dies. Large artistic horseman with view of city below. OXON between spires and R behind tail. I.m. Floriated cross. Reverse with scrolls instead of lines and floral decoration between words of legend. 1644 OXON.   ER

N.B.—There are a number of nineteenth century copies of No. 2407 and some of the existing specimens may perhaps be later strikings.

Halfcrown   Similar to Crown, but no mark of value. The three plumes above the "Declaration" are of Oxford type and equal size unless otherwise stated.

SHREWSBURY HORSE (Near hind leg raised).

2408   With groundline. Shrewsbury obverse die. 1642.   VR

2409   No plume behind king. Shrewsbury obverse die. 1642.   VR

            With groundline. Oxford plume behind king. I.m. Plume.

2410   *Reverses.* Shrewsbury die.   Shrewsbury   plumes   above   s
        " Declaration ". 1642.

2411   Oxford die. 1642.   s

2412   No groundline, otherwise as No. 2411.   I.m. Oxford or fat   N
        Shrewsbury plume. 1642.

OXFORD HORSE   (Similar to Shrewsbury but off hind leg raised).

        No groundline. I.m. Plume.
2413   *Reverses.* Three Oxford plumes. 1643.   R

2414   Three Shrewsbury plumes. 1643.   R

2415   With groundline. I.m. Plume or none. 1643.   R

BRIOT'S HORSE.

        Grass below. I.m. Plume.
2416   *Reverses.* Three even plumes. I.m. Rosette or pellets. 1643,   s
                   1643 OX.

2417   Large central plume. I.m. Pellets. 1643, 1643 OX. s

2418   Grass below. I.m. Small Shrewsbury plume.   s
        Reverse.   Large central plume. I.m. Lozenge* or pellet. 1644
                   OX.

        Lumpy ground. I.m. Rosette.
2419   *Reverses.* Three even plumes. I.m. Rosette. 1643 OX.   s

2420   Large central plume. I.m. Rosette or none. 1643 OX, s
                   1644 OX.

2421   Large central plume. I.m. Rosette. Plumes at side   s
                   side of date. 1644 OX.

        Lumpy ground. I.m. Rosette and plume.
2422   *Reverses.* Three even plumes. I.m. 5 pellets. 1643.   s

2423   Large central plume. I.m. Rosette or none. 1643   s
                   OX, 1644 OX.

        Plain ground. I.m. Plume.
2424   *Reverses.* Three even plumes. I.m. Lozenge,* rosette, or 5   s
                   pellets. 1644 OX, 1645 OX.

2425   Large central plume. I.m. Billet,* 1 or 5 lozenges,* s
                   1 or 5 pellets. 1644 OX.

2426   Large central plume with small Shrewsbury plume   s
                   at sides. I.m. Rosette with two lozenges* at each
                   side. 1644 OX.

2427   Similar to No. 2426, with small Shrewsbury plume   s
                   at each side of date. I.m. Shrewsbury plume. 1644
                   OX.

---

* Coins with this initial mark also have the same symbol between the words of the legend and beside the three plumes and the date.

LARGER HORSE (Similar to Briot's but larger and clumsier).

2428   Plain ground. I.m. Plume.
       Reverse. I.m. 5 lozenges,* or pellet. 1644 OX. Rosette.*   R
       1645 OX.

       Lumpy ground. I.m. Shrewsbury plume and lozenge.
       Lozenge stops.
2429   *Reverses.* Three even plumes. I.m. Lozenge.* 1644 OX.   S

2430   Large central plume. I.m. 1, 2, or 4 lozenges,* or   S
              pellet. 1644 OX.

2431   Lumpy ground. I.m. Plume.   R
       Reverse. I.m. Rosette.* 1645 OX.

       Pebbly ground. I.m. Plume.
2432   *Reverses.* I.m. 5 pellets. 1645 OX, 1646 OX.   S

2433   I.m. 5 pellets. Pellets by plumes and dividing   S
              figures of date. 1646 OX.

2434   I.m. 5 pellets. Annulets by plumes and dividing   S
              figures of date. 1646 OX.

       Grass below. I.m. Plume.
2435   *Reverses.* I.m. Rosette.* 1645 OX.   S

2436   I.m. 1 or 5 pellets. 1645 OX, 1646 OX.   S

Halfcrown   2437   *Obv.*   Horseman similar in style to Tower Type IV.   ER
(? Pattern)   *Rev.*   EXURGAT etc. " Declaration " and 1642 in a continuous
                                scroll, forming two circles around an oval shield. I.m.
                                Plume.

Shilling   *Obv.*   Crowned bust left with XII behind.
                       Rev.   EXURGAT etc. " Declaration " in three lines in a com-
                                partment with three plumes above and date below. All
                                reverses of 1642 and most of 1643 have lines between the
                                " Declaration ". From 1643 onwards these are omitted
                                with the exception of one die dated 1644.

2438   Shrewsbury obverse die. I.m. Plume without coronet or   VR
       bands. 1642.

2439   Bust with smaller head, large lace collar, and new crown.   R
       I.m. Plume. 1642, 1643.

       Similar to No. 2439, but coarser work. I.m. Plume.
2440   *Reverses.* Three Oxford plumes. 1643.   S

2441   Three small Shrewsbury plumes. 1643.   R

       Fine bust with scalloped edges to lace collar. I.m. Plume.
2442   *Reverses.* Three Oxford plumes. 1643.   S

2443   Three small Shrewsbury plumes. 1643.   S

2444   Large bust of fine work. I.m. Plume. 1643, 1644 OX.   R

       Smaller bust with " bent " crown.[117] I.m. Plume.

---

[117] The bent appearance of the crown, which is from the same punch as No. 2444, is due to double-striking into the die.

2445	*Reverses.* I.m. Rosette and pellets. 1643 (Rosette stops), 1644 OX.	S
2446	I.m. Two pellets. 1644 OX.	S
	Bust similar to No. 2444. Double lozenge stops. I.m. Shrewsbury plume.	
2447	*Reverses.* I.m. 1 or 4 lozenges.* 1644 OX.	VR
2448	I.m. Pellets (lozenges in field). 1044 OX (*sic.*).	VR
	Bust similar to No. 2444. Single lozenge stops. I.m. Shrewsbury plume with two lozenges.	
2449	*Reverses.* Three even plumes. I.m. 2 or 4 lozenges.* 1644 OX.	S
2450	Three even plumes. I.m. Pellets (lozenges in field). 1044 OX (*sic.*).	S
2451	Plume with small Shrewsbury plume each side. I.m. Lozenge.* 1644 OX.	S
2452	Three small Shrewsbury plumes. I.m. Pellet. 1644 OX.	S
2453	Three even plumes. I.m.? 1645 OX.	S
2454	Three small Shrewsbury plumes. I.m. Floriated cross with annulets* at sides. 1646. (Annulet between each figure).	VR
2455	Three small Shrewsbury plumes. I.m. Pellet.* 1646. (Pellet between each figure).	S
	Rawlins' dies. Fine bust with R on truncation. Double lozenge stops. I.m. Shrewsbury plume and lozenge.	
2456	*Reverses.* I.m. Rosette and lozenges. Rosettes by plumes and and lozenges as stops and by date. 1644 OX.	ER
2457	I.m. Pellet. 1644.	ER

N.B.—For pattern shillings of Oxford—see Nos. 2712–2714. * Symbols marked thus also appear in the legend and field as on the halfcrowns.

Sixpence	Types and legends similar to Shilling, but VI behind head. Aberystwyth obverse die. I.m. Book.	
2458	*Reverses.* Three Oxford plumes. 1642, 1643.	R
2459	Three Shrewsbury plumes. 1643.	S
2460	Shrewsbury plume with lis each side. 1644 OX.	ER

N.B.—A sixpence has been recorded with obverse i.m. Plume dated 1642 (Morrieson Type B—quoting Hawkins No. 1 and Ruding XXIV, 5). No existing specimen of this has been traced by the author.

Groat	Types and legends similar to Shilling, but IIII behind head. Plume before face.	
2461	Aberystwyth obverse die. I.m. Book. *Reverse.* Shrewsbury plume with lis each side. I.m. Lozenge and two pellets. 1644 OX.	N
	Oxford die. I.m. Floriated cross.	
2462/1	*Reverses.* Similar to No. 2461. I.m. Pellet. 1644 OX.	S
2462/2	Three even plumes. I.m. Two pellets. 1644.	VR

	2463	Large single plume. Scroll above "Declaration". 1645.	S
		No plume before face.	
	2464	Large bust with crown cutting inner circle. I.m. Lis. Reverse similar to No. 2461. I.m. Pellets. 1644 OX.	S
		Bust similar in style to No. 2464, but descending to lower edge of coin. Legend starts at bottom left. No i.m.	
	2465	*Reverses.* Similar to No. 2461. I.m. Pellets. 1644 OX.	R
	2466	Similar to No. 2463. 1645.	R
		Rawlins' dies. Similar to No. 2465, but no inner circle and R below shoulder.	
	2467	*Reverses.* Similar to No. 2461. I.m. Pellets. 1644 OX.	R
	2468	Large single plume above "Declaration" which is in a cartouche with lion's head. 1645, 1646.	R

Threepence 2469 *Obv.* Oxford die as No. 2471 below.
Rev. Aberystwyth die. CHRISTO etc. Oval garnished shield with plume above. I.m. Book.

Threepence Types and legends similar to Shilling, but with III behind head.

	2470	Aberystwyth obverse die. Plume before face. I.m. Book. *Reverse.* Shrewsbury plume with lis each side. I.m. Pellet. 1644 OX.	S
		Rawlins' die. Small bust without plume. R below shoulder. I.m. Lis.	
	2471	*Reverses.* Lis with small lis each side. I.m. Pellet. 1644.	N
	2472	Three even lis. I.m. Pellet. 1644.	N
	2473	Similar to No. 2471, without R and crown cuts inner circle. Reverse as No. 2471. 1646 (over 1644).	S

Halfgroat 2474 *Obv.* Crowned bust left with II behind. S
Rev. Aberystwyth type. IUSTITIA etc. Large plume with bands. I.m. Lis.
Obverse i.m.s.—Small lis, cross, mullet, pellet.

Halfgroat 2475 *Obv.* Similar to No. 2474. I.m. Lis. R
Rev. EXURGAT etc. "Declaration" in three lines between two straight lines; above, Shrewsbury plume with small lis each side; below, 1644 OX. I.m. Lis.

Penny Similar to No. 2474, but with I behind bust.

	2476	Aberystwyth die. Bust with large lace collar. I.m. Book. *Reverse.* Small plume. I.m. Pellet.	R
	2477	Aberystwyth die. Narrower bust as on the sixpences. I.m. Book. *Reverse.* Large plume. I.m. 4 pellets.	R
	2478	Fine bust similar to No. 2471. I.m. Lis. *Reverse.* Small plume. I.m. Mullet, pellet.	R
	2479	Wider bust similar to halfgroats. I.m. Lis. *Reverse.* Small plume. I.m. Lis.	R

Penny   2480   Similar to No. 2475, but with I behind bust and without OX ER
                          below date.

N.B.—For other coins of Oxford—see patterns Nos. 2711–2714.

BRISTOL MINT (1643–45).

DENOMINATIONS—**GOLD : Unite, Half-unite.**

SILVER : Halfcrown, Shilling, Sixpence, Groat, Threepence, Halfgroat, Penny.

MINT MARKS

Bristol monogram   Acorn? (perhaps a pear)   Plumelet (small Shrewsbury type)

NOTES

The early halfcrowns and shillings are very similar to Oxford coins of the same period, but they may be distinguished by one or more of the following features.

(i)   Reverse legend starting at nine o'clock.
(ii) LI(B) instead of LIBER in the Declaration.
(iii) Bristol plumes are generally broader and thicker than Oxford ones and have larger bands.

GOLD

Unite   2481   Type and legends similar to Oxford unite No. 2389, but obverse ER
                          i.m. is Bristol monogram, and reverse has a plume between two
                          plumelets.   1645.
                          Reverse mark—Plumelets before EXURGAT, or Br. before REL.

Half-unite   2482   Similar to No. 2481, but X behind head.   Initial marks: Br. ER
                          between two plumelets/Br.

SILVER

Halfcrown   *Obv.*   Equestrian figure of king left with plume (with bands
                          unless stated) behind.
                 Rev.   EXURGAT etc.   " Declaration " in two lines between two
                          straight lines, with three plumes above and date below.

           2483   Oxford obv. die without groundline.   I.m. Oxford plume.   S
                   Reverse.   Three Bristol plumes.   I.m. Pellet.   1643.

                   Oxford obv. die with ground line.   I.m. Pellet.
           2484   *Reverses.*   Similar to No. 2483.   1643.   S

           2485   Similar to No. 2483 omitting lines by " Declaration ".   S
                          1643.

           2486   Br. mongram as i.m.   1643.   S

                   Bristol horseman (King wears flat crown).   I.m. Uncertain
                   (? Acorn).

2487	*Reverses.* Similar to No. 2483. 1643.	S
2488	Br. monogram as i.m. 1643, 1644.	S
2489	Shrewsbury plume behind king and as i.m. *Reverses.* Br. monogram as i.m. 1643, 1644.	S
2490	Br. monogram below date. I.m. Pellet. 1644.	S
2491	Br. monogram beneath horse. I.m. Plume or pellet. *Reverses.* Br. monogram below date. I.m. Pellet. 1644, 1645.	S
2492	I.m. Br. monogram. 1644, 1645.	S

Shilling

Obv. Crowned bust left with XII behind.
Rev. Similar to halfcrown but " Declaration " in three lines.

2493	Oxford obv. die. I.m. Oxford plume. *Reverses.* I.m. Pellets. 1643.	S
2494	Br. monogram as i.m. 1643, 1644.	S
2495	Crude bust with stellate lace border to collar. I.m. Shrewsbury plume. *Reverses.* I.m. Pellets. 1643.	S
2496	Br. monogram as i.m. 1644.	S
2497	Bristol bust with rounded lace collar. I.m. Br. monogram (horizontal). *Reverse.* Br. monogram below date. I.m. Pellets. 1644, 1645.	S
2498	Bristol bust wearing square lace collar with scalloped edges. I.m. Pellet. *Reverse.* Br. monogram below date. I.m. Pellets. 1645.	S
2498/1	Bust of similar style with smaller face and taller crown. I.m. Pellet. *Reverse.* Br. monogram as i.m. 1645.	ER
2499	Plumelet before face otherwise as No. 2498. *Reverses.* Br. monogram as i.m. 1644, 1645.	S
2500	Similar to No. 2497. 1644.	S
2501	Plume and two plumelets above " Declaration " otherwise as No. 2497. 1644.	S

Sixpence

Similar to shilling but VI behind head.

2502	Coarse bust without plumelet. I.m. Pellet. *Reverse.* Three Shrewsbury plumes. I.m. Br. monogram. 1643.	R
2503	*Obv.* similar to No. 2499. *Reverse.* Three small Bristol plumes. I.m. Br. monogram (horizontal). 1644.	R

Groat

Types and legends similar to Shilling but IIII behind bust.

2504	No mark before face. I.m. Pellet. *Reverse.* Three plumes with bands. I.m. Pellet. 1644.	S
2505	Plumelet before face. I.m. Pellet. *Reverses.* Three Shrewsbury plumes. I.m. Br. 1644.	S

2506	Plume with plumelet each side. Br. below date. I.m. Pellet. 1644.	S

Threepence   *Obv.*   Crowned bust left with plume before and III behind.
                     Rev.   Type and legend similar to Shilling.

2507   Aberystwyth obv. die. I.m. Book.   R
        Reverse.   Three plumelets. I.m. Pellet. 1644.

2508   Plume with bands before face. I.m. Pellet.   S
        Reverse.   Similar to No. 2507. 1644.

2509[118]   Plumelet before face. I.m. Pellet.   S
        Reverse.   Single plumelet above and no line below " Declara-
        tion ". I.m. Pellets. 1645.

Halfgroat   2510   *Obv.*   Crowned bust left with II behind. I.m. Pellet.   VR
                        Rev.   EXURG DEUS DISSIP INIMICI. " Declaration " in three
                        lines between two straight lines with Br. below.

Penny   2511[118]   *Obv.*   Bust similar in style to No. 2510 with I behind. I.m.   ER
                        Pellet.
                        Rev.   IUSTITIA THRONUM FIRMAT. Large plume with bands.

B. Sir Richard Vyvyan's Mints (1642–6).

TRURO MINT (1642–43).

DENOMINATIONS—**GOLD : Unite.**

SILVER : Halfpound, Crown, Halfcrown, Shilling.

INITIAL MARKS

Rose   Bugle

GOLD

Unite   2528   *Obv.*   Crowned bust with XX behind. I.m. Rose.   ER
                    Rev.   FLORENT CONCORDIA REGNA. Crowned oval gar-
                    nished shield with crowned C R at sides. I.m. Rose.

Unite   2529   *Obv.*   Similar to No. 2528.   ER
                    Rev.   CULTORES SUI DEUS PROTEGIT. Crowned oval gar-
                    nished shield. I.m. Rose.

SILVER

Halfpound?   2530   *Obv.*   King on horseback left, looking towards the viewer, and   ER
                         with sash tied in a bow. I.m. Rose.
                         Rev.   CHRISTO etc. Oval garnished shield. I.m. Rose.

N.B.—This coin is struck from silver crown dies on a thick flan weighing
913·5 grains.

---

[118] These coins may have been struck at the " A, B and plumes " mints, or both there and at Bristol.

Crown		*Obv.* King on horseback left. I.m. Rose.	
		Rev. CHRISTO etc. Oval garnished shield. I.m. Rose.	
	2531	King's sash in two loose ends and he looks forward.	S
		King's sash in a bow and he looks towards viewer.	
	2532	*Reverses.* Normally garnished shield.	S
	2533	" Barrel " garniture i.e. twelve even scrolls.	R
Halfcrown	2534	*Obv.* King facing viewer, holding baton, mounted on spirited horse galloping over arms. I.m. Rose.	VR
		Rev. CHRISTO etc. Oval garnished shield with 1642 in curved cartouche below. I.m. Rose.	

N.B.—A number of these coins have for some time been considered later strikings. However, it is now thought that they may be contemporary strikings by machinery (cf. BNJ 30 (1960–1) pp. 149–58).

Halfcrown		*Obv.* King on horseback left, sash in two loose ends. I.m. Rose (except 2541).	
		Rev. CHRISTO etc. Oblong garnished shield with C R at sides or above. I.m. Rose (except No. 2541).	
	2535	Horseman similar to No. 2534 without arms below. *Reverse.* C R at sides of shield.	VR
		Galloping horse, king holds sword, upright or sloping forward.	
	2536	*Reverses.* C R at sides of shield.	VR
	2537	C R above shield.	VR
	2538	Trotting horse, king looks at viewer, sword upright. *Reverse.* C R at sides of shield.	R
		Walking horse with lowered head, king looks to front.	
	2539	*Reverses.* C R at sides of shield.	R
	2540	C R above shield.	R
	2541[119]	Walking horse with groundline. I.m. Bugle. *Reverse.* C R above shield. I.m. Four pellets.	ER
Shilling		*Obv.* Crowned bust left with XII behind. I.m. Rose.	
		Rev. CHRISTO etc. Garnished shield—details below. I.m. Rose.	
		First bust. Good style; large XII.	
	2542	*Reverses.* Oblong garnished shield.	ER
	2543	Oval garnished shield with C R at sides.	ER
	2544	Round shield garnished with eight even scrolls.	ER
		Second bust. Linear style with lank hair and round shoulder; smaller XII.	
	2545	*Reverses.* Similar to No. 2543.	ER
	2546	Similar to No. 2544.	ER
	2547	Round shield garnished with five small scrolls and one long scroll.	VR

[119] This attribution is not certain. The initial mark appears to be a bugle and the style is neat and close to early Truro coins (cf. SCBI 33, p. xxxvii, n. 1).

TRURO OR EXETER MINT.

DENOMINATIONS—**SILVER : Halfcrown.**

INITIAL MARKS

Rose

Halfcrown

Obv. King on horseback left. I.m. Rose.
Rev. **CHRISTO** etc. Garnished shield as below. I.m. Rose.

King's sash tied in a bow.

2548	*Reverses.* Oblong garnished shield with C R at sides.	VR
2549	Round shield garnished with eight similar scrolls.	S
2550/1	Round shield garnished with five small scrolls and one long scroll.	S
2550/2	Round shield with angular garniture.	ER

King's sash flying out behind.

2551	*Reverses.* Similar to No. 2549.	VR
2552	Oblong shield with curved sides and narrow garnishing.	ER

Briot's horse with groundline.

2553	*Reverses.* Similar to No. 2549.	R
2554	Similar to No. 2552.	ER
2555/1	Similar to No. 2550/1.	R
2555/2	Similar to No. 2550/2.	ER

EXETER MINT (1643–46).

DENOMINATIONS—**SILVER : Crown, Halfcrown, Shilling, Sixpence, Groat, Threepence, Halfgroat, Penny.**

INITIAL MARKS

Ex. **Ex**   Rose   Castle

Crown

Types and legends similar to Truro (crowns) but with date in rev. legend.

Same obv. die as No. 2532. I.m. Rose.

2556	*Reverses.* Date divided by i.m. Rose. 1644.	S
2557	Date to left of i.m. Rose. 1644.	S
2558	Date to left of i.m. Ex. 1645.	VR

	King's sash in two loose ends. I.m. Castle.	
2559	*Reverses.* Date to left of i.m. Rose. 1645.	VR
2560	Date to left of i.m. Ex. 1645.	R
2561	Date to left of i.m. Castle. 1645.	S

Halfcrown

Obv. King on horseback left—details below. I.m. Rose.
Rev. CHRISTO etc. Round garnished shield. Date at end of legend.

Similar to No. 2534.

2562	*Reverses.* Date to left of i.m. Rose. 1644.	ER
2563	Date to left of i.m. Castle. 1645.	ER

Short, portly figure of king on ill-proportioned horse.

2564	*Reverses.* Date divided by i.m. Rose. 1644.	ER
2565	Date to left of i.m. Rose. 1644.	ER
2566	Briot's horse with groundline.	R
	Date to left of i.m. Rose. 1644.	

King's sash flying out behind; horse with twisted tail.

2568	*Reverses.* Date to left of i.m. Rose. 1644, 1645.	R
2569	Date to left of i.m. Castle. 1645.	R
2570	Date to left of i.m. Ex. 1645.	R

Halfcrown

Obv. Similar to No. 2568.
Rev. EXURGAT etc. "Declaration" in two lines between two straight lines, with three plumes above and date below.

2571	Ex below date. Rev. i.m. Ex. 1644.	ER
2572	Nothing below date. Rev. i.m. Ex. 1644, 1645.	ER

Shilling

Similar to Truro No. 2547 but with date after rev. legend.

2573	Date divided by i.m. Rose. 1644.	R
2574	Date to right of i.m. Rose. 1644.	R
2575	Date to left of i.m. Rose. 1644, 1645.	R

Shilling

2576	*Obv.* Similar to Truro No. 2545.	ER
	Rev. EXURGAT etc. "Declaration" in three lines between two straight lines, with three plumes above and 1645 below.	

Sixpence

Obv. Crowned bust left with VI behind. I.m. Rose.
Rev. CHRISTO etc. Round garnished shield. Date at end of legend.

2577	Date divided by i.m. Rose. 1644.	R
2578	Date to left of i.m. Rose. 1644.	VR

Groat

2579	*Obv.* Crowned bust left with IIII behind. 1644 at beginning of legend. I.m. Rose.	S
	Rev. CHRISTO etc. Oval garnished shield. I.m. Rose.	

| **Threepence** | 2580 | *Obv.* | Crowned bust left with III behind. I.m. Rose. | S |
| | | *Rev.* | CHRISTO etc. Square shield over cross fleury; 1644 above. I.m. Rose. | |

| **Halfgroat** | 2581 | *Obv.* | Crowned bust left with II behind. I.m. Rose. | R |
| | | *Rev.* | THRO IUSTI FIRMAT 1644. Oval garnished shield. I.m. Rose. | |

| **Halfgroat** | 2582 | *Obv.* | As No. 2581. | R |
| | | *Rev.* | THRO IUSTI FIRMAT 1644. Large rose. I.m. Rose. | |

| **Penny** | 2583 | *Obv.* | Crowned bust left with I behind. I.m. Rose. | VR |
| | | *Rev.* | THRO IUS FIRMAT 1644. Large rose. I.m. Rose. | |

C. Other attested Royalist Mints.

YORK MINT (1643–44).[120]

DENOMINATIONS—**SILVER : Halfcrown, Shilling, Sixpence, Threepence.**

INITIAL MARKS

Lion (on all coins)

Halfcrown		*Obv.*	Equestrian figure with general characteristics of Tower Type No. III.	
		Rev.	CHRISTO etc. Shield—for details, see below.	
	2309		Type 1. Groundline below horse. Square garnished shield with C R at sides.	VR
	2310		Type 2. Obverse as No. 2309. Oval garnished shield.	VR
	2311		Type 3. No groundline. Oval garnished shield.	R
	2312[121]		Type 4. Similar to No. 2311 but EBOR below horse. (Struck in varying degrees of base silver).	R
	2313		Type 5. Taller horse with EBOR beneath. Crowned square shield with crowned C R at sides (flowers in legend).	S
	2314		Type 6. Obverse as No. 2313. Crowned oval shield with crowned C R at sides (flowers in legend).	N
	2315		Type 7. Similar to No. 2313 but horse's tail between legs. Crowned oval shield with lion's skin garniture, head and paws showing.	N

---

[120] A die-study of this mint appears in BNJ 54 (1984) pp. 210–41.

[121] These coins are now considered to be forgeries—probably late eighteenth century.

Shilling		*Obv.* Bust similar to No. 2231 with XII behind.	
		Rev. CHRISTO etc. Shield—for details, see below.	
	2316	Type 1. Square shield over long cross fleury with EBOR above.	N
	2317	Type 2. Bust in plain armour and mantle. Reverse similar to No. 2316. Coarser workmanship.	S
	2318	Type 3. Bust as No. 2316. Oval garnished shield with EBOR below.	R
	2319	Type 4. Similar to No. 2318 but shield crowned.	N
	2320	Type 5. Similar to No. 2318 but shield crowned and with lion's skin garniture.	N
Sixpence		*Obv.* Bust similar to No. 2231 with VI behind.	
		Rev. CHRISTO etc. Crowned oval garnished shield.	
	2321	(a) Nothing beside shield.	R
	2322	(b) C R at sides of shield.	S
Threepence	2323	Similar to No. 2136 but with III behind head.	N

N.B.—No. 2324 has been reattributed to Chester mint (see below).

CHESTER MINT (1644).

DENOMINATIONS—**GOLD : Unite.**

SILVER : Halfcrown, Shilling, Threepence.

INITIAL MARKS

Cinquefoil		Plume (Gold)		Prostrate gerb	
Plume				Sword and three gerbs[122]	

GOLD

| **Unite**[123] | 2324 | *Obv.* Bust similar to Tower Group F. | ER |
| | | *Rev.* FLORENT CONCORDIA REGNA. Crowned oval garnished shield with C R at sides. I.m. Plume. | |

---

[122] cf. BNJ 52 (1982) p. 244.
[123] For reattribution to this mint cf. BNJ 31 (1962) p. 165.

SILVER

Halfcrown   *Obv.*   King on horseback left.
                           Rev.   CHRISTO etc. Shield (details below).

2627/1   CHST below horse: plume behind king. Oval garnished shield.   R
           I.m. Sword and three gerbs.

2627/2[124]   CH engraved into die below horse. Almost round shield with   ER
           1644 above.

2628[125]   No marks by king or horse. Crowned oval shield with lion-skin   R
           garniture. I.m.'s Prostrate gerb, none/cinquefoil, none with
           triangle of pellets after REGNO.

2629[125]   Obverse without marks or initial mark. Crowned square shield   R
           with crowned C R at sides. I.m. Cinquefoil.[126]

Halfcrown   2630   *Obv.*   King on horseback left. I.m. Sword and three gerbs.   VR
                       Rev.   EXURGAT etc. " Declaration " in two lines between four
                                straight lines with three plumes above and 1644 below. I.m.
                                Plume, triangle of pellets.

Shilling[125]   *Obv.*   Crowned bust left with XII behind. I.m. Triangle of pellets.
                        Rev.   CHRISTO etc. Shield (details below). No initial mark.

2630/1   Crowned oval shield with lion-skin garniture.   ER

2630/2   Square shield over long cross fleury.   ER

2630/3[127]   Square shield without cross.   ER

Threepence   2631   *Obv.*   Crowned bust with III behind. No. i.m.   ER
                        Rev.   CHRISTO etc. Square shield. I.m. Prostrate gerb.

HEREFORD MINT.

There is evidence for a mint at Hereford, but no coins can be firmly attributed to it. It has been suggested that the " cannon ball erasing SA " (No. 2602), " CH " (No. 2627/2) and the " Garter " Nos. 2358–9) halfcrowns are possible candidates (cf. SCBI 33, pp. xl–xli and xliv–xlv).

---

[124] These coins are different in style from other Chester halfcrowns and their attribution is uncertain. Hereford has been suggested as a possibility.

[125] It has been suggested that these coins were struck at an uncertain mint probably in Yorkshire (cf. SNC 79 (1971) p. 98). However current opinion still favours Chester as the most likely mint (cf. BNJ 52 (1982) pp. 245–6).

[126] A coin of this type with i.m. None/quatrefoil of pellets is considered to be a forgery.

[127] The top of the reverse is not visible on the only known specimen and it is possible that there may be an i.m. (cf. BNJ 54 (1984) p. 293).

D. Unattested Royalist Mints.

" A ", " B " AND " PLUMES " MINTS (1645–6).

The following coins were attributed to Lundy Island and subsequently to Appledore and Barnstaple (or Bideford). Mr. Boon convincingly dismisses both and suggests Ashby de la Zouche and Bridgnorth (SCBI 33, pp. xli–xlii). The writer is not convinced that the letters A and B are necessarily the initial letters of the towns in which these coins were minted.

DENOMINATIONS—SILVER : Halfcrown, Shilling, Sixpence, Groat, Threepence, Halfgroat.

MINT MARKS

A. **A** **⊅**   B. **B**

Halfcrown

Obv. Equestrian figure left with plume behind. I.m. Shrewsbury plume.

Rev. EXURGAT etc. " Declaration " in two lines with three plumes above and date below.

A below horse.

2512	*Reverses.* Altered Bristol die. A (over Br) below date. I.m. A (over Br). 1645.	VR
2513	A below date. I.m. A. 1645.	VR
2514	Nothing below date. I.m. A. 1645.	VR
2515	B below date. Scroll above " Declaration ". I.m. A. 1646.	VR

Plumelet below horse.

2516	*Reverses.* Plume between two small S. plumes. Scroll above " Declaration ". I.m. S. plume. 1646	R
2517	Similar to No. 2516 with plumelet below date. 1646.	R

Shilling

Obv. Crowned bust left with XII behind.

Rev. Similar to halfcrown but with " Declaration " in three lines.

2518	No plume before face. I.m. Plume. *Reverse.* A below date. I.m. A. 1645.	VR

Plumelet before face. I.m. Plume.

2519	*Reverses.* A below date. I.m. A. 1645.	R
2520	Large central plume. Scroll above " Declaration ". I.m. Plumelet. 1646.	R
2521	Larger S. plume before face. I.m. S. plume. *Reverse.* Plume with plumelet each side. Scroll above " Declaration ". I.m. Pellet. 1646.	R

Sixpence   Similar to Shilling but with VI behind head.

       2522   Plumelet before face. I.m. A (horizontal).   VR
              Reverse. Three plumelets. I.m. Pellet. 1645.

       2523   Larger S. plume before face. I.m. B.   N
              Reverse. S. plume with plumelet each side. Scroll above
                     " Declaration ". I.m. Pellet. 1646.

Groat   Legends and types similar to Shilling but IIII behind head and
                 plumelet before.

       2524   (a) Similar to No. 2522. 1645.   ER

       2525   (b) Obverse as No. 2524 but i.m. Plumelet.
              Reverse. Similar to No. 2521. 1646.   S

Threepence   2526   *Obv.* Crowned bust left with plumelet before and III behind.   S
                        I.m. Plumelet.
              Rev. EXURGAT etc. " Declaration " in three lines with scroll
                      and single plumelet above and 1646 below. I.m. Pellet.

Halfgroat   2527   *Obv.* Crowned bust left with II behind. I.m. Pellet.   ER
              Rev. IUSTITIA THRONUM FIRMAT. Large plume with bands
                    dividing date, 1646.

       N.B.—The threepence No. 2509 and penny No. 2511 listed under Bristol
       mint may in fact belong to this series.

" HC " MINT.[128]

DENOMINATIONS—**SILVER : Halfcrown.**

INITIAL MARKS

One pear (Obverse)   Three pears (Reverse)

Halfcrown   2626   *Obv.* King on horseback left. I.m. One pear.   R
              Rev. CHRISTO etc. Oval garnished shield with H C (Hartle-
                    bury Castle?) in garniture below. I.m. Three pears.

" W " MINT (1644).[129]

DENOMINATIONS—**GOLD : Unite.**

                       SILVER : Halfcrown.

---

[128] Probably Hartlebury Castle, Worcestershire.

[129] Attributed to Weymouth for many years, it is now thought that these coins were probably struck at Worcester (cf. SCBI 33, pp. xliii–xliv).

MINT MARKS

Castle		Lions two	
Helmet		Lis	
Leopard's head?		Rose	In legend
Lion (sometimes in legend)		Star	

GOLD

Unite 2584 *Obv.* Crowned bust left with **XX** behind. No i.m.   ER
Rev. **FLORENT CONCORDIA REGNO** (annulet stops). Crowned garnished oval shield with lion's paw at each side. No. i.m.

SILVER

Halfcrown *Obv.* King on horseback left.
Rev. Crowned shield—for details of shape etc. and legend, see below.

W below horse. I.m. Two lions.

2585 *Reverses.* **CHRISTO** etc. Square shield. I.m. Helmet, castle.   R

2586 **CHRISTO** etc. Oval garnished shield. I.m. Helmet.   R

W below horse, grass indicated. I.m. Castle.

2587 *Reverses.* **CHRISTO** etc. Square shield. I.m. Helmet, none.   R

2588 **CHRISTO** etc. Oval draped shield. Lis or lions in legend. I.m. None.   R

2589 **CHRISTO** etc. Oval shield draped with chains. **C R** at sides. Roses in legend. I.m. None.   R

2590 **FLORENT** etc. Oval garnished shield (same rev. die die as No. 2584).   VR

Horse with tail between legs and mane blown forward, no marks below and no i.m.

2591 *Reverses.* **CHRISTO** etc. Square shield. I.m. Helmet.   VR

2592 **CHRISTO** etc. Oval draped shield. Lis, roses, lions, or stars in legend. I.m. None.   R

2593 **FLORENT** etc. Oval garnished shield.   VR

Briot's horse with groundline. I.m. Leopard's head?

	2594	*Reverses.* CHRISTO etc. Draped oval shield. Roses in legend. I.m. None.	R
	2595	Similar to No. 2594 with C R at sides of shield.	R

2596   Crude style, without ground; horse's tail straight. I.m.   R
Leopard's head?
Rev.   CHRISTO etc. Oval draped shield. Lis, lions, or stars in
legend. I.m. None.

2597   Horse with thin wavy tail. I.m. Leopard's head?   R
Rev.   CHRISTO etc. Oval draped shield. Stars in legend.
I.m. None.

Halfcrown   2598   *Obv.*   Same die as No. 2585.   VR
Rev.   EXURGAT etc. "Declaration" in two lines, between
two straight lines, with three plumes above and 1644
below.

"SA" MINT (1644).[130]

DENOMINATIONS—**GOLD : Unite.**

     SILVER : Halfcrown.

INITIAL MARKS

Boar's head		Lis	
Helmet		Rose (in legend)	

GOLD

Unite   2599[131]   Similar to No. 2584 but with no lion's paws at sides of shield   ER
which divides crowned C R. I.m. Lis?/none.

SILVER

Halfcrown   *Obv.*   King on horseback left. I.m. Lis.
Rev.   Crowned shield. For details of shape etc. and legend,
see below.

     SA below horse.

	2600	*Reverses.* CHRISTO etc. Oval garnished shield. I.m. Helmet.	ER
	2601	FLORENT etc. Oval garnished shield. I.m. None.	ER

---

[130] Attributed originally to Salisbury and later to Sandsfoot Castle, it is now thought that these coins may
have been struck at Shrewsbury (Salopia).
[131] cf. BNJ 25 (1947) p. 227.

2602[132]	Large pellet or cannon ball erasing **SA** below horse.	VR
	Reverse. **CHRISTO** etc. Oval garnished shield. I.m. None (lis in legend), helmet.	

Horse with mane blown forward, and wavy tail sometimes between legs.

2603	*Reverses.* **CHRISTO** etc. Large round shield with crude garniture. I.m. Helmet.	VR
2604	**CHRISTO** etc. Small uncrowned square shield with lion's paw above and at sides. I.m. Helmet.	VR
2605	**CHRISTO** etc. Small oval garnished shield. I.m. None (lis, roses, or nothing in legend), helmet, boar's head.	R
2606	**FLORENT** etc. Oval garnished shield. I.m. None.	VR

Cruder work with little or no mane before horse.

2607	*Reverses.* **CHRISTO** etc. Round shield with garniture of scrolls, lis etc. Usually lis in legend. I.m. None.	R
2608	Similar to No. 2607, but garniture of chains.	R
2609	Grass beneath horse.	R
	Reverse. **CHRISTO** etc. Round shield with garniture of scrolls etc. I.m. Lis, none.	
2610	Ground beneath horse.	R
	Reverse. **FLORENT** etc. Oval garnished shield. I.m. None.	

" W " OR " SA " MINT (1644).

DENOMINATIONS—**SILVER : Shilling, Sixpence, Groat, Threepence, Halfgroat.**

INITIAL MARKS

Bird		Helmet	
Boar's head		Lion	
Cannon ball and lis		Lis	

---

[132] This coin may have been struck at Hereford.

Castle

Pear?[133]

Scroll

Rose

Shilling

Obv. Crowned bust left with XII behind.
Rev. CHRISTO etc. Shield. For details, see below.

No i.m. on obverse.

2611 *Reverses.* Square shield. I.m. Castle. — VR

2612 Square shield with C (castle) R above, and orna- VR
ments in legend. I.m. Helmet and lion.

2613 Oval draped shield. I.m. Lion, pear? — VR

Crude style. I.m. Bird.

2614 *Reverses.* Square shield with lion's paw at sides and above. VR
I.m. Boar's head.

2615 Similar to No. 2614, but C (lis) R above. I.m. VR
Scroll.

2616 Oval garnished shield. Lis in legend. I.m. Lis. — VR

Crude style. I.m. Lis.

2617 *Reverses.* Similar to No. 2614. I.m. Helmet. — VR

2618 Similar to No. 2615. I.m. Scroll. — VR

2619 Round shield garnished with scrolls, lis, and pellets. VR
I.m. Lis (also in legend), three lis, helmet, helmet
and lis, cannon ball and four lis.

Shilling

Crowned bust right with XII behind. I.m. Pear?

2620/1 *Reverses.* CHRISTO (rose) AUSPICE (rose) REGNO (lis). ER
Crowned oval garnished shield.

2620/2 Similar to No. 2595 (Halfcrown die). ER

Sixpence 2621 *Obv.* Crude bust left with VI behind. I.m. Castle. VR
Rev. CHRISTO etc. Square shield with lion's paw above and
at sides.
Reverse. I.m. Castle, boar's head.

Groat

Obv. Crude bust left with IIII behind.
Rev. CHRISTO etc. Oval garnished shield. I.m. Helmet.

2622 *Obverse.* I.m. Lis. R

2623 *Obverse.* I.m. Rose. R

Threepence 2624 *Obv.* Crude bust left with III behind. I.m. Lis. R
Rev. CHRISTO etc. Oval garnished shield.
Reverse. I.m. Lis, helmet.

---

[133] This mark is uncertain and has been described as a bunch of grapes.

Halfgroat	2625	*Obv.*	Crude bust left with II behind. I.m. Lis.	R
		Rev.	CHRISTO etc. Oval garnished shield.	
		Reverse.	I.m. Rose, castle, cross and four annulets.	

"GARTER" MINT (1645).[134]

Halfcrown		*Obv.*	Equestrian figure with grass below horse. I.m. Lis.	
		Rev.	CHRISTO etc. Crowned oval shield within Garter with lion to left and unicorn to right. Crowned C R beside crown.	
	2358		Without date.	ER
	2359		With date 1645 below shield.	VR

E. Irregular coins and forgeries.

| **Halfcrown**[135] | 2350 | *Obv.* | CAROLUS D G MAGN BRITAN FRAN ET HIB REX. Horseman similar to Tower Type V. I.m. Flower. | ER |
| | | *Rev.* | Similar to Aberystwyth Halfcrown. | |

Interlinked Cs

| **Halfcrown**[136] | 2632 | *Obv.* | King on horseback left. I.m. Interlinked Cs. | ER |
| | | *Rev.* | CHRISTO etc. Oval garnished shield. I.m. Interlinked Cs. | |

N.B.—See No. 2710 for a coin formerly described as a pattern halfgroat of Aberystwyth. It is no longer considered to be a pattern and its mint and even value (due to clipping) is uncertain.

SIEGE PIECES

The following are usually struck from pieces of plate of irregular shape, and sometimes bear a part of the original design or hallmark. The shapes in which they are found are given after the denomination.

---

[134] Formerly attributed very doubtfully to "Combe Martin" mint, it has been suggested that these halfcrowns may have been struck at Hereford (cf. SCBI 33, p. xlv).

[135] Formerly attributed to Aberystwyth mint, the obverse is a copy of Briot's milled halfcrown (cf. No. 2299) and the reverse copies an Aberystwyth coin. The crude workmanship and poor lettering indicate that it is probably a forgery.

[136] Formerly doubtfully attributed to Coventry and later to Corfe Castle, this coin is now considered to be a forgery (cf. SCBI 33, pp. xlv–xlvi).

CARLISLE (Besieged October 1644 to June 1645. Coins struck in May 1645).

DENOMINATIONS—**SILVER : Three Shillings (Round), Shilling (Round or octagonal).**

Three Shillings		*Obv.*	Crowned **C R** with rosette on each side and **IIIs** below.	
		Rev.	**OBS CARL** 1645, as follows:	
	2633		In three lines with rosette above and below.	E R
	2634		In two lines with rosette below.	E R
Shilling		*Obv.*	Crowned **C R** with triangle of pellets on each side and **XII** below.	
		Rev.	**OBS CARL** 1645, as follows:	
	2635		In three lines with rosette above and below.	V R
	2636		In two lines with rosette below.	V R

COLCHESTER (June to August 1648).

DENOMINATIONS—**GOLD : Ten Shillings (Round).**

Ten Shillings	2637	*Obv.*	Gateway of Colchester between crowned **C R**; below, **OBS COL.** 16 ^s_x 48 in two lines.	E R
		Rev.	Incuse impression of obverse die.	

N.B.—This piece is probably a concoction.

NEWARK (Besieged several times—surrendered 6 May 1646).

DENOMINATIONS—**SILVER : (Diamond shaped): Halfcrown, Shilling, Ninepence, Sixpence.**

Halfcrown	2638	*Obv.*	Large crown between **C R**; below, **XXX**.	R
		Rev.	**OBS NEWARK** and date in three lines. 1645, 1646.	
Shilling			Types similar to No. 2638, but **XII** on obverse.	
	2639		Crude crown with straight band and low arch. **NEWARKE** 1645.	V R
	2640		Normal crown with curved richly jewelled band and high arch. **NEWARK(E)** 1645, **NEWARK** 1646.	S
Ninepence	2641		Types similar to No. 2638, but **IX** on obverse. **NEWARK(E)** 1645, **NEWARK** 1646.	R
Sixpence	2642		Types similar to No. 2638, but **VI** on obverse. **NEWARK** 1645, 1646.	R

PONTEFRACT (June 1648 to March 1649).

DENOMINATIONS—**GOLD : Unite (Octagonal).**

SILVER : Two Shillings (Diamond), Shilling (Diamond, round, or octagonal).

GOLD

Unite (138½ grains)	2643	*Obv.*	DUM SPIRO SPERO. Large crown over **C R**.	ER
		Rev.	CAROLUS SECUNDUS 1648. Castle gateway with flag dividing **P C**; a cannon projecting from right tower; **OBS** vertically left.	
Unite (94 grains)	2644	*Obv.*	CAROL II D G MAG B F ET H REX. Large crown with HANC DEUS DEDIT 1648 in three lines below.	ER
		Rev.	POST MORTEM PATRIS PRO FILIO. Castle gateway as on No. 2643.	

SILVER[137]

Two Shillings (150 grains)	2645	*Obv.*	Similar to No. 2643.	ER
		Rev.	Castle gateway with **P C** at sides of central tower and **OBS** vertically to left; a hand holding a sword protruding from right tower; below, 1648.	
Shilling (80 grains)		*Obv.*	Similar to No. 2643.	
		Rev.	Castle gateway; below, 1648.	
	2646		Similar to No. 2645.	R
	2647		**OBS** to left and **P XII C** to right of gateway.	R
Shilling	2648		Similar to No. 2643.	R
Shilling	2649		Similar to No. 2644 (Some bear a pistol[138] or coronet as rev. i.m.).	R

N.B.—Nos. 2643, 2644, 2648, and 2649 which bear the name of Charles II were struck after the execution of his father on 30th January 1649.

SCARBOROUGH (July 1644 to July 1645).

The value of the following coins was decided by the intrinsic value of the roughly shaped piece of silver from which they were made. This produced a large number of odd denominations. In view of the number of these and the fact that many are unique, they have not been listed in the usual manner, but are divided into three types.[139]

---

[137] As the weights vary considerably and the pieces are not marked with the denomination. it is difficult to be certain of the intended value.

[138] cf. BNJ 37 (1968) p. 213.

[139] Many forgeries exist often struck on flans made from modern coins, traces of which can sometimes be seen (cf. SNC 88 (1980) pp. 175, 264–5).

DENOMINATIONS—**SILVER :** **Five Shillings and Eightpence, Five Shillings,**
Three Shillings and Fourpence, Three Shillings, Two
Shillings and Tenpence, Two Shillings and Sixpence,
Two Shillings and Fourpence, Two Shillings and
Twopence, Two Shillings, One Shilling and Ninepence,
One Shilling and Sixpence, One Shilling and Four-
pence, One Shilling and Threepence, One Shilling
and Twopence, One Shilling and One Penny, One
Shilling, Elevenpence, Tenpence, Eightpence, Seven-
pence, Sixpence, Fourpence.

Type I   2650   View of the castle and the value in shillings and pence stamped in   ER
                        incuse. Some have **OBS** Scarborough 1645 engraved on the rev.,
                        but this is perhaps of a later date.

S D	S	S D	S
(a) v.viii.	(b) v. and s c.	(c) iii.iv.	(d) iii.

S D	S D	S D	S D
(e) ii.vv.	(f) ii.vi.	(g) ii.iiii.	(h) ii.ii.

S	S D	S D	S D
(i) ii.	(j) i.ix.	(k) i.vi.	(l) i.iiii.

S D	S	D	D
(m)i.iii.	(n) i.	(o) vi.	(p) iii.

Type II[140]   2651   View of broken castle with legend " Caroli Fortuna Resurgam ".   ER
                        No mark of value. Round or octagonal flans. " Shillings " only.

Type III   2652   Castle gateway stamped in relief with value in incuse.   ER

S
(a) ii. sometimes with gateway stamped twice.

S D	S D	S D	S D
(b) i.vi.	(c) i.iiii.	(d) i.iii.	(e) i.ii.

S D	S	D	D
(f) i.i.	(g) i.	(h) xi.	(i) x.

D	D	D
(j) ix.	(k) vii.	(l) vi.

PATTERNS

NON-PROVINCIAL

GOLD

I. High relief (Probably by Abraham Vanderdoort).

Five-unites   2653   *Obv.*   CAROLUS D G MAG BRIT FRAN ET HIBERNIAE REX.   ER
(Juxon medal)   Uncrowned bust left with long hair and pointed beard,
                                 wearing a falling lace collar.
                        Rev.   FLORENT CONCORDIA REGNA.   Crowned oval gar-
                                 nished shield with crowned **C R** at sides.
                                 No inner circles. I.m. Rose.

---

[140] Although these pieces are apparently attested by Sir Hugh Cholmley's account of the siege, it seems
likely that they were either struck as souvenirs shortly after the siege or are eighteenth century concoctions
(cf. SNC 90 (1982) pp. 229–31).

Three-unites	2654	*Obv.* Crowned bust left wearing draped armour. Inner circle. *Rev.* Similar to No. 2653 but C R uncrowned. I.m. Plume.	ER

Unite
(Gold silver tin
or pewter)

Similar to No. 2653 with abbreviated obv. legend.

2655	No mark of value. I.m. Lis.	VR
2656	XX behind head. I.m. Plume.	VR

Unite	2657	Similar to No. 2654 with XX behind head. I.m. Plume.	VR
Unite	2658	Similar to No. 2657 but dated 1630 and bust reaches to edge of coin. I.m. Heart.	ER

II.   Low relief (N. Briot).

Unite or shilling
(Gold or silver)

Rev. AUSPICIIS REX MAGNE TUIS.   Square shield crowned and garnished, with crowned C R at sides; above crown, 1630 with B to 1. and small St. George and Dragon to r.

	2659	CAROLUS D G MAGN BRITANN FRANC ET HIB REX. Uncrowned bust left. I.m. Briot's anemone.	ER
	2660	CAROLUS D G MAGN BRITANN FRANC ET HIBE REX. Crowned bust left. I.m. B.	VR
	2661	CAR D G MAGN BRITAN FR ET HIB REX. (Starts at bottom left). Uncrowned bust left reaching to bottom edge. I.m. B (at beginning of legend).	ER
	2662	Legend as No. 2661. Crowned bust left reaching to bottom edge. I.m. B (at end of legend).	ER

Unite (Silver)	2663	*Obv.* Crowned bust left. *Rev.* ARCHETYPUS MONETAE AURAE ANGLIAE. Crowned square shield with crowned C R at sides and 1635 above. I.m. B.	ER

N.B.—For similar pattern for silver coins, cf. No. 2677.

Unite or **shilling**[141] (Silver)	2664	*Obv.* CAR D G MAG BRIT FR ET HIB REX. (Starts at bottom left). Crowned bust right reaching to bottom edge; below, B. *Rev.* FIDEI DEFENSOR. Crowned shield with Garter.	ER

III.   Resembling or adopted for current coinage.

Angel	2665	Similar to No. 2145 but with obv. legend CAROLUS D G MAGN BRITANN FRAN ET HIB REX. I.m. None/B.	ER
Unite	2666	Similar to Tower Group C (cf. No. 2151). I.m. Heart sideways/ Heart.	ER
Unite	2667	*Obv.* Similar to Group D (cf. No. 2152). I.m. Plume. *Rev.* Similar to Group C (cf. No. 2151). I.m. Plume.	ER

---

[141] The status of these " coins " is uncertain because of their weight.

Double Crown	2668	Similar to No. 2158 with i.m. Trefoil.	ER
Double Crown	2669	Similar to Group D with i.m. Large rose on obv.	ER

SILVER

Crown[141]

Obv.   CAROLUS D G MAG BRITANNIAE FRAN ET HIB REX FIDEI DEFENSOR. Bust left. I.m. Flower.

Rev.   HAUD ULLI VETERUM VIRTUTE SECUNDUS. King on horseback left.

	2670	Uncrowned bust with linear inner circle.	ER
	2671	Crowned bust.	ER

Crown[141]   2672

Obv.   CAROLUS D G MAG BRIT FRAN ET HIB REX FIDEI DE. Shields of England, France, Scotland, and Ireland in cruciform pattern; crown above first shield.

Rev.   Similar to No. 2670 with B and wreath in exergue.   ER

Halfcrown[142]   2673

Obv.   O REX DA FACILEM CURSUM. King on horseback right; below groundline. N.BRIOT F.

Rev.   ATQUE AUDACIBUS ANNUE COEPTIS. Crowned oblong garnished shield dividing date, 1628.   R

Shilling   2674

Obv.   Uncrowned bust left in lace collar, armour and scarf, with XII behind.

Rev.   CHRISTO etc. Oval garnished shield with C R above. Initial mark: Plume.   ER

Shilling[143]   2675
(Gold or silver)

Obv.   Bust right wearing radiate crown; below, prostrate B.

Rev.   REGIT UNUS UTROQUE. Sceptre and trident in saltire with crowned C R at sides; below, a rose.   R

Shilling?[143]   2676

Obv.   CAROLUS D G ANG SCO FRAN ET HIB REX FIDEI DEFENSOR. Crowned shield within the collar of the Order of the Thistle, all within the Garter.

Rev.   Similar to No. 2675 but without C R; in exergue, 1628.   R

Shilling   2677   Similar to No. 2663 but rev. legend ARCHETYPUS MONETAE ARGENTAE ANGLIAE.   ER

Groat   2678

Obv.   Crowned bust left with rose and IIIID behind.

Rev.   CHRISTO etc. Square shield on long cross with 1634 above.   R

Threepence

Obv.   Crowned bust left. I.m. Bell.

Rev.   SALUS REIPUBLICAE SUPREMA LEX. Oval garnished shield with 1634 above. I.m. Bell.

	2679	Rose behind bust.	R
	2680	Rose and III behind bust.	R

---

[142] Possibly a medal for the La Rochelle expedition in 1628.
[143] Possibly a medal to mark the king's demands for an increased army and navy.

| **Threepence** | 2681 | *Obv.* | CAR D G MAG BRIT FR ET H R. Crowned bust left, reaching to bottom edge, with rose and IIID behind. | R |
| | | *Rev.* | SALUS etc. Square shield on cross fourchée with 1634 above. | |

| **Halfgroat** | 2682 | *Obv.* | Similar to Tower Group B. I.m. Heart. | ER |
| | | *Rev.* | IUSTITIA THRONUM FIRMAT. Square shield. I.m. Heart. | |

| **Halfgroat** | 2683 | *Obv.* | Similar to No. 2681 but with rose and IID behind. | R |
| | | *Rev.* | IUSTITIA etc. Square shield on cross fourchée. | |

Halfgroat		*Obv.*	CAR D G ANG SCO FR ET HIB REX. Uncrowned bust right wearing ruff.	
		Rev.	REGIT UNUS UTROQUE. Sceptre and trident in saltire.	
	2684		Nothing beside sceptre and trident.	N
	2685		Crowned C each side of sceptre and trident (Var. legend as No. 2681 and I.m. Rose).	S

| **Halfgroat** (Gold or silver) | 2686 | *Obv.* | Similar to No. 2684. | R |
| | | *Rev.* | FLOREBIT IN AEVUM. Rose radiate. I.m. Small rose. | |

| **Halfgroat** (Silver or copper) | 2687 | *Obv.* | CAR D G MAG BRIT FRAN ET HI R(EX). Bust as on No. 2684. (Also known with obverse of No. 2684). | N |
| | | *Rev.* | FIDEL DEFENSOR. Two Cs interlocked with crown above. Sometimes with B below the two Cs. | |

| **Halfgroat** (Silver or copper) | 2688 | *Obv.* | No legend. Rose with large crown above and B below between crowned C R. | R |
| | | *Rev.* | No legend. Rose or thistle with large crown above and 1640 below, between crowned C R. | |

| **Six Farthings** | 2689 | *Obv.* | Legend and bust as No. 2681 but no rose or mark of value. | VR |
| | | *Rev.* | CHRIS AUSPICE REGN. Rose with VI F below. | |

| **Five Farthings** | 2690 | | Similar to No. 2689 but V F on rev. | VR |

| **Penny** | 2691 | | Similar to No. 2683 but I D behind head. | VR |

| **Penny** | 2692 | *Obv.* | CAR D G MAG BRIT FR ET H REX. Crowned C. | VR |
| | | *Rev.* | Similar to No. 2686. | |

| **Halfpenny** | 2693 | *Obv.* | CAROLUS REX. Crowned rose with C R beside crown. I.m. Lis. | VR |
| | | *Rev.* | A HALF PENI. Similar to obverse. | |

| **Halfpenny** | 2694 | *Obv.* | No legend. Crowned C R. | R |
| | | *Rev.* | No legend. Rose. | |

| **Halfpenny** | 2695 | *Obv.* | CAROLUS D G MAG BRIT. Radiate draped bust left. | VR |
| | | *Rev.* | FRAN ET HIBER REX. Crown with C $\frac{1}{2}$ D R below. | |

Resembling or adopted for current coinage.

| **Halfcrown** | 2696 | | Similar to Tower Group III (cf. No. 2209). Rose stops and scrolls by i.m. on rev. I.m. Portcullis. | ER |

| **Shilling** | 2697 | Similar to Tower Group D (cf. No. 2223), but without inner circles. I.m. Rose. | ER |

| **Shilling** | 2698 | Similar to Tower Group D (cf. No. 2225). Rose stops on rev. I.m. Portcullis. | ER |

Sixpence　　2699　　*Obv.*　Similar to Tower Group C (cf. No. 2238).　　　　　　　　ER
　　　　　　　　　　　　Rev.　CHRISTO AUSPICE REGNO. Shield as on Group D with C R at sides and plume above. I.m. Plume.

Sixpence　　2700　Similar to Tower Group D (cf. No. 2241). I.m. Portcullis.　　ER

Groat　　　2701　Legends and types similar to sixpences of Tower Group D (cf. No. 2241) but no mark of value behind head. I.m. Bell.　ER

Halfgroat　2702　Similar to Tower Group D (cf. No. 2254). I.m. Rose.　　　ER

Penny　　　2703　Similar to Tower Group D (cf. No. 2267). I.m. Rose.　　　ER

N.B.—The above are all well struck on round flans. There also exist a number of current type coins, bearing the initial mark of their type, which are similarly struck. These may be patterns but are more probably proofs.

COPPER

Farthing　2704　*Obv.*　FARTHING TOAKENS. Crossed sceptres crowned with a rose in centre and three lis around.　　　　　　　　　R
　　　　　　　　　　　Rev.　TYPUS MONETAE ANGL AERIS. Crossed sceptres crowned with three lions around.

Farthing　2705　*Obv.*　CITTIE OF LONDON. Crowned rose and 1644 between two swords.　　　　　　　　　　　　　　　　R
　　　　　　　　　　　Rev.　Similar to No. 2704.

Farthing　2706　*Obv.*　CAROLUS D G M B REX. Crowned rose with C R at sides. I.m. Lis.　　　　　　　　　　　　VR
　　　　　　　　　　　Rev.　A FARTHING PLEDGE. Crowned rose with C R at sides.

Farthing　2707　*Obv.*　CAROLUS D G MAG BRIT. Helmeted bust left reaching to edge of coin. I.m. Rose.　　　　　　　　R
　　　　　　　　　　　Rev.　FRA ET HIBER REX. Oval garnished shield.

Farthing　2708　*Obv.*　Square shield. I.m. Mullet.　　　　　　　　　　　VR
　　　　　　　　　　　Rev.　EXURGAT DEUS DISSIPENTUR INIMICI. Crowned portcullis.

Farthing?　2709　*Obv.*　No legend. Three crowns connected by a knot.　　R
　　　　　　　　　　　Rev.　Similar to obv.

N.B.—This piece is probably a medalet.

Uncertain Mint

Halfgroat?[144]
(Silver)
2710   *Obv.*   Plume with **C R** at sides and **II** below.   ER
           Rev.   CHRISTO AUSPICE REGNO.   Oval shield.

Oxford Mint

Triple Unite
(Gold)
2711   Types and legends similar to No. 2382 but with different style   ER
bust from other triple unites and a very small lis as obv. i.m.
Rev. legend and " Declaration " on a continuous scroll. 1643.

Shilling
(Silver)
2712   *Obv.*   Crowned bust left, wearing figured armour with a lion's   ER
head on shoulder, and small plain collar; behind, **XII**.
I.m. Shrewsbury plume between two lozenges.
           Rev.   EXURGAT etc.   "Declaration" in three lines between
two scrolls with Shrewsbury plume between two Oxford
plumes above and 1644 **OX** below.   I.m. Four lozenges.
Lozenge stops on both sides.

Shilling
(Silver)
2713   *Obv.*   Crowned bust right in armour with plain collar and scarf   ER
looped up in front, behind **IIX**.   I.m. Shrewsbury plume
with lozenge to left.
           Rev.   EXURGAT etc.   "Declaration" in three lines between
two straight lines with three Oxford plumes above and
1644 **OX** below.   I.m. Lozenge with : at each side.
Lozenge stops on both sides.

Shilling
(Silver)
2714   *Obv.*   Legend commences at bottom left.   Bust similar to No.   VR
2713 reaching to edge of coin, behind, **XII**.
           Rev.   EXURGAT etc.   "Declaration" in three lines within a
cartouche with a large Shrewsbury plume above and 1644
below.
Small module.   No inner circles or i.m.

---

[144] This coin is no longer regarded as a pattern and one cannot even be sure of its denomination in view of the clipped condition of the sole surviving example. Its former association with Aberystwyth is tenuous and it is possibly the production of an uncertain Civil War mint (cf. SCBI 33, p. xlviii & no. 1181).

COMMONWEALTH

1649–1660

DENOMINATIONS—**GOLD** : **Unite, Double-crown, Crown.**

SILVER : **Crown, Halfcrown, Shilling, Sixpence, Halfgroat, Penny, Halfpenny.**

INITIAL MARKS

Sun (1649–57) 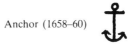 Anchor (1658–60) ⚓

| **Standard Type** | *Obv.* | **THE COMMONWEALTH OF ENGLAND.** Shield of St. George within wreath formed of a palm and laurel branch. I.m. on obverse only. |
| | *Rev.* | **GOD WITH US.** (Date). Conjoined shields of St. George and Ireland with mark of value above. |

GOLD

Unite Standard type with mark of value, **XX.**

| 2715 | I.m. Sun.   1649, 1650, 1651, 1652, 1653, 1654, 1655, 1656, 1657. | S |
| 2716 | I.m. Anchor.   1658, 1660. | VR |

Double-crown Standard type with mark of value, **X.**

| 2717 | I.m. Sun.   1649, 1650, 1651, 1652, 1653, 1654, 1655, 1656, 1657. | R |
| 2718 | I.m. Anchor.   1660. | VR |

Crown Standard type with mark of value, **V.**

| 2719 | I.m. Sun.   1649, 1650, 1651, 1652, 1653, 1654, 1655, 1656, 1657. | R |
| 2720 | I.m. Anchor.   1658, 1660. | VR |

SILVER

Crown Standard type with mark of value, **V.**

| 2721 | I.m. Sun. 1649, 1651, 1652, 1653, 1654, 1656. | R |

Halfcrown Standard type with mark of value, **II. VI.**

| 2722 | I.m. Sun. 1649, 1651, 1652, 1653, 1654, 1655,[145] 1656. | S |
| 2723 | I.m. Anchor. 1658, 1660. | VR |

---

[145] cf. BNJ 38 (1969) p. 190.

Shilling		Standard type with mark of value, XII.	
	2724	I.m. Sun. 1649, 1651, 1652, 1653, 1654, 1655, 1656, 1657.	N
	2725	I.m. Anchor. 1658, 1659, 1660.	R
Sixpence		Standard type with mark of value, VI.	
	2726	I.m. Sun. 1649, 1651, 1652, 1653, 1654, 1655, 1656, 1657.	N
	2727	I.m. Anchor. 1658, 1659, 1660.	VR
Halfgroat	2728	*Obv.* No legend or i.m. Types as standard type.	N
		Rev. No legend or date. Types as standard type. Mark of value, II.	
Penny	2729	Similar to No. 2728, but mark of value, I.	N
Halfpenny	2730	*Obv.* No legend. Shield of St. George.	N
		Rev. No legend. Shield of Ireland.	

PATTERNS

SILVER

Halfcrown (Silver or copper)		Similar to No. 2722, but of neater workmanship and struck by machinery. Inscribed edge as below.	
	2731	IN THE THIRD YEARE OF FREEDOME BY GODS BLESSING RESTORED 1651.	R
	2732	TRUTH AND PEACE 1651 (olive branch) PETRUS BLOND-AEUS INVENTOR FECIT (palm branch).	R
Halfcrown	2733	*Obv.* THE COMMONWEALTH OF ENGLAND. Shield of St. George within a laurel wreath.	VR
		Rev. GAURDED WITH ANGELES 1651. Angel facing holding the conjoined shields of St. George and Ireland.	
		Edge TRUTH AND PEACE 1651 (mullet stops).	
Shilling	2734	Similar to No. 2733, but thinner and with plain or grained edge.	VR
Sixpence[146] (Gold, silver, or copper)	2735	*Obv.* TRUTH AND PEACE (mullet stops). Shield of St. George.	VR
		Rev. TRUTH AND PEACE (mullet stops). Shield of Ireland.	
		Edge Plain, with stars, or inscribed TRUTH AND PEACE 1651.	

N.B.—There also exist machine struck shillings and sixpences of the standard type but smaller module with grained edges, which were patterns by Blondeau.

COPPER

| **Farthing** | 2736 | *Obv.* FARTHING TOKENS OF ENGLAND. Shield of St. George. | VR |
| | | *Rev.* FOR NECESSITY OF CHANGE 1649. Shield of Ireland. | |

---

[146] Possibly a pattern farthing.

| **Farthing** | 2737 | *Obv.* | THE FARTHING TOKENS FOR. Shield of St. George. | VR |
| (Copper or Brass) | | *Rev.* | THE RELEFE OF THE PORE. Shield of Ireland. | |

| **Farthing** | 2738 | *Obv.* | THUS UNITED INVINCIBLE. Three pillars united. | VR |
| | | *Rev.* | AND GOD DIRECT OUR COURSE (COURS or CORSE). Ship. | |

| **Farthing** | 2739 | *Obv.* | THE COMMONS PETICION. Shields of St. George and Ireland. | ER |
| | | *Rev.* | THE POORES RELEFE. Shields of St. George and Ireland with E R below. | |

| **Farthing** | 2740 | *Obv.* | PITTY THE POORE 1652. Shields of St. George and Ireland. | VR |
| (Silver, brass, or copper) | | *Rev.* | SUCH GOD LOVES. Shields of St. George and Ireland with E R below. | |

| **Farthing** | 2741 | *Obv.* | ENGLANDS FARDIN. (Various renderings). Shield of St. George with wreath above. | VR |
| | | Rev. | FOR NECESSARY CHA(NGE). Shield of Ireland with wreath above. | |

| **Farthing** | 2742 | *Obv.* | $\frac{1}{4}$ OUNCE OF FINE PEWTER. Shield of St. George with T K in wreath above. | R |
| (Pewter) | | *Rev.* | FOR NECESSARY CHANGE. Shield of Ireland with wreath above. | |

| **Farthing** | 2742/1 | *Obv.* | THE FARTHING TOKEN OF THE. Shield of Ireland. | VR |
| (Tin) | | *Rev.* | COMMONWEALTH OF ENGLAND. Shield of St. George. | |

| **Farthing** | 2742/2 | *Obv.* | GOD IS OUR SUN AND SHIELD. Sun. | VR |
| | | *Rev.* | OUR FOUNDATION IS A ROCK. A TOKEN. 1651. Rock beaten by waves. | |

OLIVER CROMWELL

PATTERNS

| **Standard Type** | | *Obv.* | OLIVAR D G RP ANG SCO ET HIB &c PRO. Laureated bust left (undraped on gold; draped on silver). | |
| | | *Rev.* | PAX QUAERITUR BELLO. Crowned shield with date above. | |

GOLD

| **Fifty Shillings?** | 2743 | Standard type dated 1656 with edge inscribed PROTECTOR LITERIS LITERAE NUMMIS CORONA ET SALUS. | ER |
| **Broad** | 2744 | Standard type dated 1656 with grained edge (also known in silver[147] and pewter). | S |

---

[147] This exists with a plain edge.

SILVER

Crown 2745 Standard type dated 1658 with edge inscribed HAS NISI PERI- N
TURUS MIHI ADIMAT NEMO (also known in gold).

Halfcrown 2746 Standard type dated 1656 or 1658 with edge inscribed as No. N
2745 (also known in gold dated 1658).

Shilling 2747 Standard type dated 1658 with grained edge (also known in N
copper and pewter).[148]

Sixpence 2748 Standard type dated 1658 with grained edge (also known in ER
pewter).

N.B.—The following imitations of Cromwell's coins were made at a later
date. The differences from the original coins are shown.

(i) Tanner's dies made c. 1738.
Half-broad (Gold) 1656. No original strikings of this denomination known.
Crown (Silver) 1658. Top leaf of laurel wreath between A and N.

(ii) Low Countries' dies made before 1700.
(a) Struck only in the Low Countries.
Crown (Silver, silver gilt, pewter, or lead) 1658. N of ANG reversed.
(b) Some possibly struck in the Low Countries before 1700, but most struck
probably at the Royal Mint in London, c. 1738.
Half-broad (Gold or copper) 1656, 1658. Without &c on obverse. Shilling
(Silver or copper) 1658. Without &c on obverse and N of ANG reversed.
Some on thick flans have been called " two-shillings ".
Sixpence (Silver) 1658. Without &c on obverse; top leaf of laurel wreath points
to P; no berries in wreath. Some on thick flans have been called " ninepences ".

COPPER

Farthing 2749 *Obv.* OLIVAR PRO ENG SC IRL. Laureated bust left. VR
Rev. THUS UNITED INVINCIBLE. Three pillars united.

Farthing 2750 *Obv.* Similar to No. 2749. VR
Rev. CHARITIE AND CHANGE. Crowned shield.

Farthing 2751 *Obv.* Similar to No. 2749. VR
Rev. AND GOD DIRECT OUR CORSE. Ship.

Farthing[149] 2752 *Obv.* OLIVER PRO ENG SCO & IRE. Laureated bust left. VR
(Silver or I.m. Mullet.
copper) *Rev.* Similar to No. 2750.

---

[148] A nine-sided proof in pewter exists.

[149] A similar coin with the reverse reading CONVENIENT CHANGE 1651 (listed as No. 2752 in the first
edition) is a forgery.

CHARLES II

1660–1685

DENOMINATIONS—**GOLD : Unite, Double-crown, Crown.**

SILVER : Halfcrown, Shilling, Sixpence, Groat, Threepence, Halfgroat, Penny.

GOLD

Standard Type

Obv. CAROLUS II D G MAG BRIT FRAN ET HIB REX. Laureated and draped bust left. I.m. Crown.

Rev. FLORENT CONCORDIA REGNA. Crowned oval garnished shield with C R at sides.

Unite Standard Type.

2753	No mark of value.	R
2754	Mark of value XX behind head.	R

Double-crown Standard Type.

2755	No mark of value.	VR
2756	Mark of value X behind head.	VR

Crown Standard Type.

2757	No mark of value	VR
2758	Mark of value V behind head.	VR

SILVER

Standard Type

Obv. CAROLUS II D G MAG BRIT FRAN ET HIB REX. Crowned bust in armour left. I.m. Crown (except No. 2774).

Rev. CHRISTO AUSPICE REGNO. Square shield on cross fleury. Nos. 2761, 2764, 2767, 2772, 2775 only have i.m. Crown.

Halfcrown Standard Type.

2759	No mark of value or inner circles.	VR
2760	Mark of value, XXX. No inner circles.	VR
2761	Mark of value, XXX. Inner circles.	S

Shilling Standard Type.

2762	No mark of value or inner circles.	S
2763	Mark of value, XII. No inner circles.	R
2764	Mark of value, XII. Inner circles.	N

Sixpence		Standard Type.	
	2765	No mark of value or inner circles.	S
	2766	Mark of value, VI. No inner circles.	R
	2767	Mark of value, VI. Inner circles.	N
Groat	2768	Standard Type with mark of value, IIII, and inner circles.	N
Threepence	2769	Standard Type with mark of value, III, and inner circles.	N
Halfgroat		Standard Type.	
	2770	No mark of value or inner circles.	N
	2771	Mark of value, II. No inner circles.	S
	2772	Mark of value, II. Inner circles.	C
Penny		Standard Type.	
	2773	No mark of value or inner circles.	N
	2774	No mark of value, inner circles or initial mark.	N
	2775	Mark of value, I. Inner circles.	C

N.B.—There are also the following machine made coins in this series. Halfgroat. Similar to No. 2771, sometimes with bust to edge of coin.

Penny. Standard Type with mark of value, I. No inner circles. Bust sometimes to edge of coin.

PATTERNS

GOLD

Broad (Gold, silver or copper)	2776	*Obv.*	CAROLUS II D G MAG BR FR ET HI REX. Laureated bust in armour right.	R
		Rev.	MAGNA OPERA DOMINI 1660. Square shield crowned.	

N.B.—The reveres of this pattern is also known combined with the obverse of the coronation medal.

Broad (Gold or silver)	2777	*Obv.*	CAROLUS II REX. Laureated draped bust right.	R
		Rev.	MAGNALIA DEI 1660. Shields of England, Scotland, France, and Ireland in cruciform, with crowned interlocked Cs over II in each angle.	
		Edge	REVERSUS SINE CLADE VICTOR SIMON FECIT. Or sometimes grained or plain.	
Broad (Silver)	2778	*Obv.*	Similar to the reverse of No. 2777.	R
		Rev.	PROBASTI ME DNE SICUT ARGENTUM. Crowned garnished shield.	
		Edge	REVERSUS etc.	
Broad (Silver)	2779	*Obv.*	As reverse of No. 2776.	R
		Rev.	As reverse of No. 2777.	
		Edge	REVERSUS etc.	

| **Broad** | 2780 | *Obv.* | Laureated and draped bust left. | R |
| | | *Rev.* | FLORENT CONCORDIA REGNA.   1662.   Crowned square shield. | |

COPPER

| **Farthing** | 2781 | *Obv.* | SUCH GOD LOVES.   Crowned bust of Charles I left. I.m. Rose. | ER |
| | | *Rev.* | THUS UNITED INVINCIBLE.   Three pillars interlinked. | |

| **Farthing** | 2782 | *Obv.* | Similar to No. 2781. | VR |
| | | *Rev.* | TRUTH AND PEACE.   Crowned rose with crowned C R at sides and 1660 below.   I.m. Rose. | |

| **Farthing** (Silver) | 2783 | *Obv.* | CAROLUS II REX.   Crowned bust left.   I.m. Rose. | VR |
| | | *Rev.* | As No. 2781. | |

| **Farthing** (Copper or silver) | 2784 | *Obv.* | As reverse of No. 2782. | |
| | | *Rev.* | As reverse of No. 2781. | |

N.B.—The above is a selection of the patterns struck during this reign. They are included, as they were struck during the period covered by this book.

METROLOGY

The following are the weights and values of the main denominations from Edward I to Charles II. They are inserted only where a change takes place in one or both. The largest denomination is shown for each series of the gold and the penny for the silver. The relative data for multiples and divisions of the coins quoted may be easily calculated from the figures given.

Weights are given in grains troy (1 grain = 0·0648 grammes).

The fineness of silver is the number of ounces of pure silver in the pound (12 ounces) of coin, e.g. 11 oz. 2 dwt. = 0·925 fine. The fineness of gold is the number of carats of pure gold in 24 carats e.g. 23 ct. 3·5 gr. = 0·9948 fine.

STANDARD GOLD (23 carats 3·5 grains)									SILVER PENNY
Edward I. 1279									22·2
	NOBLE								
Edward III. 1344	6/8	136·7							20·3
1346	6/8	128·6							20
1351	6/8	120							18
Henry IV. 1412	6/8	108							15
	RYAL		**ANGEL**						
Edward IV. 1464	10/–	120	6/8	80					12
					SOVEREIGN				
Henry VII. 1489					20/–	240			
							CROWN GOLD (22 carats) SOVEREIGN		
Henry VIII. 1526			7/6	80	22/6	240			$10\frac{2}{3}$
1544			8/–	80			Debased issue (below)		
Edward VI. 1550			10/–	80	30/–	240	20/–	$174\frac{6}{11}$	8*
Mary. 1553	15/–	120							
Elizabeth. 1601							20/–	$171\frac{83}{87}$	$7\frac{23}{31}$
	SPUR RYAL				**ROSE RYAL**		**UNITE ETC.**		
James I. 1604	15/–	$106\frac{2}{3}$	10/–	$71\frac{1}{9}$	30/–	$213\frac{1}{3}$	20/–	$154\frac{26}{31}$	
1611	16/6	$106\frac{2}{3}$	11/–	$71\frac{1}{9}$	33/–	$213\frac{1}{3}$	22/–	$154\frac{26}{31}$	
1619	15/–	$98\frac{2}{11}$	10/–	$65\frac{5}{11}$	30/–	$196\frac{4}{11}$	20/–	$140\frac{20}{41}$	
Charles I. 1625			10/–	$64\frac{64}{89}$					
Charles II. 1660							20/–	$131\frac{3}{4}$	

N.B.—All silver coins in the above list are 11 oz. 2 dwt. fine except those marked * which are 11 oz. 1 dwt. (1550–3), 11 oz. (1553–60) and 11 oz. 2 dwt. (after 1560).

DEBASED COINAGE

	SOVEREIGN		SHILLING		GROAT		PENNY	
Henry VIII. 1544	23 ct.	200 gr.	9 oz.	120 gr.				
1545	22 ct.	192 gr.			6 oz.	40 gr.	⅓ oz.	10 gr.
1546	20 ct.	192 gr.	4 oz.	120 gr.	4 oz.	40 gr.	⅓ oz.	10 gr.
Edward VI. 1549	22 ct.	$169\frac{7}{17}$ gr.	8 oz.	60 gr.				
			6 oz.	80 gr.				
1550			3 oz.	80 gr.			4 oz.	12½ gr.
Mary. 1553							3 oz.	12 gr.

THE ECCLESIASTICAL MINTS

Details are given below of the archbishops and bishops occupying the sees of the three main privilege mints, during the periods in which their coins bore specific marks. In order to complete the lists the names of ecclesiasts, for whom no specially marked coins are known, have been included. Personal marks appearing on the coins are shown by the relative archbishop's or bishop's name. The pence struck at the York privilege mint only bear a quatrefoil in the centre of the reverse as a distinguishing mark until c. 1465 A.D., and the mint was usually closed when the royal mint in that town was striking.

The first date shown is the granting of the temporalities which is more relevant to numismatists than the election or consecration.

CANTERBURY

Archbishop Thomas Bourchier (1454–1486). Bourchier knot on breast; I.m. Pall.
,,   John Morton (1486–1500). M in centre of reverse.
,,   William Warham (1504–1532). WA on reverse or by bust.
,,   Thomas Cranmer (1533–1555). TC on reverse or by bust.

DURHAM

Bishop Robert de Insular (1274–1283). No marks.
,,   Antony Bek (1283–1311).[150] Cross moline.
,,   Richard Kellawe (1311–1316). Crozier end on reverse.
,,   Ludovic de Beaumont (1317–1333). Lion rampant with two or three lis.
,,   Richard de Bury (1333–1345). Crown in centre of reverse.[151] Crozier end on reverse.
,,   Thomas Hatfield (1345–1381). Crozier end on reverse.
,,   John Fordham (1381–1388).
,,   Walter Skirlaw (1388–1406).
,,   Thomas Langley (1406–1437). Star by crown or no marks.
,,   Robert Nevill (1438–1457). Rings on reverse.
,,   Lawrence Booth (1457–1476).[152] Cross and B by bust. Rings on reverse. BD, BV, D, V, etc. beside bust, by crown, or on reverse. B and trefoil, nothing or lis by bust. D on reverse.
,,   William Dudley (1476–1483). DV or V by bust. D in centre of reverse.
,,   John Sherwood (1485–1494). S on breast, D in centre of reverse. Later, DS beside reverse shield.
,,   Richard Fox (1494–1501). RD or DR beside reverse shield.
,,   William Senhouse (1502–1505). Coinage suspended.
,,   Christopher Bainbridge (1507–1508). Coinage suspended.
,,   Thomas Ruthall (1509–1523). TD above or beside shield on reverse.
,,   Thomas Wolsey (1523–1529). DW or TW and cardinal's hat on reverse.
,,   Cuthbert Tunstall (1530–1559). CD beside reverse shield.

[150] Temporalities suspended July (effective Sep.) 1302–July 1303 and end 1305–July 1307 (dies restored May 1309).
[151] The attribution of pence with this mark is uncertain and they may have been struck by Beaumont (cf. SCBI 39, pp. 61–2).
[152] Temporalities suspended Dec. 1462–Apr. 1464.

YORK

Archbishop William Wickwaine (1279–1285).
  ,,   John le Romeyne (1286–1296).
  ,,   Henry Newark (1297–1299).
  ,,   Thomas Corbridge (1300–1304).
  ,,   William Greenfield (1306–1315).
  ,,   William Melton (1317–1340).
  ,,   William Zouche (1342–1352).
  ,,   John Thoresby (1353–1373).   } Quatrefoil in centre of reverse.
  ,,   Alexander Neville (1374–1388).
  ,,   Thomas Arundel (1388–1396).
  ,,   Robert Waldby (1397–1398).
  ,,   Richard Lescrope (1398–1405).
  ,,   Henry Bowet (1407–1423).
  ,,   John Kempe (1426–1452).
  ,,   William Booth (1452–1464).
  ,,   George Nevill (1465–1476).[153] **G** and key or **G** and rose by bust.
  ,,   Lawrence Booth (1476–1480). **B** and key by bust.
  ,,   Thomas Rotherham (1480–1500). **T** and key, cross, or trefoil by bust. Later, keys on reverse.
  ,,   Thomas Savage (1501–1507). Keys by bust.
  ,,   Christopher Bainbridge (1508–1514). Keys or **XB** on reverse (rarely both).
  ,,   Thomas Wolsey (1514–1530). **TW** by bust or on reverse. Cardinal's hat and keys on reverse.
  ,,   Edward Lee (1531–1544). **EL** or **LE** by bust or on reverse.

---

[153] Temporalities suspended Apr. 1472–Summer 1475.

CROSSES

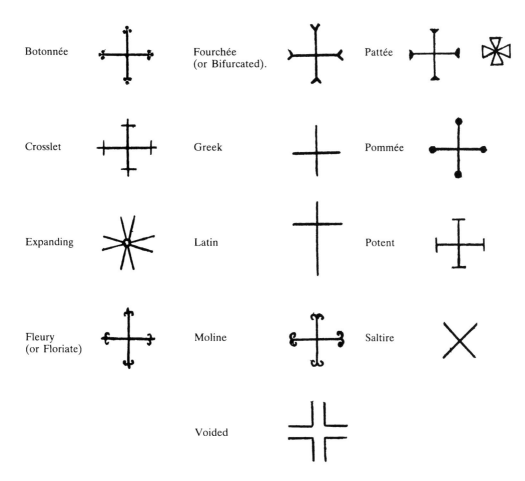

Botonnée	Fourchée (or Bifurcated).	Pattée	
Crosslet	Greek	Pommée	
Expanding	Latin	Potent	
Fleury (or Floriate)	Moline	Saltire	
	Voided		

TRANSLATIONS OF LEGENDS

A DOMINO FACTUM EST ISTUD ET EST MIRABILE IN OCULIS NOSTRI This is the Lord's doing and it is marvellous in our eyes (Psalm cxviii. 23).

AMOR POPULI PRAESIDIUM REGIS The love of the people is the king's protection.

BELLO ET PACE In war and peace.

CAROLI FORTUNA RESURGAM I, the fortune of Charles, shall rise again.

CHRISTO AUSPICE REGNO I reign under the auspices of Christ.

CULTORES SUI DEUS PROTEGIT God protects his worshippers.

DOMINE NE IN FURORE TUO ARGUAS ME O Lord, rebuke me not in Thine indignation (Psalm vi. 1).

DOMINE, DEUS, REX O Lord God, (heavenly) king (Gloria).

DUM SPIRO SPERO Whilst I live, I hope.

EXALTABITUR IN GLORIA He shall be exalted in glory (comp. Psalm cxii. 9).

EXURGAT DEUS DISSIPENTUR INIMICI Let God arise (and) let His enemies be scattered (Psalm lxviii. 1).

FACIAM EOS IN GENTEM UNAM I will make them one nation (Ezek. xxxvii. 22).

FLORENT CONCORDIA REGNA United kingdoms flourish.

HANC DEUS DEDIT God has given this (i.e. the crown).

HAS NISI PERITURUS MIHI ADIMAT NEMO Let no one remove these (letters) from me under penalty of death.

HENRICUS ROSAS REGNA IACOBUS Henry (united) the roses, James the kingdoms.

INIMICOS EIUS INDUAM CONFUSIONE As for his enemies I shall clothe them with shame (Psalm cxxxii. 19).

IESUS AUTEM TRANSIENS PER MEDIUM ILLORUM IBAT But Jesus, passing through the midst of them, went His way (Luke iv. 30).

IUSTITIA THRONUM FIRMAT Justice strengthens the throne.

LUCERNA PEDIBUS MEIS VERBUM EST Thy word is a lantern unto my feet (Psalm cxix. 105).

MIRABILIA FECIT He hath done marvellous things (Cantate).

MUNUS DIVINUM A divine offering.

O CRUX AVE SPES UNICA Hail! O Cross, our only hope.

PAX QUAERITUR BELLO Peace is sought by war.

PER CRUCEM TUAM SALVA NOS CHRISTE REDEMPTOR By Thy cross, save us, O Christ, our Redeemer.

POST MORTEM PATRIS PRO FILIO After the death of the father for the son.

POSUI DEUM ADIUTOREM MEUM I have made God my Helper (comp. Psalm liv. 4).

PROTECTOR LITERIS LITERAE NUMMIS CORONA ET SALUS A protection to the letters (on the face of the coin), the letters (on the edge) a garland and a safeguard to the coinage.

QUAE DEUS CONIUNXIT NEMO SEPARET What God hath joined together, let no man put asunder (Matt. xix. 6).

REDDE CUIQUE QUOD SUUM EST Render to each that which is his own.

RELIGIO PROTESTANTIUM LEGES ANGLIAE LIBERTAS PARLIAMENTI The religion of the Protestants, the laws of England, the liberty of Parliament.

RUTILANS ROSA SINE SPINA A dazzling rose without a thorn.

SCUTUM FIDEI PROTEGET EUM The shield of faith shall protect him.

TALI DICATA SIGNO MENS FLUCTUARI NEQUIT Consecrated by such a sign the mind cannot waver.

TIMOR DOMINI FONS VITAE The fear of the Lord is a fountain of life (Prov. xiv. 27).

TUEATUR UNITA DEUS May God guard these (i.e. the kingdoms) united.

VERITAS TEMPORIS FILIA Truth, the daughter of Time.

The above translations are taken from the British Museum's " Handbook of the Coins of Great Britain and Ireland ", 1899.

BIBLIOGRAPHY

A selection of the major works consulted in the preparation of this volume is given below. For the sake of brevity, it has been necessary to curtail the list and reference is confined mainly to books and articles which cover a reign or series. In most cases any further information required will be found in the British Numismatic Journal or the Numismatic Chronicle. Both contain important articles giving the results of the most recent research as well as details of hoards and previously unpublished coins and are indispensable to the student and collector. Volumes of the Sylloge of Coins of the British Isles, often devoted to a single reign or series, are based on the latest classification (often refined) and provide an invaluable source of illustrations of the coins of the period covered. Important notes also often appear in Spink's Numismatic Circular and Seaby's Coin and Medal Bulletin, while catalogues of important auction sales are often profusely illustrated and provide an essential supplement to the standard works of reference.

GENERAL

BRITISH NUMISMATIC JOURNAL (BNJ), 1903–

G.C. BROOKE. English Coins. 1966 (Revised edition).

I.D. BROWN & M. DOLLEY. A Bibliography of the Coins of Great Britain and Ireland. 1500–1967, 1971.

Sir John CRAIG. The Mint.

H.A. GRUEBER. Handbook of the Coins of Great Britain and Ireland in the British Museum. 1970 (Revised edition).

E. HAWKINS. The Silver Coinage of England. 1887.

R.L. KENYON. Gold Coins of England. 1970 (with addendum).

NUMISMATIC CHRONICLE (NC), 1836–

C. OMAN. The Coinage of England. 1931.

R. RUDING. Annals of the Coinage. 1840.

B.A. SEABY LTD. Coin and Medal Bulletin (SCMB).

SPINK & SON LTD. Numismatic Circular (SNC).

C.H.V. SUTHERLAND. English Coinage, 600–1900. 1973.

SYLLOGE OF COINS OF THE BRITISH ISLES (SCBI).

J.D.A. THOMPSON. Inventory of British Coin Hoards, 600–1500. 1956.

J.H. WATSON. Ancient Trial Plates. 1963.

Illustrated Sale Catalogues—Christies, Glendining & Co. Ltd., Sotheby's and Spink & Son Ltd.

MEDIAEVAL

E. and J.S. FOX. Numismatic History of the Reigns of Edward I, II and III. BNJ 6 (1969) p. 197; 7 (1910) p. 91; 8 (1911) p. 137; 9 (1912) p. 181; 10 (1913) p. 95.

E. BURNS. Coinage of Scotland, 1887. Vol. I, p. 186 (Montrave hoard).

C.E. BLUNT. The Mint of Berwick-on-Tweed under Edward I, II and III. NC (1931) p. 28.

J. SHIRLEY FOX. The Pennies and Halfpennies of 1344–51. NC (1928) p. 16.

J.J. NORTH.   Edwardian English Silver Coins 1279–1351 (The J.J. North Collection).   SCBI 39.

L.A. LAWRENCE.   The Coinage of Edward III from 1351.   NC (1926) p. 417; (1929) p. 106; (1932) p. 96; (1933) p. 15.

W.J.W. POTTER.   The Gold Coinage of Edward III.   NC (1963) p. 107; (1964) p. 305.

W.J.W. POTTER.   The Silver Coinage of Edward III from 1351.   NC (1960) pl. 137; (1962) p. 201.

P.D. MITCHELL.   Catalogue of the Gordon V. Doubleday Collection of Coins of Edward III. Glendinings 7th & 8th June 1972.

F.A. WALTERS.   The Coinage of Richard II.   NC (1904) p. 326.

F. PURVEY.   The Pence, Halfpence and Farthings of Richard II.   BNJ 31 (1962) p. 88.

W.J.W. POTTER.   The Silver Coinages of Richard II, Henry IV and Henry V.   BNJ 29 (1958–9) p. 334; 30 (1960–1) p. 124.

F.A. WALTERS.   Henry IV.   NC (1905) p. 247.

L.A. LAWRENCE.   The Coinage of Henry IV.   NC (1905) p. 83.

C.E. BLUNT.   The Heavy Gold Coinage of Henry IV.   BNJ 24 (1941–4) p. 22.

C.E. BLUNT.   Unrecorded Heavy Nobles of Henry IV and Some Remarks on that Issue.   BNJ 36 (1967) p. 106.

C.E. BLUNT.   Some New Light on the Heavy Silver Coinage of Henry IV.   Transactions of the International Numismatic Congress (1936). p. 360.

G.C. BROOKE.   The Privy Marks of Henry V.   NC (1903) p. 44.

F.A. WALTERS.   The Coinage of Henry V, Henry VI and Edward IV.   NC (1902) p. 224; (1903) p. 286; (1906) p. 172; (1909) p. 132; (1910) p. 117; (1911) p. 153; (1914) p. 330.

R. CARLYON-BRITTON.   The Sequence of Mintmarks preceding, during and succeeding the Restoration of Henry VI.   BNJ 17 (1923–4) p. 125.

C.A. WHITTON.   The Heavy Coinage of Henry VI.   BNJ 23 (1938–40) p. 59, p. 206, p. 309; 24 (1941–4) p. 118; see also BNJ 34 (1965) p. 118.

W.J.W. POTTER.   The Heavy Groats of Henry VI.   BNJ 28 (1955–7) p. 300.

D.F. ALLEN.   The Coinage of Henry VI restored; Some Notes on the London Mint.   NC (1937) p. 28.

C.E. BLUNT and C.A. WHITTON.   The Coinage of Edward IV and Henry VI restored. BNJ 25 (1945–8) p. 4, p. 130, p. 291.

H. SYMONDS.   Mint Accounts and Documents of Edward IV.   NC (1926) p. 99.

H. MONTAGU.   The Coinage of Edward V.   NC (1895) p. 117.

C.E. BLUNT.   The Coinage of Edward V with Some Remarks on the Later Issues of Edward IV.   BNJ 22 (1934–7) p. 213.

E.J. WINSTANLEY.   The Angels and Groats of Richard III.   BNJ 24 (1941–4) p. 179.

T.G. WEBB WARE.   Dies and Designs: The English Gold Coinage 1465–1485, Part I.   BNJ 55 (1985) p. 95.

M. MITCHINER and A. SKINNER.   English Tokens. c. 1200 to 1425, BNJ 53 (1983) p. 29; c. 1425 to 1672, BNJ 54 (1984) p. 86.

TUDOR

L.A. LAWRENCE. The Coinage of Henry VII. NC (1918) p. 205.

R. CARLYON-BRITTON. On Some Early Silver Coins of Henry VII. BNJ 24 (1941–4) p. 28.

W.J.W. POTTER and E.J. WINSTANLEY. The Coinage of Henry VII. BNJ 30 (1960–1) p. 262; 31 (1962) p. 109.

R. CARLYON-BRITTON. The Last Coinage of Henry VII. BNJ 18 (1925–6) p. 1.

D.M. METCALF. Coins of Henry VII (Asmolean Museum Part III), SCBI 23.

C.A. WHITTON. The Coinages of Henry VIII and Edward VI in Henry's Name. BNJ 26 (1949–51) p. 56, p. 171, p. 290. (Addenda etc. BNJ 27 (1552–4) p. 201).

W.J.W. POTTER. Henry VIII—The Sequence of Marks in the Second Coinage. BNJ 28 (1955–7) p. 560; 33 (1963) p. 140.

H.A. PARSONS. Notes on the "Wolsey" Coins of Henry VIII. BNJ 25 (1945–6) p. 60.

H. SYMONDS. The Bristol Mint of Henry VIII and Edward VI. NC (1911) p. 331.

H.W. MORRIESON. The Silver Coins of Edward VI. BNJ 12 (1916) p. 137.

W.J.W. POTTER. The Coinage of Edward VI in His Own Name. BNJ 31 (1962) p. 125.

H. SYMONDS. Edward VI and Durham House. NC (1914) p. 138.

J. BISPHAM. The Base Silver Shillings of Edward VI. BNJ 55 (1985) p. 134.

H. SYMONDS. The English Coinages of Edward VI (Documentary evidence). BNJ 11 (1915) p. 123.

H. SYMONDS. The Coinage of Mary Tudor. BNJ 8 (1911) p. 179.

H. SYMONDS. The Mint of Queen Elizabeth. NC (1916) p. 61.

H.A. PARSONS. The Hammered Silver Coinage of Elizabeth. SNC (1947).

I.D. BROWN. Some Notes on the Coinage of Elizabeth I. BNJ 28 (1955–7) p. 568.

I.D. BROWN and C.H. COMBER. Portrait punches used on the Hammered Coinage of Queen Elizabeth I. BNJ 58 (1988) p. 90.

D.G. BORDEN and I.D. BROWN. The Milled Coinage of Elizabeth I. BNJ 53 (1983) p. 108.

STUART

H. SYMONDS. Mint Marks and Denominations of the Coinage of James I. BNJ 9 (1912) p. 207.

H.W. MORRIESON. The Silver Coins of James I. BNJ 4 (1907) p. 165; 9 (1912) p. 230.

F.R. COOPER. The English Silver Crowns of James I. BNJ 39 (1970) p. 145.

J.J. NORTH and P.J. PRESTON-MORLEY. Coins of Charles I (The J.G. Brooker collection) SCBI 33.

H. SCHNEIDER. The Tower Gold of Charles I. BNJ 28 (1955–7) p. 330; 29 (1958–9) p. 101, p. 382; 30 (1960–1) p. 302; 58 (1988) p. 74.

G.R. FRANCIS. Silver Coins of the Tower Mint of Charles I. BNJ 12 (1916) p. 181; 13 (1917) p. 75; 14 (1918) p. 57; 15 (1919–20) p. 79.

H.W. MORRIESON. Tables of the Silver Coins of the Tower Mint of Charles I. BNJ 18 (1925–6) p. 159.

F.R. COOPER. Silver Crowns of the Tower Mint of Charles I. BNJ 37 (1968) p. 110.

M.B. SHARP. The Tower Shillings of Charles I and their Influence on the Aberystwyth Issue. BNJ 47 (1977) p. 102; see also BNJ 50 (1980) p. 136.

B.R. OSBORNE. The Tower Coins of Charles I. BNJ 54 (1984) p. 164.

E. BESLY. The York Mint of Charles I. BNJ 54 (1984) p. 210.

H.W. MORRIESON. The Coins of Aberystwyth 1637–42. BNJ 10 (1913) p. 181.

H. SYMONDS. A Glance Inside the Mint of Aberystwyth in the Reign of Charles I. BNJ 8 (1911) p. 203.

H.W. MORRIESON. The Coinage of Coombe Martin, 1647–48. BNJ 20 (1929–30) p. 153. —now classified as Aberystwyth, Dovey Furnace.

G.C. BOON. Cardiganshire Silver and the Aberystwyth Mint in Peace and War. National Museum of Wales, 1982.

H.W. MORRIESON. The Coins of Shrewsbury Mint 1642. BNJ 12 (1916) p. 195; 14 (1918) p. 87.

H.W. MORRIESON. The Coins of Oxford 1642–46. BNJ 16 (1921–2) p. 129; 20 (1929–30) p. 137.

R.D. BERESFORD-JONES. The Oxford Mint and the Triple Unites of Charles I. BNJ 27 (1952–4) p. 334.

R.D. BERESFORD-JONES. The Oxford Mint 1642–46. Unites and Half Unites. BNJ 28 (1955–7) p. 604.

H.W. MORRIESON. The Coinage of Bristol 1643–45. BNJ 18 (1925–6) p. 135.

H. SYMONDS. Bristol Types after 1645. NC (1912) p. 140.

H.W. MORRIESON. The Coinage of Lundy 1645–6. BNJ 19 (1927–8) p. 131—now classified as " A ", " B " and " Plumes " mints.

Mary COATE. The Royalist Mints of Truro and Exeter 1642–46. NC (1928) p. 213.

R.C. LOCKETT. Notes on the Mints of Truro and Exeter under Charles I. BNJ 22 (1934–7) p. 227.

F.R. COOPER. The Silver Crowns of Truro and Exeter under Charles I. BNJ 46 (1976) p. 51.

D.F. ALLEN. The Weymouth and Salisbury Mints of Charles I. BNJ 23 (1938–40) p. 97— now classified as " W " and " SA " mints.

J.R. VINCENT. Unpublished Information upon Charles I Weymouth Mints. BNJ 28 (1955–7) p. 169—now classified as " W " mint.

H. SYMONDS. " S.A. ". NC (1913) p. 119.

R. LYALL. The Chester Mint and the Coins attributed to that Mint. SNC 79 (1971) p. 98.

Helen FARQUHAR. Nicholas Briot and the Civil War. NC (1914) p. 169.

P. NELSON. The Obsidional Money of the Great Rebellion. BNJ 2 (1905) p. 291.

W.J. ANDREW. Contemporary Evidence . . . of Obsidional Money. BNJ 11 (1915) p. 207.

H. SYMONDS. Scarborough (Colchester) Siege-pieces. NC (1918) p. 122.

T.H.B. GRAHAM. The Silver Coinage of Cromwell. NC (1908) p. 62.

D.F. ALLEN. The Coinage of Cromwell and its Imitations. BNJ 24 (1941–4) p. 191.

M. LESSEN. A Summary of the Cromwell Coinage. BNJ 35 (1966) p. 163.

H. SCHNEIDER. The Hammered Gold Coinage of Charles II. BNJ 36 (1967) p. 122.

T.H.B. GRAHAM.   Charles II's Hammered Silver Coinage.   NC (1911) p. 57.

W.J. HOCKING.   Simon's Dies in the Royal Mint Museum.   NC (1909) p. 56.

D. ALLEN.   Warrants and Sketches of Thomas Simon.   BNJ 23 (1938–40) p. 441.

PATTERNS AND COPPER COINS

C.W. PECK.   English Copper, Tin and Bronze Coins in the British Museum, 1558–1958. Second Edition. 1964.

C.W. PECK.   The Royal Farthing Tokens of James I.   BNJ 27 (1952–4) p. 313.

A.E. WEIGHTMAN.   The Royal Farthings of James I and Charles I.   BNJ 3 (1906) p. 181.

E. ROGERS.   The Rose Farthing Tokens.   BNJ 18 (1925–6) p. 93.

G.F. CROWTHER.   A Guide to English Pattern Coins. 1887.

INDEX

INDEX

PLATES

PLATE I

PLATE I

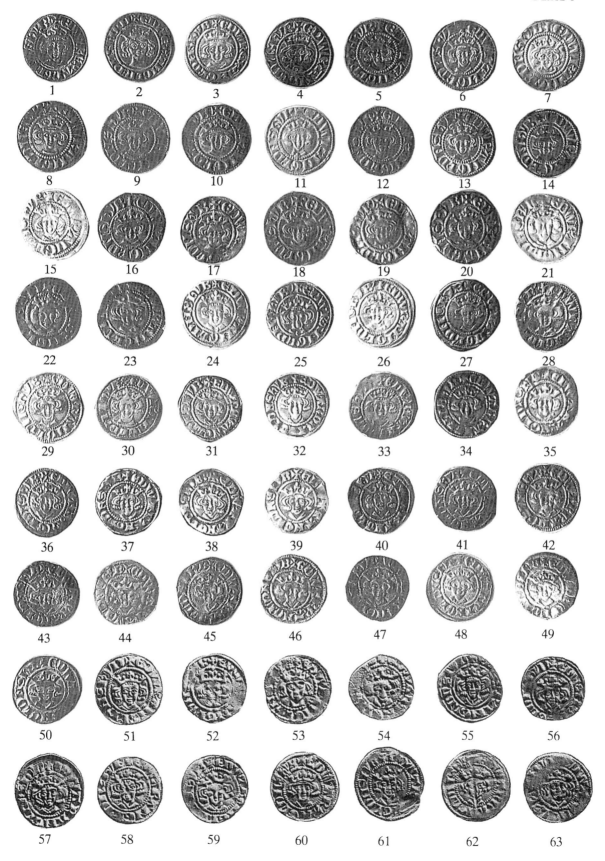

1   2   3   4   5   6   7

8   9   10   11   12   13   14

15   16   17   18   19   20   21

22   23   24   25   26   27   28

29   30   31   32   33   34   35

36   37   38   39   40   41   42

43   44   45   46   47   48   49

50   51   52   53   54   55   56

57   58   59   60   61   62   63

PLATE II

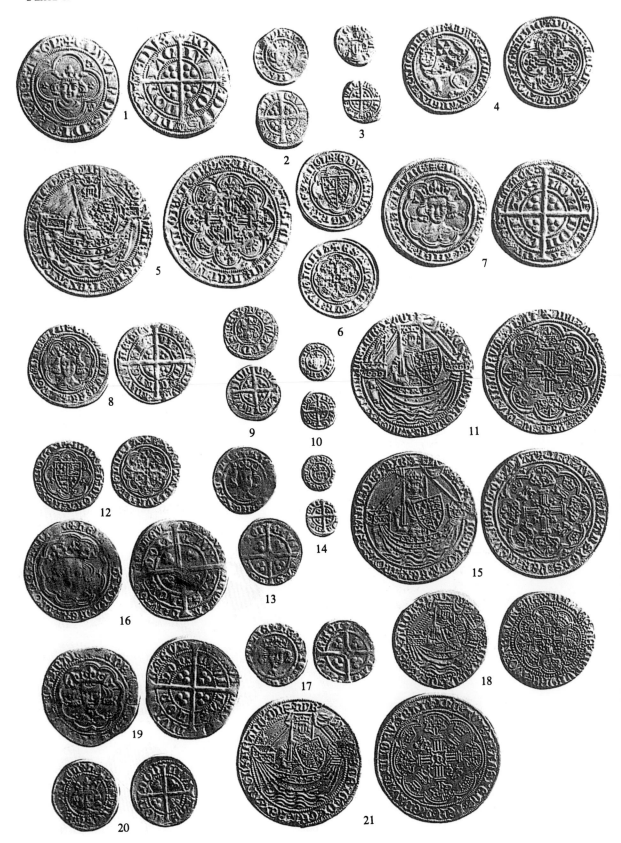

PLATE II

PLATE III

PLATE III

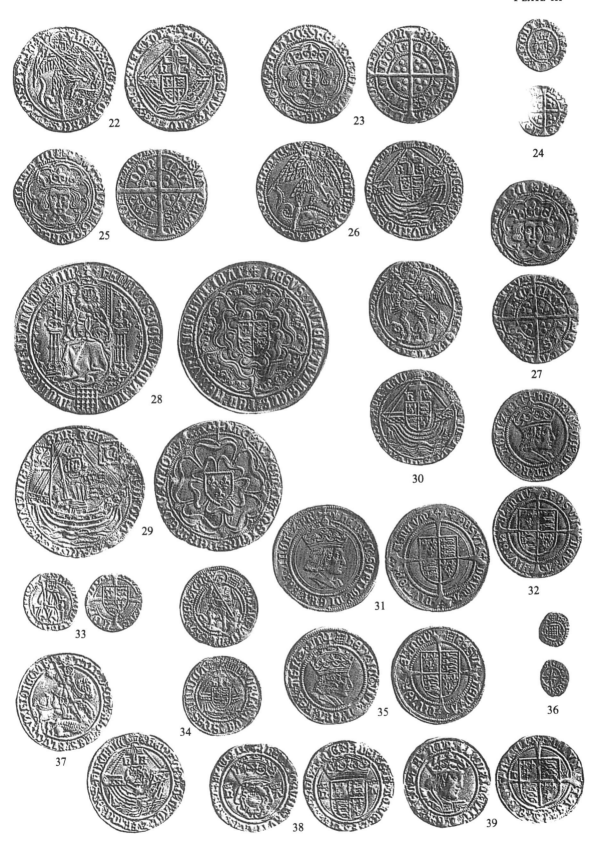

22

23

24

25

26

27

28

29

30

31

32

33

34

35

36

37

38

39

PLATE IV

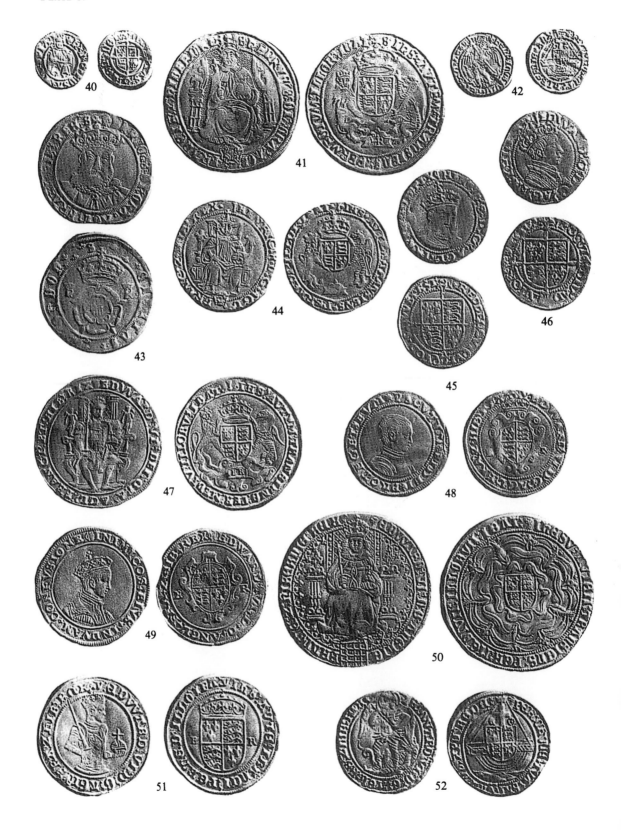

40

41

42

43

44

45

46

47

48

49

50

51

52

PLATE IV

PLATE V

PLATE V

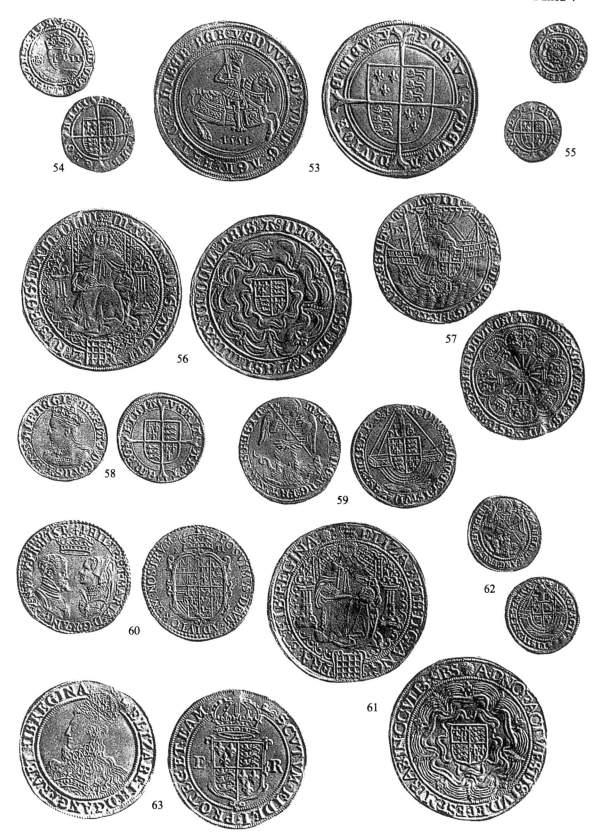

54

53

55

56

57

58

59

60

61

62

63

PLATE VI

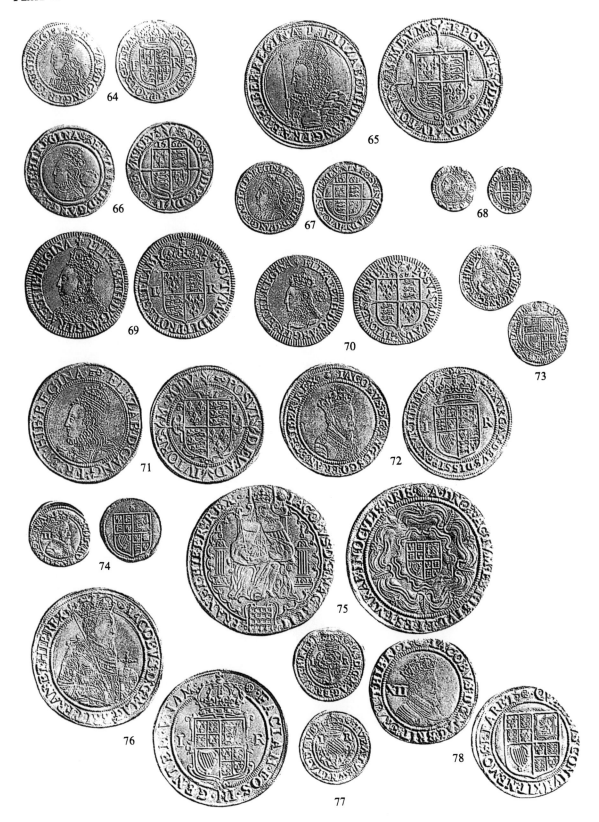

PLATE VI

PLATE VII

PLATE VII

PLATE VIII

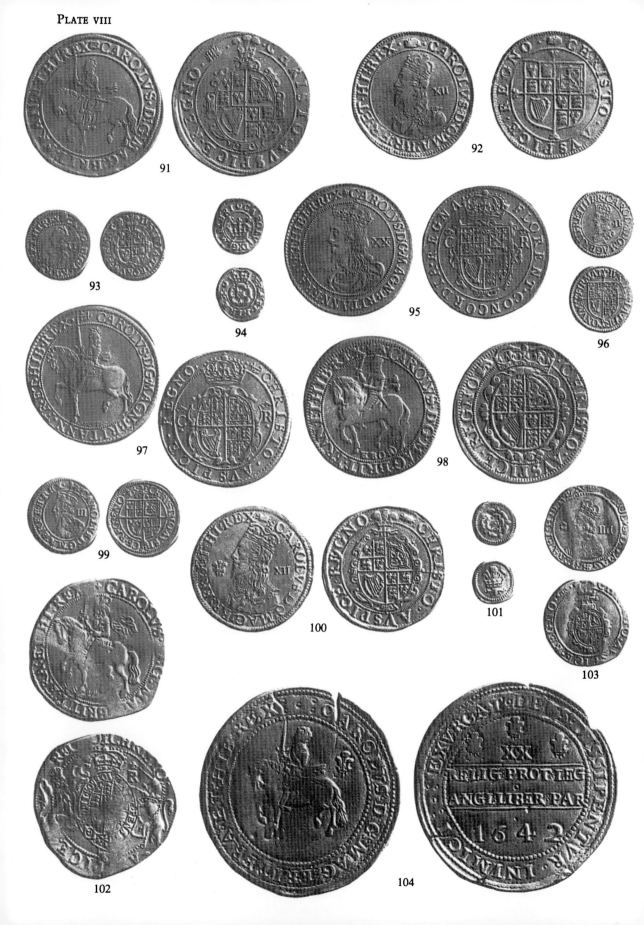

91

92

93

94

95

96

97

98

99

100

101

102

103

104

PLATE VIII

PLATE IX

PLATE IX

105

106

107

108

109

110

111

112

113

114

115

PLATE X

116

117

118

119

120

121

122

123

124

125

PLATE X

PLATE XI

PLATE XI

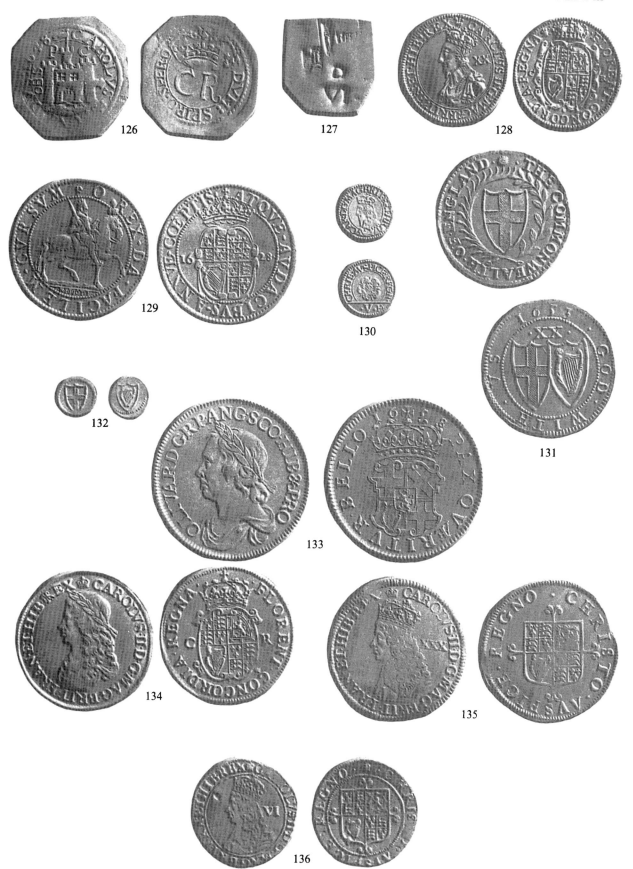

126

127

128

129

130

131

132

133

134

135

136

NOTES